Unfree
Speech

Unfree Speech

The Folly of Campaign Finance Reform

With a new preface by the author

BRADLEY A. SMITH

PRINCETON UNIVERSITY PRESS • PRINCETON AND OXFORD

Fourth printing, and first paperback printing,
with a new preface, 2003
Paperback ISBN 0-691-11369-6

**The Library of Congress has cataloged the cloth edition
of this book as follows**
Smith, Bradley A.
Unfree speech : The folly of campaign
finance reform / Bradley A. Smith
p.   cm.
Includes bibliographical references and index.
ISBN 0-691-07045-8 (alk. paper)
1. Campaign funds—United States.
2. Campaign funds—Law and legislation—
United States. I. Title.
JK1991 .S56   2001
324.7′8′0973—dc21   00-059818

British Library Cataloging-in-Publication Data
is available

This book has been composed in Sabon
Text design by Carmina Alvarez

Printed on acid-free paper. ∞

www.pupress.princeton.edu

Printed in the United States of America

10 9 8 7 6 5 4

In memory of

the signers of the Declaration

of Independence, who pledged

their fortunes

to the cause of liberty,

and

dedicated to Julie,

for everything

Contents

Preface to the Paperback Edition

Since the manuscript for this book was completed in the spring of 2000, much has happened in the world of campaign finance. Most notable may be the enactment of the Bipartisan Campaign Reform Act of 2002 (BCRA), also known as the McCain-Feingold or Shays-Meehan bill after its primary sponsors, John McCain and Russell Feingold in the Senate and Christopher Shays and Marty Meehan in the House. The legislation is a variation of earlier, unsuccessful efforts by the same sponsors, which are discussed at points in the body of this work, especially in chapter 9.

Previous efforts to pass these campaign speech regulations had failed, largely due to the determination and ability of Senator Mitch McConnell of Kentucky. Despite being regularly skewered in both the national and Kentucky press for his principled opposition to speech regulation, for a decade the Kentucky senator repeatedly frustrated efforts to further regulate political speech. As the final debate wound down in the Senate, with the result known in advance, Senator McConnell vowed, "After years of making my constitutional arguments to this body, I am eager to . . . take my argument to the branch of government charged with the critical task of interpreting our constitution. . . . This is the very moment for which the Bill of Rights was enacted."

True to his word, within hours of the bill being signed into law by President George W. Bush, McConnell filed suit in federal court. Ultimately, he would be joined by literally dozens of plaintiffs from across the political spectrum, including citizens' groups, state and national political parties (both major and "third"), legislators from both major parties, and several individuals. Amongst them, the various plaintiffs sought to overturn virtually every provision of the law on constitutional grounds. To lead the fight, McConnell put together a legal team featuring such luminaries as the liberal First Amendment expert Floyd Abrams and the conservative hero and former judge, solicitor general, and Whitewater prosecutor Kenneth Starr. The legislation's primary sponsors joined the government in defending the lawsuit, assembling their own "dream team" of lawyers headed by Seth Waxman, solicitor general for President Clinton. As of this writing, the lawsuit, styled *McConnell v. Federal Election Commission*, is pending in federal district court. By the time this paperback edition is published, or shortly thereafter, the United States Supreme Court will issue its decision, which may again dramatically change the constitutional landscape of campaign finance law.

In light of these and other events discussed below, the obvious question is whether this book is still relevant. Despite my self-interest in saying so, my answer is an unqualified "yes." As I wrote in the preface to the hardcover edition, "[a]lthough the book draws on a variety of recent and current examples to make its points, it is not intended to be anecdotal or 'current' in the sense of being a book about . . . campaign finance regulation in the 1990s. Its tales are intended to make points that are relatively timeless." Recent legislative and judicial actions may change the political and legal landscape, but they have not changed the fundamental philosophical, empirical, and constitutional issues at the heart of this book. Indeed, they beg what is one of the fundamental issues raised in the book:

"Where is it intended to end?" For even before the president signed the bill into law, advocates of greater regulation were promising still further reaching "reform."

The Bipartisan Campaign Reform Act of 2002

The new law is the most far-reaching federal campaign finance legislation ever. It features three main components, each of which are discussed in the body of this book. First, it prohibits national political party committees, such as the Republican National Committee or the Democratic National Senatorial Committee, their officers and agents, and federal officeholders from soliciting, receiving, and spending funds not subject to federal contribution limits. To prevent evasion of this rule, it also prohibits state and local parties, and their officers and agents, from spending any soft money on a variety of state campaign activities, including voter registration and get-out-the-vote drives, that might affect federal elections. Since, arguably, everything done to encourage voting in a state race can affect any federal races also on the ballot, the result is to substantially federalize state campaign finance law.

One likely consequence of this soft money "ban" is that other groups and organizations will step in and take over many functions traditionally carried out by political parties. In an almost certainly futile effort to prevent this, the law covers any organizations "directly or indirectly established, financed, maintained, or controlled" by a political party. The phrase is sweepingly broad and would potentially subject virtually every group that engages in political activity to investigation by the federal government in order to determine if it is, indeed, "indirectly established, financed, maintained, or controlled" by a party.

The law also seeks to limit the speech of other citizens and groups by sharply curtailing the right to run ads on political issues, if those ads also mention a candidate for federal office. In *Buckley v. Valeo*, discussed at length in chapters 5, 6, 7, 9, and 10, the Supreme Court had held that the First Amendment right to free speech, and concerns over vagueness and overbreadth, prohibited Congress or the states from regulating ads that did not specifically advocate the election or defeat of candidates for office (what is today known as "express advocacy"). As discussed in chapter 9, the Court did so with the full recognition that ads which discussed issues and candidates, but stopped short of specifically advocating the election or defeat of candidates (known as "issue advocacy"), would, if the other limits remained in place, emerge as substitute methods of campaigning.[1] Thus the rise of so-called soft money and issue advocacy was both a predictable and judicially predicted consequence of the Federal Election Campaign Act (FECA). Though *Buckley* was decided in 1976, issue advocacy did not become especially important as a means of campaigning until the 1990s. By the 2000 campaign, both political parties and many other groups and individuals were engaged in ad campaigns attacking or praising the records of candidates for office based on their positions on issues, but without urging people to vote for or against any particular candidate. Proponents of the McCain-Feingold legislation referred to these ads as "sham" issue ads.

Supporters of bans on issue ads have spent a great deal of time and effort in recent years trying to "prove" that these "sham" issue ads in fact influence elections.[2] I consider this a wasted effort, since *(a)* no one has ever really denied this, *(b)* influencing elections is one purpose of discussing issues, and *(c)* the Supreme Court explicitly recognized this possibility in *Buckley*. Indeed, these regulatory advocates, by their own admission, have come up with no other objective way to separate "genuine" issue ads from "sham" issue ads. For example, one study notes that most "genuine" issue ads list a toll-free phone number to call, while most "sham" issue ads do not. However, the study also admits that many "sham" issue ads do include phone numbers, while many "genuine" issue ads do not.[3] Nor does any of this explain why the First Amendment should ever be interpreted to allow the government to determine whose speech is a "sham" and whose speech is not. Indeed, it seems more probable that the purpose of the First Amendment was precisely to keep the federal government out of determining whose speech is a "sham" that can be limited or prohibited, and whose speech is "genuine" and should therefore remain unregulated.

Nevertheless, through a complex set of provisions, BCRA prohibits unions and corporations, including nonprofit groups such as the NAACP or National Right to Life, from running broadcast ads that mention a candidate for federal office within thirty days of a primary or sixty days of a general election. This idea, which has been kicked around in "reform" circles for several years, is also discussed in chapter 9. The theory is that the thirty- and sixty-day cut-offs establish a "bright line" that eliminates the constitutional problem of vagueness. However, it does nothing to address the issues of overbreadth and underbreadth, or the basic question of whether the government may restrict speech close to an election, when it would seem most valuable.

Furthermore, under the Act, anyone who would run such an ad is placed under new restrictions, including advance disclosure of his or her intent to run an ad, just the type of provision that courts have found to be an unconstitutional prior restraint on speech. The bill also restricts the rights of political parties and, indirectly, of nonprofit organizations to run ads that "promote, support, attack, or oppose" a candidate for federal office at any time.

A third key provision of the law instructs the Federal Election Commission (FEC) to adopt a new definition of "coordination." This is important because if a person or group coordinates its activities with a party or candidate's campaign, or if a party coordinates its activities with its candidates, then the activities of the coordinating entity are treated as contributions to the campaign. This makes those activities subject to federal contribution limits—in other words, "coordinated" speech is subject to added legal restrictions. BCRA requires the FEC to adopt a definition of coordination that does not require "agreement or formal collaboration" between the entities involved. Just how a group might coordinate its activities without "agreement" or "formal collaboration" is hardly clear. However, the sweeping definition apparently contemplated by Congress raises the same constitutional problems of vagueness and overbreadth that have so bedeviled the pro-regulation lobby on the question of issue ads.[4] For example, if a group worked closely with a particular senator on a piece of legislation, would any activity conducted by the group praising that senator be considered coordinated, even if never discussed with the senator or his campaign? Could a group be deemed to "coordinate" its activities if it gained general information on the candidate's strategy through the press and planned its activities to compliment the candidate's campaign? What if a group hired a former staffer from the campaign?

Would it matter if the staffer was fired before being hired by the group? Or suppose the candidate, a longtime supporter of the group, hired a staffer from the group to run his campaign? If any of these situations would meet the legal standard for coordination, they could severely restrict the rights of citizens to communicate with candidates and the public. BCRA repealed the FEC's former regulation, which found coordination only when a communication was undertaken at the request of a candidate, when the candidate exercised control over the communication, or when the candidate's campaign and the speaker had engaged in "substantial discussion" over the communication. However, beyond instructing the FEC not to require "agreement or formal collaboration" in conduct or "express advocacy" in content, Congress offered little guidance. As of this writing, the FEC has yet to adopt a new definition, though it will have done so by the time this edition is in print.

Unfortunately, there is not room in this brief preface to analyze all of these and other provisions of the bill in detail. However, the basic principles behind each of these provisions, including both policy and constitutional objections, are already discussed in the book. Readers who wish to consider BCRA can extrapolate appropriately.

Calls for More Regulation

By any standard, BCRA is far reaching legislation. It federalizes much state and local activity, and, while not banning all avenues of speech, it sharply curtails the rights of citizens to publicly criticize, and in some cases even mention, officeholders and candidates. Yet even before the new law had taken effect, its sponsors and supporters were noting that it would not accomplish its objectives and that far more regulation would be required. Shortly after the bill passed, lead sponsor Senator Russell Feingold declared, "It is only a beginning. It is modest reform. . . . There will be other reforms." Senator Paul Wellstone, instrumental in the provision limiting ads that even mention a candidate's name in the sixty days before an election, vowed, "This legislation is a first step." Pro-regulation columnist E. J. Dionne chimed in that the passage of the bill was only "the end of the beginning" of their efforts. A representative of the Indiana Alliance for Democracy wrote that while the bill was "an important first step, it does not solve all the problems of money in politics." A typical comment was that of *Philadelphia Inquirer* columnist Mark Bowden, who said that the bill "scratches at the surface."[5]

Many of these speakers and writers made clear that their ultimate goal is full "public," or tax-financed, elections. This is so even though voluntary support for the federal presidential system, which is discussed in chapter 2, continues to fall, and the system is unlikely to have enough cash on hand to meet its obligations to provide funds to eligible candidates in any timely fashion in 2004. The nonpartisan, pro-"reform" Campaign Finance Institute has called the system "broken" and "a train wreck," primarily because the system lacks the flexibility to keep up with the world of campaigning—exactly the problem that in chapter 5 I suggest is endemic to tax-financed systems.[6] Indeed, shortly after the passage of BCRA, Senators McCain and Feingold introduced legislation to provide for "free" television time, which, as explained in chapter 9, is simply a mutant form of tax financing. However, tax-financed elections, discussed in chapters 5 and 9, will no more solve the alleged problems of corruption and equality than will McCain-Feingold, unless accompanied by still further restrictions on private speech.

Besides tax financing of elections, Senators McCain and Feingold and their House colleagues Representatives Shays and Meehan have also indicated support for replacing the Federal Election Commission with a "tougher" enforcement agency. Exactly what they mean is unclear, but other supporters of such "reform" are calling for an agency modeled after the FBI. At a press conference announcing this proposal, Common Cause president Scott Harshbarger argued that law enforcement should treat campaign finance "like murder." Of course, Mr. Harshbarger wasn't arguing for life sentences without parole and no bail, but his comments are revealing of the increasingly hard-edged antipathy to political speech that has taken hold in the so-called reform community. Indeed, Harshbarger added that more people "need to go to jail" for campaign finance violations, i.e., for engaging in political speech and activity.[7] With this attitude, it is not surprising that the recently passed BCRA legislation adds new criminal penalties for violations of the law. While FECA has long included some criminal provisions, BCRA makes it increasingly possible in the United States to be jailed for engaging in nontreasonous political speech.

Yet, these steps are not the end, either, because, as discussed in chapter 9, they still won't solve the alleged problems of corruption and inequality. They will fail because, even if all of BCRA is upheld as constitutional, citizens will continue to speak out on political issues. They will run ads more than sixty days before an election. They will run print ads rather than broadcast ads. New groups, run by old party operatives, will spring up to carry on the activities of parties in all but name.

Other sources of influence will go further underground. For example, in October of 2001 the Brennan Center, a special interest group advocating campaign finance regulation, raised over $800,000 at a dinner in New York. Co-chaired by Senators Hillary Clinton and Charles Schumer, and featuring Senator John McCain as the guest of honor, the dinner was underwritten by corporate donors. Sponsors included over two dozen large law firms, many with substantial Washington lobbying practices, plus corporate giants such as Coca Cola, Enron, Phillip Morris, Bear Stearns & Co., The Limited, and others. Such activities are not required to be disclosed, and generally occur with little press scrutiny. Post-BCRA, this could be the future—corporations hoping to curry favor with lawmakers or get a few moments to discuss an issue may simply sponsor the interest groups that they know favor and work with the officeholders. If the arguments for "reform" are true, especially the concern over the "appearance of corruption," won't this have to be stopped as well? Surely the potential for corruption and the appearance of corruption exist when large corporations and lobbyists contribute to a group honoring a senator and promoting the senator's legislative agenda.

So where is it intended to end? That question remains unanswered in the wake of BCRA.

Recent Supreme Court Cases

In addition to the passage of BCRA, important new developments since publication of the hardcover edition have occurred in the courts and in the states. In the courts, the most prominent case is *Federal Election Commission v. Colorado Republican Federal Campaign Committee*, also known as "*Colorado II*" to distinguish it from the 1996 case of the same name, mentioned in chapter 9.[8] In *Colorado II*, the U.S. Supreme Court upheld FECA's limits on coordinated expenditures by political parties. As all of the coordinated expenditures made by a party would come from regulated "hard" money, and as parties are not themselves "special inter-ests" but broad organizations that the candidates join voluntarily, the corrupting influence of such expenditures is not readily apparent. But the Court apparently accepted the theory of "conduit corruption," discussed in chapter 9. Coupled with the Court's 2000 decision in *Nixon v. Shrink Missouri Government PAC* (briefly discussed in chapter 7), the decision indicates that the Court is simply lowering the bar, without saying so, on the state's burden to justify restrictions on political speech.[9] The case may be effectively superseded by the litigation in *McConnell v. FEC*, or it may be a sign that the Court will uphold the new limits of BCRA. It may be worth noting that in 2001 the U.S. District Court for the District of Alaska, the first federal court to squarely face a ban on soft money, found such a ban to be unconstitutional. A Washington state appellate court has also found a soft money ban to be unconstitutional.[10]

In another noteworthy case, *Republican Party of Minnesota v. White*,[11] the Supreme Court held that a Minnesota statute limiting the ability of candidates for judicial offices to state their views on legal or political issues was unconstitutional. This decision indicates that the Court still sees little danger of corruption from political speech generally and may be sympathetic to the *McConnell* plaintiffs, at least on the question of "issue ads."

"Clean Elections" in the States

Meanwhile, in the states, efforts to promote tax-financed elections are running into difficulties. In the late 1990s, so-called clean election laws, which provide full public funding on a voluntary basis (but with powerful disincentives for any candidate to refuse the tax subsidy), were adopted by four states: Vermont, Maine, Massachusetts, and Arizona. However, in the elections of 2000, "clean elections" proposals were soundly de-feated by voters in Oregon and Missouri, and no such initiatives appeared on state ballots in 2002. At the same time, all of the existing "clean elec-tions" programs, and most other state-level government financing efforts as well, have run into trouble.

Arizona attempts to fund its clean elections system, in part, with voluntary tax check-offs, as in the federal system, and a dollar-for-dollar tax credit for voluntary contributions up to $500. As with the federal system, attempts to convince taxpayers to dedicate a portion of their taxes to government-financed elections through these tax check-offs have largely failed. Even the dollar-for-dollar tax credit has generated relatively little funding. And the primary source of funds—a tax surcharge on every fine, civil or criminal (including, for example, parking tickets), which had provided nearly two-thirds of the funding—was struck down as unconstitutionally compelled speech by the Arizona Court of Appeals in June 2002, though the decision is under appeal as of this writing. Meanwhile, those hoping that tax financing would reduce "special interest" influence suffered a blow when an early analysis by an Arizona think-tank, the Goldwater Institute, found "no meaningful difference in the way subsidized and unsubsidized legislators voted."[12]

In both Arizona and Vermont, taxes on lobbyists which were used to partially fund the systems were struck down by courts as unconstitutional burdens on the right to petition the government.[13] In Kentucky, the state legislature has refused to fund its system of matching contributions, demanding instead that the funds be spent for other government purposes. Likewise, in Massachusetts the state legislature refused to provide funds for the clean elections system, until finally forced to auction off state property under court order. Support for tax financing remains low in the polls. Indeed, in a rather humorous episode, the director of Massachusetts Voters for Clean Elections complained that the legislature was trying to "lead voters to a particular answer" by placing a nonbinding referendum on the ballot asking voters: "Do you support taxpayer money being used to fund political campaigns for public office in the Commonwealth in the amount of up to $90 million per statewide election cycle?" Unlike, of course, asking voters if they favor "clean elections." One reason for the low public support is the difficult issue, discussed in chapter 5, of calibrating payments to include popular candidates while excluding fringe candidates. In both Maine and Massachusetts, gubernatorial candidates of the tiny Green Party have qualified for hundreds of thousands of dollars in taxpayer subsidies for their campaigns. Wisconsin's system, discussed in chapter 5, remains underfunded and rarely utilized. None of these particular problems are incurable, but they do indicate that these types of issues are a constant political reality for tax-financed systems, making them unlikely to be successful. Coupled with the fact that noncandidate spending cannot be controlled, thus leaving alive the alleged problems of corruption and equality, they illustrate that government-financed campaigns are not the answer.[14]

Recent Scandals

No update, however brief, would be complete without some mention of recent scandals that helped fuel the passage of BCRA. Two stand out: the Clinton pardons and the Enron scandal. Both are too complex to be fully recorded here, but they can be briefly described as follows.

In the closing hours of his administration, President Bill Clinton issued a number of pardons, several apparently outside of the usual channels. Many observers felt some of the pardons were inappropriate, especially one given to Mark Rich, a fugitive financier. Rich's ex-wife, Denise Rich, who lobbied for the pardon, had been a major donor to the Clinton library, a major Democratic Party fundraiser and donor, and had given the Clintons a personal gift of furniture valued in excess of $7000. Rich's pardon was also facilitated by former Clinton White House counsel Jack Quinn, who was hired by Rich to lobby on his behalf. Many people argued that campaign finance reform would prevent such questionable deals.[15] In fact, while BCRA would have prohibited Denise Rich's million-dollar contributions to the Democratic Party, nothing in BCRA would prohibit gifts to presidential libraries, or personal gifts, or hiring a high-powered lawyer with White House connections. Nor would Denise Rich be precluded from spending her money to directly support Democratic candidates, rather than giving it to the Democratic Party for that purpose. In short, it seems rather far-fetched to think that BCRA, or even more extreme proposals to limit contributions, will stop such efforts at influence peddling. The American people were not unaware of, or at least without the information necessary to evaluate, Mr. Clinton's character at the time of both the 1992 and 1996 presidential elections and the 1998–99 impeachment battles. Nor were news organizations such as the *New York Times*, which endorsed his candidacy. To express shock over

Mr. Clinton's actions, and then to demand that because of them the rights of millions of honest, politically active citizens be restricted, while the *Times*'s editorial influence is left unchecked, seems the height of hypocrisy.

Enron was the seventh largest corporation in the United States when it suddenly declared bankruptcy in the fall of 2001. Right up until the moment of its bankruptcy, Enron was a major contributor to a wide variety of civic, charitable, and public policy causes (including campaign finance reform advocacy groups) and a major donor to both the Democratic and Republican parties. Its political action committee (PAC), funded by small, voluntary contributions from its employees, shareholders, and their families, contributed to many candidates' campaigns, as did various Enron employees individually. As the company careened toward bankruptcy, Enron made political appeals to be bailed out through favorable regulation, but the appeals fell on deaf ears.

There can be no doubt that Enron played politics at both the state and federal level, lobbying hard for either more regulation or more deregulation, depending upon what was in its best interest at the time. But reporting on Enron and campaign finance ranged from facile to ignorant. For example, voters were frequently told that Enron had contributed over $3.5 million in soft money between 1989 and 2001. With no context, readers wouldn't know that that figure amounted to approximately two-tenths of 1 percent of total party soft money raised, or not even enough to adequately fund a single U.S. House race in each election cycle. Similarly, the $1.37 million in hard money given by Enron's PAC and by individual Enron employees amounted to approximately eight one-hundredths of 1 percent of total hard money contributions. Of course, in its hour of need, Enron's contributions brought it no assistance. But how much could they have mattered in any event? Even Representative Shays, in perhaps an unguarded moment, noted that Enron, one of the nation's largest employers, would have political influence if it never gave a dime, "by the fact of who it is and what it does." Nevertheless, Enron—like essentially all scandals—was trotted out as a need for campaign finance reform.[16]

What should we make of these developments? These are the two big "campaign finance" scandals to have occurred since this book was published. Yet it seems doubtful, to say the least, that anything in BCRA, or the addition of "free TV," or a "tougher" FEC, or indeed, even the most extreme proposals noted in this book, such as proposals to limit paid political speech to that meted out by the government in the form of vouchers (see chapter 8), would have undercut the influence of either the Riches or Enron, or would have prevented either scandal. If these are the best justifications for campaign finance reform—as House Minority Leader Richard Gephardt stated of Enron—then what can we really expect these limits on speech to accomplish?

Corruption and the Appearance of Corruption

One criticism that has been leveled at *Unfree Speech* is that it does not convincingly enough show that campaign contributions such as Enron's are not corrupting. But that is not really the argument made. The book accepts the premise that campaign contributions can influence the behavior of elected officials. What I question, however, is whether it is accurate to consider all, or even most, such influence to be "corruption." Further, I argue that, assuming some such influence might be "corrupting," it is unproven that legislators are corrupted in any systematic manner, or that corruption in the form of campaign contributions is a major problem. Additionally, I argue that there are very good intuitive reasons to doubt the common wisdom that campaign contributions have much impact on the behavior of those elected to office, once elected. Equally important, the thesis of *Unfree Speech* is that efforts to solve such corruption problems as might exist are damaging to the body politic and contrary to First Amendment rights.

Still, the Supreme Court has accepted both corruption and "the appearance of corruption" as a basis to override what it admits are core First Amendment rights. This latter is important for, lacking much evidence of actual corruption that would be addressed by campaign finance restrictions, Congress has justified its regulation primarily on the grounds that it must prevent "the appearance of corruption." Yet what are the American people to think when, in 2002, the wife of the U.S. Senate majority leader is a highly paid lobbyist for big business—as are the wives of at least two other U.S. senators? The ranks of Washington lobbyists also include the children and other immediate relatives of lawmakers, and many spouses of lawmakers sit on corporate boards. In the spring of 2002, it was reported that one prominent senator's wife gave nearly two dozen speeches in 2001, receiving, on average, $16,000 per speech, for no immediately obvious reason other than her spousal position.[17] I do not mean to say that any of these individuals are necessarily corrupt. I do mean to say that in light of such facts, if it is the appearance of corruption we are after, why are we worried if a person gives $2500 to the campaign of a candidate, or spends $500 of his own money on some radio ads? Don't those other types of activities—which personally enrich lawmakers and their families—do far more to create the appearance of corruption than campaign contributions? Thus, campaign finance laws remain both overinclusive and underinclusive. They limit or prohibit a great deal of core First Amendment speech that is not corrupting, and they do little or nothing to address the scandals, and the appearances of corruption, often used to justify them.

Finally, a personal note. As I stated in the preface to the hardcover edition, shortly before finishing this book, I was nominated to a seat on the Federal Election Commission. I was eventually confirmed by the Senate, 64–35, and took office in June of 2000. What I have learned while serving—and I have learned much—has deepened my belief that campaign finance reform is a trip down the wrong road, and a trip that demands an answer to the question, "What is the destination?" If the passage of BCRA is only a "first step," what is the end?

In two years, I have seen many complaints come before the commission. Most of them are partisan complaints, often with only the flimsiest legal or factual basis: campaign finance litigation as a campaign strategy, as noted in chapter 4 of this work. Others are simply silly. For example, I have watched the commission pursue sons for giving too much money to their fathers, parents for giving too much to their children, and husbands for contributing too much to their wives. I have watched people face complaints for such trivial grassroots political expressions as homemade signs parked on cotton trailers.

My concerns about disclosure requirements, voiced in chapter 10, have grown—it is clear that disclosure is one of the most burdensome aspects of the law for small political groups and independent actors. I have watched as the FEC charged individuals with FECA violations for failing to place proper disclaimers on as little as $300 in radio ads. I have read the letters from volunteer campaign treasurers, personally liable for improperly filed reports, vowing never to take part in politics again.[18]

Life on the Federal Election Commission may be summed up as follows: We see many complaints. Many of them are obviously not violations of the Federal Election Campaign Act. Some clearly are violations. And many are difficult cases on the margin. But virtually none have anything to do with special interest influence or the prevention of corruption. Indeed, the clearest violations of the law often have the least connection to any real or perceived corruption. That is the dirty little reality that scholars, policy makers, "good government" supporters of more regulation, and the Supreme Court, with its mantra-like invocation of the "appearance of corruption," need to face.

Unfree Speech is a book that walks a thin line. I hope it is viewed as a serious piece of scholarship. But it is not neutral scholarship—my research and writing in the field has left me with a clear point of view, and that viewpoint is conveyed in both the title and contents of the book. Two years on the Federal Election Commission, seeing the law from another point of view, have only deepened those convictions.

Fredericksburg, Virginia
September 9, 2002

Notes

1. *Buckley v. Valeo*, 424 U.S. 1, 42 (1976).
2. See, for example, Ken Goldstein and Paul Freedman, "Lessons Learned: Campaign Advertising in the 2000 Elections," (forthcoming) *Political Communication* 19 (2002); Craig B. Holman and Luke P. McLaughlin, *Buying Time 2000* (New York: Brennan Center for Justice, 2002); David B. Magleby, ed., *The Other Campaign: Soft Money and Issue Advocacy in the 2000 Congressional Elections* (Lanham, M.D.: Rowman & Littlefield, 2001); Jonathan S. Krasno and Daniel E. Steltz, *Buying Time: Television Advertising in the 1998 Congressional Elections* (New York: Brennan Center for Justice, 2000); David B. Magleby, ed.,

Outside Money: Soft Money and Issue Advocacy in the 1998 Congressional Elections (Lanham, M.D.: Rowman & Littlefield, 1999).

3. Krasno and Steltz, *Buying Time*, pp. 9–11.

4. See, for example, *F.E.C. v. Christian Coalition*, 52 F. Supp. 2d 45 (D.D.C. 1999); Federal Election Commission, *MUR 4624, The Coalition (Statement of Reasons, Commissioner Bradley A. Smith)* (2001).

5. See quotes in William M. Welch and Jim Drinkard, "Supporters Turn to Defending, Extending Victory," *USA Today*, March 21, 2002, 6A; Nick Anderson, "Campaign Reform Passes Congress," *Los Angeles Times*, March 21, 2002, A1; E. J. Dionne, Jr., "Campaign Reform: The Next Steps," *Washington Post*, March 22, 2002, A27; Stefanie Miller, "Clean Elections Law is Next Step in Campaign Reform," *Indianapolis Star*, March 10, 2002, 4D; Mark Bowden, "Campaign Reform? Not Quite; The McCain-Feingold Bill Scratches the Surface," *Philadelphia Inquirer*, March 31, 2002, 1B.

6. See Federal Election Commission, *2002 Recommendations to Congress* (2002); Campaign Finance Institute, *Press Release, Blue Ribbon Panel to Study Financing Presidential Nominations*, July 18, 2002 (quoting Executive Director Michael Malbin and Trustee Bill Brock).

7. See Democracy 21, *No Bark, No Bite, No Point: The Case for Closing the Federal Election Commission and Establishing a New System for Enforcing the Nation's Campaign Finance Laws* (Washington, D.C.: Democracy 21, 2002). Mr. Harshbarger's quotes are taken from my personal notes of the press conference.

8. 121 S. Ct. 2351 (2001).

9. *Shrink PAC*, 528 U.S. 377 (2000); See J. Clark Kelso, "Mr. Smith Goes to Washington," *Journal of Election Law* 1 (2002): 77–78.

10. *Jacobus v. Alaska*, Case No. A97-0272CV (D. Alaska 2001); *Washington State Republican Party v. Washington State Disclosure Commission*, 4 P.3d 808 (Wash. 2000)(state court striking down Washington state ban on party soft money).

11. 122 S. Ct. 2528 (2002).

12. *May v. McNally*, 376 Ariz. Adv. Rep. 31(June 17, 2002); Robert J. Franciosi, *Is Cleanliness Next to Godliness? Arizona's Clean Elections Law after Its First Year* (Phoenix, A.Z.: Goldwater Institute, 2001).

13. *Vermont Society of Association Executives v. Milne*, 779 A. 2d 20 (Vermont 2001); See *May v. McNally*, 376 Ariz. Adv. Rep. 31, n.2 (June 17, 2002)(noting unreported ruling striking down Arizona lobbying tax was not appealed).

14. See Alan Greenblatt, "That Clean-All-Over Feeling," *Governing Magazine* (July 2002): 40; Ellen S. Miller and Nick Penniman, "The Road to Nowhere," *American Prospect*, August 12, 2002, 14; Rick Klein, "A Deal May Fund Clean Elections: Some Want Issue Returned to Voters," *Boston Globe*, June 12, 2002, A1.

15. For a general, though highly partisan, discussion of the pardon scandal, see Barbara Olson, *The Final Days* (Washington, D.C.: Regnery Publishing, 2001). For a sampling of comments alleging a connection to campaign finance reform, see Mary Leonard, "Clinton Exit Gives Party Shudders," *Boston Globe*, January 31, 2001, A1 (quoting John McCain as saying the pardon of Rich "is an argument for campaign finance reform"); National Public Radio, *All Things Considered*, January 24, 2001 (comments of Daniel Schorr, "Maybe if we ever get campaign finance reform, we can be rid of clemency for sale."); Editorial, "An Important Step Forward," *St. Louis Post-Dispatch*, January 24, 2001, B18.

16. For a quick review of the scandal, see Dana Milbank and Peter Behr, "Enron Asked for Help From Cabinet Officials," *Washington Post*, January 11, 2002, A1; for giving by Enron and its employees, see *www.opensecrets.org/news/enron/enron_totals*, the website of the Center for Responsive Politics; for Shays quote, see Liz Marlantes and Gail Chaddock, "Enron's Reach in Congress," *Christian Science Monitor*, January 15, 2002, 1.

17. See Judy Keen, "In Capital, Business and Politics Firmly Entwined," *USA Today*, July 31, 2002, 1A; Amy Keller, "Clinton Wasn't Only Spouse to Make Big Bucks," *Roll Call*, June 17, 2002, 26.

18. For some of these stories, see Bradley A. Smith, "Regulation and the Decline of Grassroots Politics," *Catholic University Law Review 50* (2000): 1–12; Bradley A. Smith, "McCain-Feingold Will Hurt the Little Guy," *Wall Street Journal*, March 20, 2001, A14.

Preface

On February 9, 2000, as I was working toward completion of this book, I was nominated to fill a vacancy on the Federal Election Commission, the independent federal agency that oversees enforcement of federal campaign finance laws. This created an outcry of sorts, unprecedented for a nominee to this rather obscure government agency. Senator Dick Durbin of Illinois dubbed me a "nihilist." Scott Harshbarger, the president of Common Cause, called my nomination a throwback "to the dark days of Watergate." Editorial writers compared nominating me to public office to nominating pornographer Larry Flynt, former Ku Klux Klansman David Duke, and murderer Ted Kaczynski (aka the "Unabomber") to public office. From there it often got worse.

Most telling, however, were the comments of Vice President Al Gore. Opposing the nomination of his own president, the vice president declared, "the last thing we need is an FEC commissioner who publicly questions not only the constitutionality of proposed [campaign finance] reforms, but also the constitutionality of current limitations." It is, in a sense, because of Gore and those who think like him that I wrote this book. For I would have thought that an appreciation of free speech and a concern for the actual effects of regulation in practice would be vitally important for the head of federal agency to carry out his or her duties successfully. And I had always assumed that concern about the constitutionality of legislation, whether proposed or already on the books, would be a minimal and necessary requirement for any person seeking public office, elective or appointed. That a concern about the constitutionality of regulation would be considered a disqualification for office had never before crossed my mind.

Unfortunately, in recent years the debate over campaign finance reform has lost this sense of proportion. Those who favor more regulation of the system are all too often designated to wear white hats, whereas anyone who would question the wisdom of added regulation is not merely wrong but "a nihilist" or a throwback to "the dark days of Watergate."

Few people like our current campaign finance laws. I certainly don't, and in that respect, I am a full-throated "reformer." But "reform" need not be limited to defending current regulation and calling for more. "Reform" can also mean critically examining the effects of current regulation and calling for its repeal or revision. The purpose of this book is to undertake that critical examination and to place concerns about the Constitution, the First Amendment, and freedom back at the fore of this debate. It may be that, having done so, we will continue on the path of regulation—but at least we will have examined the relevant issues.

For many years now, the bulk of both legal scholarship and popular writing on campaign finance has been a literature of regulation, not freedom. The nation's editorial pages pound a steady drumbeat in favor of proposals to restrict campaign contributions and spending, while the nation's law journals are filled with articles, often sadly divorced from any empirical analysis of campaign giving and spending, that suggest ever more creative ways to regulate political speech, on increasingly specious constitutional grounds. But as I have taught and written about election law over the last decade, I have become increasingly convinced that almost everything the American people know, or think they know, about campaign finance is wrong. Campaign spending is not exploding, but in fact is rising at a slower pace than advertising for most categories of consumer goods. Although campaign spending is important, it does not "buy" elections, and limits on spending seem to destroy electoral competition. Far from corrupting the legislature, campaign contributions seem to have remarkably little effect on legislative behavior. And far from empowering ordinary citizens and political outsiders, campaign finance regulations have struck hardest at grassroots political involvement. Furthermore, I have come to conclude that, in fact, the bulk of campaign finance regulation is unconstitutional.

In reviewing popular literature on the subject, one can find many books with titillating titles such as "The Buying of the President" and "The Best Congress Money Can Buy," but virtually none that attempts to make the case for freedom. On the academic side, it seems to me that political scientists and economists have been producing a voluminous literature that questions the validity of many of the assumptions behind campaign finance reform efforts, but this literature has remained largely detached from legislative and constitutional theories that might give it added life. Meanwhile, law professors, far too often oblivious to this literature, have continued to write in a theoretical vacuum, unwilling to challenge their fundamental assumptions about money in politics.

This book is an effort to start filling in the gulf between the empirical research of political scientists and economists and the constitutional theories now heard in the legal academy and the courts. I have attempted to write a book that is scholarly enough for the professional but accessible to the intelligent, involved layman, the political science undergraduate, or the law student without a background in empirical political research. I fear that the end result may satisfy no one, but I hope otherwise. In an effort to keep the volume slim, I have tried to focus on big-picture questions, touching the finer details long enough only to illuminate the larger points and suggest avenues for further thought. Although the book draws on a variety of recent and current examples to make its points, it is not intended to be anecdotal or "current" in the sense of being a book about the 2000 presidential campaign, or campaign finance regulation in the 1990s. Its tales are intended to make points that are relatively timeless.

At the advice of my first editor at Princeton University Press, Malcolm Litchfield, I have tried to limit the number of footnotes, removing nonessential and repetitive notes as well as citations to information that I believe is generally available, and at times I have combined many footnotes into one. Given the penchant of legal academics for footnotes, this was a nearly traumatizing experience, and I fear that some legal readers will be unsatisfied with the documentation. Nevertheless, readers familiar with political science literature and lay readers may find the work hopelessly cluttered. Readers will also note that in exploring the many aspects of campaign finance regulation, and in particular the constitutional issues involved, I have chosen the writings of a relatively small number of outstanding legal theorists as touchstones for my critiques. The work of these scholars, I believe, can fairly be said to be representative—and among the best—scholarship that supports particular points of view. Certainly there are other fine scholars working in the field, and the exclusion of detailed discussions of all such work is not intended to slight these individuals or to avoid difficult issues but is done to help achieve the book's objectives of brevity and accessibility to a nonacademic audience.

In completing this work, I am indebted to Capital University Law School, whose generous grants have supported my research and writing in the field over several summers. I thank Capital's law dean, Steven Bahls, for his material support of my work. Daniel Lowenstein and Joel Gora provided written comments on an earlier draft of the manuscript; I have benefited from many discussions with both men, and both also have my thanks for their encouragement, support, and guidance over the past several years. I have also benefited from discussions with a great many individuals, including Lillian BeVier, Jim Bopp, Richard Cordray, Ed Crane, Craig Engle, Jeff Ferriell, Brian Freeman, John Hasnas, Don Hughes, Dan Kobil, John Kozyris, Jeff Lindeman, Bill Marshall, David Mason, John McGinnis, John Norton Moore, Roger Pilon, Dan Polsby, Jamin Raskin, and many others.

Portions of this work first appeared in several law review articles. None of these articles is reprinted in its entirety, none without substantial revision, and none constitutes a chapter on its own. Moreover, portions of a particular article may appear in different chapters in the book. I thank the editors for their permission to include these excerpts, and also the editors who worked on these manuscripts for their respective journals.

- Portions of "Faulty Assumptions and Undemocratic Consequences of Campaign Finance Reform" appear in chapters 2, 3, and 4, and are reprinted with permission of the Yale Law Journal Company and Fred B. Rothman and Company from the *Yale Law Journal* 105 (1996): 1049–91.
- Portions of "Money Talks: Speech, Equality, Corruption and Campaign Finance," *Georgetown Law Journal* 86 (1997): 45–99, appear in chapters 6, 7, and 8, and are reprinted with permission of the publisher, Georgetown University and *Georgetown Law Journal*.
- Portions of "Some Problems with Taxpayer-Funded Political Campaigns," *University of Pennsylvania Law Review* 148 (1999): 591–628, appear in chapters 5 and 8 and are reprinted with permission from the University of Pennsylvania Law Review.
- Portions of "The Sirens' Song: Campaign Finance Regulation and the First Amendment," *Journal of Law and Policy* 6 (1997): 1–43, appear in chapters 2 and 9, and are reprinted with permission of the *Journal of Law and Policy* at Brooklyn Law School.

I have also benefited from being able to discuss the ideas included in this book in numerous lectures and panels over the past several years, including ones at Brooklyn Law School, Chicago-Kent College of Law, Franklin Pierce Law School, Harvard University Department of Government, Hillsdale College, Kalamazoo College, New York University School of Law, Nichols College, Notre Dame Law School, Quinnipiac Law School, the University of Connecticut School of Law, and Yale Law School. I would especially like to thank the Federalist Society for sponsoring many of the above lectures and panels, along with others at various lawyers' chapters around the country and before the society's E. L. Wiegand Free Speech and Election Law Practice Group. The Center for New

Democracy, the Institute for American Values, the Madison Society at NYU Law School, the Journal of Legislation at Notre Dame Law School, and the Center for First Amendment Rights also sponsored some of these panels and lectures.

Steven Hoersting provided valuable research assistance, helpful comments, and moral support during the down periods. Jennifer Goaziou also provided research assistance. Bryan Barch assisted in preparation of the bibliography and index. I am grateful to the students in my election law classes over the years, from whom I often learn much. Shawna Whitehead's secretarial support was invaluable to completion of the manuscript.

A special word of thanks is owed to my friend and colleague at Capital University Law School, David Mayer, who read and commented on portions of this work, was a constant source of encouragement and inspiration, and who gave the book its title.

Special thanks are also owed to Senator Mitch McConnell of Kentucky, who has often stood all but alone on the side of free speech in the United States Senate, recognizing what is at stake in this debate when others have not.

Finally, the greatest thanks are owed to my wife Julie, and my daughters Eleanor and Emmaline, who have shown patience and understanding when their husband and father was alternately distracted and missing while working on this manuscript.

Unfree
  Speech

Chapter 1

INTRODUCTION

On May 31, 1972, a two-page ad appeared in the *New York Times* that featured the headline "A Resolution to Impeach Richard Nixon as President of the United States." The ad, which cost a total of $17,850, was paid for by a group consisting of several lawyers, at least one law professor, a former United States senator, and a number of other citizens of modest prominence, calling themselves the National Committee for Impeachment. In addition to criticizing President Richard Nixon, the ad recognized an "honor roll" of several congressmen who had introduced a resolution that called for the president's impeachment. The United States Department of Justice moved swiftly, getting a federal district court to enjoin the National Committee for Impeachment and its officers from engaging in further political activity. The committee, argued the government, was violating the Federal Election Campaign Act of 1971 because its efforts had the potential to "affect" the 1972 presidential election, and the committee had not properly registered with the government to engage in such political activity.

United States v. National Committee for Impeachment was the first enforcement action ever brought under the Federal Election Campaign Act (FECA), which, as amended, remains our basic national campaign finance law. The case made plain the extent to which FECA was one of the most radical laws ever passed in the United States; for the first time in history, Congress had passed a law requiring citizens to register with the government in order to criticize its office holders.

The case also illustrates the inextricable link between political speech and political spending. For the government's hook in its effort to quiet the National Committee for Impeachment was not the committee's actual speech but its expenditure of money to advertise that speech. The government did not attempt to argue that the defendants had no right to speak out about impeachment or other subjects, or that the contents of the ad were libelous or defamatory. Rather, it argued that the Committee for Impeachment was barred by law from spending more than $1,000 to disseminate its views. But as the case shows, speech costs money. If the government can regulate or limit expenditures to fund speech, it can effectively regulate or limit the corresponding speech. Virtually any effort to communicate with a mass audience requires an expenditure of money, whether that expenditure goes to advertise in a newspaper or on television, rent a hall or pay for a permit for a public rally, publish a newsletter or handbills, or simply to purchase a soapbox and bullhorn. It was the expenditure of money—a quite modest amount, really—that made the speech of the National Committee for Impeachment potentially persuasive to voters, and that served as the foundation for the government's claimed authority to regulate that speech.

In the summer of 1976, Edward Cozzette and a handful of friends organized the Central Long Island Tax Reform Immediately Committee (CLITRIM). The group was unaffiliated with any political party or candidate. Cozzette and his friends contacted National Tax Reform Immediately, an unincorporated committee affiliated with the conservative John

Birch Society, and obtained information on the voting record of their local congressman, Representative Jerome Ambro. They then spent $135 to print copies of a bulletin that included a photo of Representative Ambro and a list of twenty-four of his votes in congress. Each vote was identified as being "for lower taxes and less government" or "for higher taxes and more government." Twenty-one of the twenty-four votes fell into the latter category. The bulletin urged readers, "if your representative consistently votes for measures that increase taxes, let him know how you feel. And thank him when he votes for lower taxes and less government." CLITRIM members distributed copies of the bulletin at a commuter rail station, shopping centers, and at a public meeting at which Representative Ambro appeared.

On August 1, 1978, the Federal Election Commission (FEC) sued CLITRIM in federal court for violating the terms of the Federal Election Campaign Act by distributing Representative Ambro's voting record in the summer of 1976.[1] Is this what Americans want in the polling data that seems to show overwhelming support for "campaign finance reform"? Is it right that a handful of Americans could be sued in court for spending $135 to publish and distribute truthful information about the voting record of a candidate for federal office? If not, what went wrong? Can it be avoided in the future?

In the end, the cases against both CLITRIM and the National Committee for Impeachment were dismissed by federal appellate courts, which ruled that the First Amendment to the Constitution prohibited enforcement of the Federal Elections Campaign Act against the defendants. Yet each case is, in essence, still alive, for in each of the last several congresses bills have been introduced, and even passed in the U.S. House or Senate, that would regulate, limit, and in some cases ban exactly the types of behavior engaged in by CLITRIM and the National Committee for Impeachment. And why not? In each case, the dismissal of the charges hinged on the fact that the literature in question did not specifically urge readers how to vote. Had either CLITRIM or the National Committee for Impeachment specifically urged readers to "vote against" a candidate for office, the Supreme Court's jurisprudence would have allowed the government actions against them to proceed. The speakers' First Amendment rights would have been pushed aside because of the allegedly "compelling" government interest in preventing corruption, or the "appearance of corruption," in the ensuing election.

But would there really have been a threat of corruption if CLITRIM had urged voters specifically to "vote against Jerome Ambro," as opposed to merely criticizing Ambro's voting record? And why should it be unlawful, as it is today, for a group of individuals to contribute more than $5,000 to a challenger's campaign that urges voters to "vote against the president this fall," but not to impress upon voters, as the National Committee for Impeachment tried to do, that the president's actions are so deleterious as to merit not merely defeat at the polls but impeachment once in office? Was the government not correct in believing that a two-page ad in the *New York Times* that urged voters to support impeachment of the president had as much potential to affect the outcome of the upcoming election as a $5,000 donation to the campaign of George McGovern, Nixon's opponent? Would McGovern, had he been elected, not have felt a debt of gratitude to the National Committee for Impeachment? Could not this debt of gratitude have had the potential to influence McGovern's actions as president? Wouldn't this be "undue" influence obtained through the expenditure of money?

Curiously, soon after the decision in *United States v. National Committee for Impeachment*, the Supreme Court held in the case of *Buckley v. Valeo* that, because of the compelling government interest in preventing "corruption" and the "appearance of corruption," the Constitution does not prohibit legislation that limits individual citizens to giving no more than $1,000 directly to a presidential candidate. But doesn't a $17,850 newspaper ad urging not the defeat but the impeachment of his opponent pose the same "threat of corruption?"

On April 27, 1988, Margaret McIntyre and two others stood outside of Blendon Middle School in the town of Westerville, Ohio, passing out handbills. Inside, employees of the Westerville public schools were holding a meeting to rally public support for an upcoming vote for higher school taxes. McIntyre, whose son attended Westerville schools, was passing out a handbill that criticized certain wasteful practices of the school board and listed various promises that the board had made, and allegedly later broken, since a previous tax-hike campaign. McIntyre had created the fliers on her home computer and paid to make several hundred copies at a local printing shop. She signed some of the fliers in her own name and others as "Concerned Parents and Taxpayers." After observing McIntyre, J. Michael Hayfield, an assistant superintendent in the Westerville school district, approached her and told her that her distribution of handbills violated state law. McIntyre, however, carried on. The tax increase was eventually defeated. Several months later, Hayfield filed charges against Margaret McIntyre for violating the Ohio Elections Code by distributing "anonymous" campaign literature, and McIntyre was fined by the Ohio Elections Commission.

The state law under which Margaret McIntyre was charged, found guilty, and fined is, unlike the FECA, relatively old; it dates back to the first wave of campaign laws passed in the United States in the early part of this century. The law was rarely enforced until the 1970s, however, when Watergate helped to foster an explosion of both new laws and media attention related to campaign finance. McIntyre's actions would seem to be the very core of First Amendment activity—true grassroots activism by a single, middle-class, suburban housewife. Yet the State of Ohio forced McIntyre to litigate against her punishment for six years before she was finally granted relief by the United States Supreme Court, which held that McIntyre's activities were constitutionally protected.[2] The Supreme Court pointed out that anonymous political activity has a long and honored place in American history, with past practitioners including, among others, Abraham Lincoln and the authors of the Federalist Papers. Unfortunately, McIntyre herself never saw her final triumph—she died during the course of the protracted legal proceedings.

During the litigation, one argument put forth by the state in defense of the statute was that enforcement was necessary in order to insure the integrity of state's campaign finance laws. After all, if campaigning can be done anonymously, how can the state keep track of who is contributing how much and to which campaigns? If it cannot do that, what is to prevent some people from spending or contributing large sums of money to support a candidate's bid for election? If a few Margaret McIntyres get caught in the way, is that not a small price to pay to assure "clean" elections? And, indeed, the Supreme Court's opinion included language to indicate that such anonymous speech might not be permitted in a candidate election—a position explicitly adopted by Justice Ruth Bader Ginsberg in a concurring opinion.

In the fall of 1998, Suffield, Connecticut resident Leo Smith was mad. The Republican majority in the U.S. House of Representatives appeared poised to impeach President Bill Clinton, and Smith didn't like it. On his computer, he designed a web page that urged viewers to "support President Clinton" and to defeat Connecticut Congresswoman Nancy Johnson, a Republican who was supporting the impeachment bid. He included links to other political sites critical of Republicans. He felt that he had done his part to participate in one of the great political debates of the day. And then Smith received a call from the campaign of Johnson's opponent, Charlotte Koskoff. Smith discerned that the Koskoff campaign was concerned that his website put both him and the campaign in violation of the Federal Election Campaign Act. Smith sought an advisory opinion from the Federal Election Commission.

In the ensuing advisory opinion, the FEC concluded that Smith's establishment of a web site counted as an independent expenditure in favor of Johnson's Democratic opponent, and so was subject to the reporting requirements of FECA.[3] There would be no more unregulated grassroots activity for Smith, lest his efforts corrupt, or create the appearance of corrupting, Representative Johnson or her opponent.

Unlike Margaret McIntyre, Leo Smith did not pursue his case to the Supreme Court, and if he had, he would probably have lost. Yet why should McIntyre's speech have greater constitutional protection than the speech of someone such as Leo Smith, simply because it related to an issue separate from any candidate campaign, whereas Leo Smith's speech criticized the actions of a person running for office and urged voters to defeat that candidate at the polls? Would it matter if Smith had spent thousands of dollars to design and promote his web site? If so, why? And if Smith's speech is subject to regulation, as the FEC claims, then we find ourselves in the curious position of providing greater constitutional protection to internet pornography, which is protected from regulation by the First Amendment, than to internet political speech.[4] Can this be how the nation's founders intended the First Amendment to be applied?

For nearly twenty years prior to 1996, Steve Forbes had written an opinion column in each issue of the business magazine that bears his family name. Before that, the column had been written by Forbes's father, and before that, by Forbes's grandfather, all the way back to the founding of the magazine in the early part of the century. In 1996, Forbes declared himself a candidate for the presidency of the United States. As a candidate, he continued to write his monthly column in *Forbes* magazine. He never discussed his candidacy, but he did discuss subjects such as abortion, taxes, term limits, the gold standard, and that most passionate of political issues, interleague baseball play. In September 1998, the Federal Election Commission instituted an action against Forbes, Inc., the publisher of *Forbes*. The FEC calculated the value of the columns to Forbes's presidential campaign at $94,900, and argued that by publishing the columns, Forbes, Inc. had violated the legal prohibition on corporate contributions to candidates. Oddly, Steve Forbes had already spent some $28 million of his personal fortune, largely made through Forbes, Inc., on his campaign.

As a candidate, the FEC argued, Forbes lost the right to speak to the public through his magazine columns, unless his campaign paid *Forbes* to publish the columns. In other words, as a candidate, Steve Forbes had fewer rights under the First Amendment than he did before declaring his candidacy. Such a theory seems preposterous, for it is hard to imagine a time when one would more want or need to exercise First Amendment rights than when one is running for office. Thus it was not altogether surprising when, just two months after filing suit, a rather embarrassed FEC, with three new commissioners on board, dropped its enforcement action against Forbes, Inc. Yet dropping the enforcement action raised questions as well. For it is clear that Forbes, Inc., or any other publisher of a newspaper or magazine, could give editorial space to writers other than the candidate to support or oppose various candidates for president or other federal office. Why should publishers have this power, but not candidates themselves? Why should a publishing corporation be able to devote substantial resources to supporting or opposing a candidate when a nonpublishing corporation cannot? This publishing dilemma raises other questions, such as whether to regard Internet web pages as publications. If a web page is considered a publication, should Leo Smith's Internet activities be exempt from reporting requirements? Or is the difference that Leo Smith has less First Amendment protection because he doesn't operate his web site for profit?

These five cases—the National Committee for Impeachment, Edward Cozzette and CLITRIM, Margaret McIntyre, Leo Smith, and Steve Forbes—are each problematic in their own way, yet they are not atypical of the world we have created in an effort to regulate campaign finance. Indeed, in many respects they barely scratch the surface of the intractable dilemmas that mark efforts to regulate campaign finance. None of the actions of any of these people posed any serious danger of political corruption, by any stretch of the imagination. It is true that the first three were all vindicated in the courts, that the FEC chose not to pursue Smith (although Smith closed his web site) and that the FEC dropped the Forbes case. Yet in each of the last several congresses laws have been drawn up, and in many cases nearly passed, that are far more restrictive of political speech than anything under which any of the above individuals were charged. If the polling data is accepted at face value, Americans approve of such restrictions on political speech and, in fact, would like to see more of it.

Meanwhile, pressure is growing for a "final solution" to the problem of First Amendment limits on government power, limits that forced the charges against the National Committee for Impeachment, CLITRIM, and Margaret McIntyre to be dismissed. In 1997, thirty-eight U.S. senators voted for a constitutional amendment that would have essentially repealed the First Amendment when it comes to political speech: the amendment would have allowed Congress to impose "reasonable" restrictions on political speech.[5] The amendment also had considerable support in the House. Richard Gephardt, the minority leader in the House and a supporter of the amendment, went so far as to tell *Time* magazine, "What we have is two important values in direct conflict: freedom of speech and our desire for healthy campaigns in a healthy democracy."[6] Similarly, New Jersey Representative Bill Pascrell, responding to a witness's comment that "the First Amendment promises us free elections," is reported to have replied, "I find that to be ludicrous."[7] Could it possibly be true? Are free speech and healthy campaigns incompatible? Is the idea that the government should not interfere with what and how much is said in political campaigns really "ludicrous"?

Or consider these comments from former Common Cause president Ann McBride. Appearing on national television in 1996, McBride stated, "at the same time there are efforts to regulate them, [you] have oil and gas companies, [you] have trial lawyers, [you] have all the major interests that have an outcome in the election and an outcome in policy being able to pour this money in . . . they want access to influence in the political process. It's corrupting."[8]

Are efforts to persuade fellow citizens how to vote "corrupting," or are they the essence of democracy? Consider the implications of McBride's statement. She is arguing, in essence, that those persons and interests that are affected by government policies and possibly subject to government regulation must give up their right to try to influence government policy. This is a far cry from "no taxation without representation." In fact, McBride seems to suggest that the very possibility of taxation ought to deprive one of the right to representation: "It's corrupting."

If the five cases discussed above indicate that something is wrong with the laws we have passed in an effort to regulate campaign finance, the words of Minority Leader Gephardt, Representative Pascrell, and Ann McBride indicate that perhaps our entire approach to the issue has gone dreadfully astray. It is hard to believe that one of the highest-ranking members of the United States House of Representatives would state that free speech and healthy campaigns are in irreconcilable conflict, without the slightest public outcry in response. It is hard to imagine how more than one-third of the U.S. Senate could vote to repeal the protections given by the First Amendment to political speech, with no more public debate or press coverage than is given to a routine highway funding bill. But it is true, and it is more believable once we recognize that this is the end result of a long and determined campaign to cheapen some types of political speech.

As long ago as 1989, Columbia Law School professor Martin Shapiro bemoaned the fact that "almost the entire first amendment literature produced by liberal academics in the past twenty years has been a literature of regulation, not freedom—a literature that balances away speech rights."[9] During the intervening years, the nature of that scholarship has grown still more radical. Today, in the pages of some of the nation's most prestigious law journals some of our most talented young legal scholars are arguing that the Constitution permits, or perhaps even requires, a ban on all partisan political speech, except to the extent authorized by a grant of government speech vouchers. If this seems like idle speculation from the ivory tower, it should be noted that what today are mainstream prescriptions for campaign finance "reform" were, just a few decades ago, considered equally radical, and that one such advocate, Edward Foley, formerly of the Ohio State University School of Law, was appointed Ohio state solicitor in 1999 by a conservative state attorney general.

When statements such as those of Richard Gephardt and Ann McBride can be made by prominent persons in national news media and create no stir at all, something has gone wrong with the way in which we think about political campaigns. This book is an effort to explain what has gone wrong, both at a political level and in constitutional doctrine. This is a book about campaign finance, but unlike most such books, it is not full of breathless innuendo about alleged "corruption" in politics, nor is it replete with cocktail party factoids aimed at making it seem as though political spending is beyond all control. Rather, this book asks the reader to reconsider the entire intellectual framework around which most of the nation's campaign finance regulation has been built. It asks the reader to begin by considering the possibility that virtually everything that the typical American knows, or thinks he knows, about campaign finance reform is wrong. And unlike most such books, it concludes not with any grand new scheme for "closing loopholes" or regulating the system, but for the readoption of a radical *old* approach to the question of campaign finance regulation.

Part I of this book explores how we arrived at our present state of campaign finance regulation, and how our existing efforts at regulation have not always worked as planned; Part II discusses the constitutional issues surrounding reform; Part III discusses the future of campaign finance regulation. In discussing this future, Part III suggests that we are rapidly approaching the day of reckoning, when we must either jettison our traditional First Amendment liberties, as Gephardt and others ask us

12

to do, or we must pull back, and return to the system of campaign finance "regulation" envisioned by the framers of the Constitution and enshrined in the First Amendment. I remain confident that when the American people understand the options available to them, they will choose the system chosen by the founders. This book is intended to present those options—plainly, if not always simply, for the issues are complex—to the people.

PART I
THE COST OF CAMPAIGNS
AND THE PRICE OF REFORM

Chapter 2

Money Talks: A Short History
of Campaign Spending,
Regulation, and Reform

To place modern issues of campaign finance in perspective, it is helpful to review, even briefly, the history of campaign finance and efforts to regulate political contributions and spending. In fact, casual observers are often shocked to discover that the regulation of political contributions and expenditures is a relatively recent phenomenon, even though the concerns that have led to such regulation have a long pedigree in American political life.

Early Days

In the colonial period and the early years of the Republic, campaign finance was not an issue. The reasons for this are neither hard to understand nor a source of hope for those who now seek to purge the political system of money. During the seventeenth and early eighteenth centuries, campaign finance was not an issue because most offices were not elected, and those that were frequently went uncontested. Even by the mid-eighteenth century, when contested elections become more common, the electorate still consisted of a relatively homogenous group of propertied white men.[1]

For example, in George Washington's first bid for the Virginia House of Burgesses in 1757, there were only 391 eligible voters; all owned real property, all were male, all were white. Nevertheless, Washington spent £39 to buy "treats" for voters, including 160 gallons of rum and other strong beverages, or more than a quart per eligible voter. In those early days, such expenses as existed usually went for food and drink, or the occasional pamphlet or piece of campaign literature, and were typically paid for by the candidate from his own pocket, which limited campaigning to the affluent. During this early period, a few states attempted to limit the practice of providing voters with food and drink. These laws did not regulate contributions to candidates or total spending by candidates, but merely regulated a type of spending by candidates that appeared to be little more than straightforward bribes for votes, the notion being that giving the man a quart of liquor is no different from paying a man $1 for his vote. But voters had come to expect such treatment, and the effort to outlaw the provision of food and drink did not meet with much success. Beyond these laws, candidates were left alone.[2] Indeed, many campaigns still provide prospective voters with free food and drink.

By the last decade of the eighteenth century, the rudiments of a party system were beginning to evolve, and both Federalist and Republican party interests turned to newspapers as a primary mechanism for political campaigning. Both sides subsidized partisan editors and publications, and arranged for copies of newspapers to be distributed free of charge. Thomas Jefferson, for one, spent considerable sums publishing partisan tracts and also raised money from Philadelphia citizens to support pro-Republican newspapers. In the 1820s, General Winfield Scott, second in command in the U.S. Army, was one prominent American who contributed substantial sums to start a partisan newspaper. Partisan pamphlets, or "circulars," were widely distributed in an effort to reach voters. Still, during this period, no truly national campaigns were waged, and many state level offices continued to be uncontested over lengthy periods.[3]

This relatively genteel system of upper-class politics began to change in the late 1820s, particularly after the campaign of 1828, in which Martin Van Buren organized the first popular mass campaign around Andrew Jackson. By this time, the electorate was growing rapidly, due to both population growth and the abolition of many property requirements for voting in the states.[4] Van Buren created a new type of campaign that involved newspapers, pamphlets, rallies, and candidate travel, in an effort to have the campaign communicate directly with large numbers of voters. It was Van Buren's democratization of the campaign process that created the need for significant spending. By the 1830s, most major offices were routinely contested by the two major parties, the Democrats and Whigs. Congressional races during this period typically cost $3,000 to $4,000, and the 1830 gubernatorial race in Kentucky was estimated to cost $10,000 to $15,000, or the equivalent of over $200,000 in 2000 dollars.

The new-style, mass-based political parties, however, still obtained financing from a small number of sources. Self-financing by candidates remained common, and well-heeled individuals began to contribute directly to campaigns. By the late 1830s, prominent New York Whigs such as Philip Hone and Thurlow Weed were helping to raise thousands of dollars for their party from friends and fellow merchants and bankers. Another development of the 1830s was the appearance of significant political spending by entities with no direct connection to a candidate. Most notable in this regard were the efforts of the United States Bank. After his victory in the presidential election of 1828, Andrew Jackson, a bitter opponent of the bank, sought to revoke the bank's federal charter. Not unlike the tobacco industry in the late 1990s, the bank was not content to sit by while the federal government sought to destroy it. Between 1830 and 1832, it spent approximately $42,000—an enormous sum at that time—on literature and advertisements in an effort to defeat Jackson in the election of 1832.[5] Though unsuccessful, the bank's efforts showed that the victims and beneficiaries of government policy will not sit idly by as their fates are decided. The bank's efforts were the forerunner of what we today call "issue advertising," that is advertising that discusses political issues with the hope that voters will oppose politicians who hold contrary views, without specifically calling for the election or defeat of any particular candidate.

Meanwhile, direct campaign spending continued to grow. In the presidential election of 1860, supporters of Abraham Lincoln reportedly spent over $100,000. Lincoln himself spent some $400 in 1860 to subsidize a Republican newspaper in Illinois. By 1872, the winning campaign of U. S. Grant cost approximately $250,000. Just four years later, in 1876, both Republican Rutherford B. Hayes and Democrat Samuel J. Tilden spent over $900,000, or more than $11 million in 2000 dollars.[6]

During both the antebellum and post–Civil War eras, a primary source of party funds was the practice of assessments on officeholders. With virtually all government jobs allotted on the basis of the "spoils" system, officeholders and government contractors were expected to contribute a portion of their salary or contract—usually 2 percent—as a condition of retaining office. The assessment system, first used by the Democrats in the 1830s, grew so rapidly that by 1878 approximately 90 percent of the Republican Party congressional committees' income came from assessments on officeholders. A bill was introduced to stop this practice as early as 1839, but it was not until the 1881 assassination of President Garfield by a disgruntled office seeker that the Pendleton Act created a civil service.[7] Although the Pendleton Act, which made it a crime for a federal employee to solicit funds from another federal employee, is often considered the first campaign finance bill, the motivation for the bill was the opposite of later efforts at reform. By limiting the ability of officeholders to extract contributions from those they appointed to office, civil service reform sought not to protect legislators or the government from the corrupting influence of contributions but rather to protect government employees from the power of government officials. Indeed, if one is concerned about the possibility that campaign contributions might corrupt officeholders, a system of finance based on assessments of party officeholders seems a benign, or even a positive idea: campaigns are financed by small contributors who care most about electoral outcomes, and there is no serious danger of quid-pro-quo corruption, at least in policymaking decisions.

The passage of the Pendleton Act, and similar laws at the state level, led to a steady decline in assessments as a source of revenue. To replace

20

this lost income, the parties increasingly relied on wealthy individuals for large donations. Wealthy donors were not entirely new, of course; in the antebellum era, the Democrats countered wealthy Whig supporters such as Thurlow Weed with their own donors, such as banker Augustus Belmont. In 1852, Belmont established the first national party committee, the Democratic National Committee, to help support the election of Franklin Pierce to the presidency. When contributions fell short of the target, Belmont made a large personal contribution. But with the decline of assessment income, these wealthy benefactors took on increased importance. For example, Belmont and his son, Augustus Belmont, Jr., remained major Democratic Party financial angels through the rest of the century, frequently contributing six-figure amounts in presidential campaigns. Other prominent Democrats in the postwar era included the party's 1876 presidential candidate, Samuel Tilden, and streetcar operator William Whitney. Tilden, a wealthy and incorruptible New York lawyer, contributed to several Democratic campaigns, including a contribution of $10,000 (the equivalent of over $100,000 today) to the 1868 campaign. Major Republican donors included, among others, railroad tycoon Jay Gould, John Jacob Astor, and department store magnate John Wannamaker.[8]

Big Money and the Beginning of Regulation

The campaign of 1888, in which Wannamaker contributed $50,000— roughly half a million in 2000 dollars—to Benjamin Harrison's presidential campaign, marked the full-scale development of a second new source of campaign cash: corporations. The Republicans were particularly aggressive in soliciting corporate cash; they sent letters to leading manufacturers detailing the benefits to them of the high tariffs that a Republican victory would guarantee, and urged contributions to assure that victory. Roughly 40 percent of Republican national campaign funds came from manufacturing and business interests in Pennsylvania, where the party's new national chairman, Matthew Quay, was party boss. State parties, both Republican and Democrat, were probably even more reliant on corporate funds.[9]

With the availability of corporate cash, campaign costs rose rapidly in the 1890s. In 1892, Chicago mayoral candidate Carter Henry Harrison reportedly spent $500,000 (approximately $8.7 million in year 2000 dollars), and a Chicago alderman candidate in 1895 raised a campaign fund of $100,000, more than $1.5 million in 2000 dollars and far more than is normally spent on such a race today. However, the latter candidate, "Hinky Dink" Kenna, lost—in part because his campaign kitty was stolen.[10]

Spending reached a peak in the presidential election of 1896, when the new Republican national chair, Ohio's Mark Hanna, systematized fund raising as no political operative had done before. To Hanna, a Republican victory over William Jennings Bryan, the "radical" proponent of silver money, was essential to the economic well-being of the country. Hanna, himself a wealthy businessman, personally contributed nearly $100,000 to help William McKinley win the Republican nomination, but Hanna recognized that far more would be needed for the general election. It was self-evident to Hanna that business would benefit from a victory by the hard-money, high-tariff Ohioan, McKinley. Thus, to Hanna it was only natural that business interests should support McKinley's campaign. Hanna methodically "assessed" the nation's leading businesses for campaign cash. Banks were generally assessed one quarter of 1 percent of their capital; other businesses were assessed flat amounts based on their ability to pay and perceived stake in the general prosperity. Scrupulously honest, Hanna saw his role as one of insulating McKinley from requests for favors. He would not accept contributions in exchange for promises of any kind—he rejected contributions that even implied a quid pro quo and refunded contributions from corporations that contributed more than their predetermined assessment. Hanna had no trouble raising funds in this manner—for the most part, businesses contributed to the McKinley campaign eagerly, not in the expectation of policy favors but out of fear of the consequences of a Bryan win, and in the firm conviction that a McKinley victory would benefit the economy generally. In this manner, Hanna raised as much as $7 million (equivalent to approximately $145 million in 1999) to support McKinley's campaign. This amount would not be reached again, even in nominal dollars, until 1936.[11]

Corporate funding remained vital to the Republicans even after Hanna left the scene. Although Theodore Roosevelt's trust-busting activities shook the faith that many businessmen had in Republican policies, corporate supporters of Roosevelt still contributed over 73 percent of the party's 1904 presidential funds. Businessmen who thought that they had "bought" Roosevelt, however, invariably came away disappointed, as Roosevelt routinely rejected corporate requests for both favors and appointments. Though heavily outgunned in raising business money, the Democrats also had major corporate contributors at the turn of the century, notably the silver mines that stood to benefit from Bryan's free-silver policy.[12]

Even as corporate money flooded into politics, large individual donors continued to grow in importance in late nineteenth and early twentieth centuries. In 1904, for example, Democratic candidate Alton B. Parker received approximately $700,000 from longtime party supporters August Belmont, Jr., and Thomas Fortune Ryan. Henry Davis, a mine owner and the party's vice-presidential nominee, also contributed heavily. At about this same time, both parties made major efforts to attract money from small donors, but had just enough success to make clear that although small donations could augment campaign funds, on the whole small donors alone would not contribute enough to run an effective national campaign. By 1928, both major parties still relied on contributions of $1,000 or more—enough to pay cash for two new cars—for nearly 70 percent of their income.[13]

During this period, campaign fund-raising began to be regulated for the first time. The first laws that would commonly be recognized today as campaign finance reform were passed in the 1897, when Nebraska, Missouri, Tennessee, and Florida banned corporate contributions. Significantly, each of these states had voted for William Jennings Bryan in the presidential election of 1896. The bans on corporate contributions were, in large part, an effort to retaliate against corporate support of Bryan's opponent, McKinley. Supporters of these measures certainly thought that they were acting to promote good government. Their idea of good government, unfortunately, involved silencing those with whom they disagreed.

The federal government did not become involved in campaign finance for another decade. Ironically, what triggered reform was an unrelated state investigation into insurance industry practices. In 1905, the state of New York held a legislative inquiry into the financial practices of the

Equitable Life Insurance Company. During the course of this investigation, it came out that the company had made large contributions to the Republican Party. Though corporate support for the GOP was well known before, the Equitable investigation took on the air of scandal. One judicial critic of corporate political contributions called such involvement "a menace to the state." The outcry eventually led to passage of the Tillman Act, the first federal ban on campaign contributions or spending. The Tillman Act, passed in 1907, banned contributions by federally chartered banks and corporations. The bill's chief sponsor, segregationist Senator "Pitchfork" Ben Tillman, argued, much as reform advocates do today, that the American people had come to believe that congressional representatives had become the "instrumentalities and agents of corporations."[14]

Although the Tillman Act may have reduced corporate participation in politics, it hardly served to eliminate it, for several reasons. First, corporations continued to donate a variety of goods and services in lieu of cash, including office space, typewriters, and free travel. Another way to donate "in-kind" services was to keep campaign officers on the corporate payroll during a campaign. Some corporate executives simply defied the law, viewing it much the same way most Americans would soon view prohibition: as something that turned reasonable and noncorrupting activity—in this case, political activism—into a crime. Other executives made large personal contributions with the knowledge that they would be reimbursed by their corporate employers. As one corporate board chairman stated nearly fifty years after passage of the Tillman Act, "A lot of corporate presidents just reach in the till and get $25,000 to contribute to political campaigns."[15] With the lack of any meaningful enforcement, such flouting of the law carried little risk. Thus the first federal foray into campaign finance had little practical effect other than to rechannel the way in which contributions were made.

In 1910, passage of the Publicity Act required the postelection disclosure, in House races, of each contributor of $100 or more (equal to about $1,667 in 2000), and of each recipient of $10 or more. Amendments passed the very next year required disclosures to be made at least ten days before the election, and extended the disclosure requirements to cover the Senate. The 1911 amendments also limited the amount that could be spent in Senate races to $10,000, and in House races to $5,000 (amounts equal to approximately $170,000 and $85,000 in 2000). Senator James Reed, who first proposed these spending limits, contended that they were necessary because only rich people could run for office, unless they were "willing to accept contributions from those institutions which may be interested in the legislation."[16]

However, like the Tillman Act of 1907, the Publicity Act had little effect, for four reasons. First, because Congress doubted its constitutional authority to regulate state and district committees under the Commerce clause, the law applied only to party committees operating in two or more states. Disclosure and spending limits could be avoided by party spending through state and district committees. Second, many observers interpreted the spending limits to apply only to the candidate, not to committees operating without the candidate's involvement. Thus these limits were easily evaded through the simple expedient of the candidate's "discreet ignorance" of what his supporters were doing. Third, the Supreme Court, in the 1921 case of *United States v. Newberry*, held that Congress lacked constitutional authority to regulate primary elections. This interpretation gutted the law in the deep South, where the Democratic nomination was tantamount to election. Finally, the law lacked any enforcement provision. The clerk of the House and the secretary of the Senate were responsible for receiving and filing reports, but neither had any authority to compel a committee to file a report, and no one was given authority to review the reports for errors. Thus the Publicity Act and its amendments did little to restrain spending other than to encourage the proliferation of committees and to redirect some spending from federal to state committees.[17]

The Beginning of Big Regulation

In 1925, in the wake of the Teapot Dome scandal, Congress again attempted to tighten the restrictions on campaign finance by passing the Federal Corrupt Practices Act. It is worth pointing out that Teapot Dome had little to do with campaign contributions. Warren Harding, the honest but unfortunate man who ended up presiding over the scandal, was, in fact, not even a "big money" candidate. In his campaign for the Republican presidential nomination, Harding relied on a small number of old friends and supporters to raise just $113,000. He was heavily outspent by his major rivals for the nomination, business favorite and retired General Leonard Wood, and Illinois governor and Pullman family in-law Frank Lowden. Even populist California Senator Hiram Johnson, who had once campaigned on the slogan "kick the corporations out of politics," outspent Harding by nearly two to one in the campaign for the nomination. And though the Republicans outspent the Democrats by a significant margin in the general election, they raised record amounts in small contributions. The oil leases at the heart of the scandal itself involved straightforward kickbacks—not campaign contributions—made to Interior Secretary Albert Fall, who was convicted under traditional bribery statutes.[18]

In the course of the Teapot Dome investigation, however, it came out that oilman Harry Sinclair had made large, though legal, political contributions in nonelection years. This allowed those contributions to escape disclosure under the Publicity Act, which only required disclosure of contributions made in an election year.[19] Although this pointed up the simple need to require disclosure of all campaign contributions, regardless of when made, the ensuing reforms were largely unrelated to the corruption that was used to justify them. It would not be the last time that efforts to regulate campaign finance reform would benefit from unrelated scandals. In any case, the Federal Corrupt Practices Act, passed in 1925, closed the nonelection-year loophole by requiring disclosure regardless of when the contributions were made. It raised the spending ceiling for some Senate races to $25,000, and required disclosure of all receipts by House and Senate candidates and by political committees operating in two or more states.[20]

Although the Corrupt Practices Act required reporting all expenditures made with a candidate's "knowledge or consent," most candidates interpreted this as applying to their personal expenditures only; they did not routinely report committee expenses. Similarly, the spending limits, which were in any event substantially out of date with the rise of radio advertising, were ignored by establishing numerous committees, each of which could spend up to the limit. National parties could avoid disclosure by running money through state committees. In addition, the disclosure provision lacked an enforcement mechanism and had no provision to correct errors. Indeed, there would not be a single successful prosecution under the act in the forty-six years it was law.[21]

Another method to get around the ban on corporate donations was pioneered by the Democratic Party in the election of 1936. The Democrats produced a book for their national convention, which contained pictures of and flattering articles on the party's candidates. Advertising space was sold to corporate sponsors, with full-page ads running $2500. Books were then sold to corporations and others at prices ranging from bargain editions selling for $2.50 to $100 deluxe editions autographed by President Franklin Roosevelt. The party raised some $250,000 in this manner, and such books became a regular fund-raising tactic of both parties in future elections through 1972.[22]

By the late 1930s, both Republicans and conservative Southern Democrats were concerned that New Deal programs were being used to create a political power base for Roosevelt. Through the government's various public works programs, large numbers of people were being added to the government payroll, but outside of the civil service protections of the Pendleton Act. Roosevelt's political opponents alleged that government employees in the Works Progress Administration were being forced to make campaign contributions. A coalition of Republicans and conservative Democrats, led by New Mexico Senator Carl Hatch, combined to pass the Hatch Act in 1939. The Hatch Act extended the ban on political contributions beyond the civil service to include any government employee. However, unlike the earlier Pendleton Act, which aimed to protect citizens from government exploitation, the Hatch Act was intended to strike at Democratic Party funding and Franklin Roosevelt's political power.[23] In 1940, the Hatch Act was amended to add a ban on donations by federal contractors or by employees of state agencies financed in whole or in part by the federal government. Also, contributions to national committees were limited to $5,000, and total spending by national committees was limited to $3 million. In the years that followed, however, the contribution limits were avoided by having amounts over $5,000 be paid to state and local committees. Spending limits were avoided through the simple expedient of establishing a variety of "nonparty" organizations and multiple committees, so that even in the year the bill was passed both parties spent more than twice the $3 million limit.

During this same period, Republicans sought to ban political spending by labor unions, which went almost entirely to support Democrats. In 1936 organized labor contributed an estimated $770,000 from union treasuries to Franklin Roosevelt's reelection campaign. In 1943, in the wake of a bitter strike by the United Mine Workers, Republicans capitalized on fears that unchecked union power might damage the war effort, to pass the Smith-Connally Act. One provision of the act prohibited labor unions from contributing to campaigns for the duration of the ongoing world war. Unions circumvented this ban by establishing the first political action committees, or PACs, which collected money from members through automatic payroll check-offs, and then used that money to make contributions to candidates. Additionally, lawyers for the Congress of Industrial Organizations (CIO) interpreted the law as applying only to contributions to candidates, and not to expenditures made independently from candidates. Therefore, they reasoned, unions were free to engage in other political activity that assisted Democratic candidates. Thus the unanticipated result of the Smith-Connally Act was actually to increase labor union involvement by institutionalizing a system for political giving—the PAC—and by focusing organized labor's attention even further on politics. As a result, the CIO-PAC alone spent almost $2 million to support Democrats in the election of 1944.[24]

In 1947, the first Republican-controlled Congress in sixteen years made the ban on union contributions permanent, but also went further to ban all union expenditures on political activity, including even internal communications with members. A portion of the Taft-Hartley Act would have prevented any communication paid for from the general treasury of the union, including, for example, an editorial endorsing a candidate in the union's house newspaper. Unions decided to challenge the law immediately, and within weeks the CIO News published an editorial endorsing a Democratic candidate in Maryland. The government brought an indictment against the CIO. Eventually the Supreme Court, in a rather twisted ruling that defied the legislative debate behind Taft-Hartley, held that the act was not intended to ban such internal communications, after all. Four justices, however, would have ruled that the act did intend to ban such communications, and that such a ban was an unconstitutional infringement of First Amendment rights.[25] It seems unlikely that any of the nine justices would have voted to upheld a ban on union communications to members. The case is important, however, because it marks the first attempt by a legislature not merely to ban contributions to a candidate but also to limit all political speech by political opponents, in this case unions.

Despite the Supreme Court's ruling in *United States v. CIO*, in 1957 the Justice Department sought to indict the United Auto Workers for violating Taft-Hartley's ban on external communications aimed at the general public. Again, the unions argued that such a ban was unconstitutional. The Supreme Court ducked the issue on procedural grounds and returned the matter to the district court, which acquitted the union in a jury trial.[26] Nevertheless, after *United States v. United Auto Workers*, the unions generally halted direct communications to the general public. After all, they didn't need to make such communications: money from automatic dues check-offs rolled into their PACs, allowing them to make sizeable contributions to candidates from the PACs rather than from the union treasuries. Meanwhile, their internal communications reached millions of members and helped the unions to organize thousands of "volunteers" to staff phone banks, register voters, and otherwise assist candidates. Still, *United States v. United Auto Workers* marked the first time that a group had been hauled into court for daring to speak directly to the public about political issues. In this respect, the case presaged today's political fights over bans on "issue advocacy," those ads which do not urge the election or defeat of specific candidates but attack the policy positions of various individuals who may be candidates for federal office. Meanwhile, unions continued to fund the administrative expenses of their PACs out of general treasury dues, arguing that these expenses were not political expenses or contributions as they did not support or oppose candidates—that was done with the money contributed to the PAC through voluntary contributions, mainly in the form of automatic dues check-offs.

Although nothing prohibited corporations from following labor's example and organizing PACs to avoid the restrictions on direct contributions to candidates, few did so. This was in part because it was doubted that corporations could legally use corporate funds even to establish and administer a PAC. More important, however, was the fact that corporate PACs seemed unnecessary since executives often made large contributions that were reimbursed by the corporation, and with the lack of enforcement many corporations simply contributed directly, in spite of the law.

Campaign spending had crept up only gradually from the turn of the century through the 1940s, dampened in part by the Great Depression and World War II, which naturally limited the resources that could be spent on political activity. In inflation-adjusted dollars, combined Republican and Democratic spending in the 1948 presidential election was the lowest since 1880. In 1952, however, yet another wave of spending growth began. Coincidentally, 1952 was the year in which a government freeze on new television stations ended, and in the years after 1952 television became an increasingly important, and expensive, part of campaigning. Combined political spending at the local, state, and federal levels grow rapidly after 1952, from $140 million for the two-year election cycle culminating in the presidential election of 1951–1952, to $200 million in 1963–1964, and to $540 million in 1975–1976.[27]

Between 1950 and the passage of the Federal Election Campaign Act amendments of 1974, a handful of candidates, such as presidential candidates Barry Goldwater in 1964 and George McGovern in 1972, were able to raise large sums from a broad base of small donors. Large contributions continued to dominate campaign funding, however, as in 1968, when insurance executive Clement Stone and his wife contributed $2.8 million to Richard Nixon's successful presidential campaign.[28]

Throughout this period, efforts were made to pass various "clean elections" bills. As usual, complaints were voiced that money has made "some citizens more equal than others," and that the political process had become "corrupt."[29] Restrictions on spending and contributions were required because "radio and television advertising eat up millions."[30] As we have seen, previous efforts to limit contributions and spending, or even to require disclosure of contributions, had been largely evaded through the exploitation of what would today be called "loopholes," so that reform had done little but rechannel contributions and spending. Thus, a push began for legislation that would be much more heavy-handed than prior reform efforts. This effort led to the passage of the Federal Elections Campaign Act in 1971 and even more far-reaching reform in 1974.

30

The Federal Election Campaign Act was passed to replace the old Federal Corrupt Practices Act. It significantly tightened disclosure requirements, eliminating most of the old loopholes in the law. Penalties were put in place for failure to make proper disclosures. Operating on the theory that disclosure would eliminate political quid pro quos, the act abolished the old, unenforced expenditure ceilings. At the same time, it limited total media spending in congressional races, and also limited the percentage of media spending that could go toward radio and television advertising.[31] Meanwhile, beginning in the spring of 1968 and accelerating once Republicans regained the White House in the elections that November, the Justice Department had again been questioning the legalities of union PAC structures and the practice of using union dues to defray PAC operating expenses. In the 1971 FECA debate, Labor, seeking to fend off what it considered to be a politically motivated effort to stifle political activity by union members, lobbied hard for a provision that expressly sanctioned the use of union dues to communicate with members and to set up and administer PACs. In the political bargaining that took place, this provision was expanded to include corporations, as well. By the time of the 1972 elections, over ninety corporate PACs were operating at the federal level.[32] By the end of the decade, over a thousand PACs were operating at the federal level. Once again, the results of reform were surprising: a measure intended to strengthen union political activity led instead to increased, and institutionalized, corporate political activity.

Watergate, Buckley v. Valeo, and the 1974 FECA Amendments

FECA had not been long in place when the Watergate scandals of 1972–1974 broke. The FECA had not made it clear whether contributions made between the last filing required under the old Federal Corrupt Practices Act and the effective date of FECA had to be disclosed. The Nixon campaign took the position that they did not, and refused to disclose contributions made during that period. When it was finally forced by court order to disclose these contributions, in September 1973, it was revealed that the committee had received over $11 million during that period, mostly in large contributions, and much within the last forty-eight hours before

FECA took effect. Included in these contributions were $100,000 from financier Robert Vesco and some $2 million in dairy industry contributions. It was also revealed that at least $10 million in illegal corporate contributions had gone to the campaign before passage of FECA, and that campaign money had been used both to fund and cover up the Watergate break-in.[33]

If these revelations, and the public reaction to them, proved anything, it was that good, enforceable disclosure laws, such as those passed in 1971, would work. Once Nixon's campaign finances and expenditures were revealed, public reaction was harsh, and undoubtedly contributed to the electoral pasting the Republicans suffered in the 1974 congressional elections. Had these disclosure provisions been in place throughout the 1968–1972 period, it seems unlikely that the Nixon administration would have risked a voter backlash by engaging in such unsavory and illegal activities. If such practices had occurred, they would have been revealed earlier, and undoubtedly used against the president in the 1972 campaign. But rather than revel in the triumph of disclosure, the reform lobby used the scandals to push for much tighter restrictions on campaign financing. They succeeded with the passage of sweeping amendments to FECA in 1974.

The Federal Election Campaign Act of 1971, coupled with the 1974 amendments to the act, set up a regime of campaign finance regulation based on four principles: enforceable disclosure provisions; public financing of presidential races; limits on contributions; and limits on spending. The disclosure provisions, enacted in 1971, we have already discussed. The added wrinkle of the 1974 amendments was to lodge the responsibility for enforcing these provisions, and making the disclosure public, in the hands of a new independent administrative agency, the Federal Election Commission. Public financing of presidential races, and contribution and spending limits on all races, were enacted as part of the 1974 amendments.

The 1974 FECA amendments first created a system of taxpayer financing for presidential races. Funding would come from a voluntary $1 checkoff on individual income tax returns (later changed to $3). Candidates who pursued their party's nomination would be eligible for "matching funds" from the federal treasury once they had raised at least $5,000 in contributions of $250 or less in each of twenty states. Candidates who met that threshold would receive a dollar-for-dollar match, up to $250 for each private contribution received. To receive federal funds in the primaries, candidates would agree to both global and state-by-state spending limits. Additionally, the amendments provided for taxpayer funding of the major party nominating conventions and of the general election. Candidates could choose not to participate in the federal funding system, but candidates who accepted federal funds would have to agree not to spend more in the general election than the amount provided by the government.

In addition to this system of presidential campaign financing, the 1974 amendments sought to limit the size of contributions to all candidates for all elected federal offices. It placed a $1,000 limit on individual contributions and a $5,000 limit on contributions by political action committees (PACs) to candidates for federal office. These limits were made applicable to each election, so that an individual or PAC could make one contribution up to the limit in a primary and a second contribution for the general election. Individuals were also limited to contributing no more than $25,000 in an election cycle. Furthermore, donors would be prohibited from spending more than $1,000 in any election cycle "relative to a clearly identified candidate." All of these limits would also apply to candidates spending money on behalf of their own candidacy.[34] However, the 1974 amendments repealed the old Hatch Act provision that barred federal contractors from establishing PACs, noting that the ban limited speech not only by corporate actors but also by unions and employees associated with federal contractors.[35]

Finally, the 1974 amendments sought to limit total spending on House and Senate races to amounts wholly inadequate for modern campaigning, especially for challengers. The act set expenditure limits at just $75,000 for House races. Adjusted for inflation, that would be approximately $220,000 in 2000, or far below the amounts needed to challenge successfully an incumbent congressperson. Limits on Senate races were based on population, starting from a base of $250,000.[36] These limits applied not only to direct candidate spending but also to any spending "relative to a clearly identified candidate." Thus, the law purported to regulate expenditures made by uncoordinated, noncandidate individuals and groups both in direct support of a candidate ("Vote for Smith") and expenditures made that would have only the indirect effect of supporting or opposing a candidate ("write to Congressman Smith and tell him you oppose his proposal to cut social security benefits").

The 1974 amendments were almost immediately challenged in court by a diverse groups of plaintiffs including, among others, Conservative Senator James Buckley, the American Civil Liberties Union, and the Libertarian Party. The story of the lawsuit *Buckley v. Valeo* is fascinating, but need not concern us here. The constitutional issues raised by *Buckley* will be discussed at length in Part II, but it will suffice to note here that the Supreme Court agreed with the plaintiffs' constitutional challenges on a number of issues.

The Court held that limits on campaign contributions do infringe on the First Amendment right to free speech, and that only the prevention of corruption or the "appearance of corruption" was a sufficiently weighty government concern to justify these infringements. The Court then held that large contributions might have the potential to lead to quid-quo-pro corruption, and that this protential justified the act's limits on contributions and provisions for disclosure. The Court struck down as unconstitutional, however, restrictions on total spending and on candidate spending from personal resources.[37] Spending the money raised pursuant to the act's contribution limits, the Court held, posed no threat of corruption, and thus the speech restraints of spending limits could not be justified by the need to prevent corruption. In other words, the Court held that spending money poses no danger of trading favors or votes for campaign cash— only the act of raising money does so.

Similarly, the Court struck down limits on spending "relative to a clearly identified candidate." The Supreme Court recognized that the vague wording, "relative to a . . . candidate," if given a broad reading, would have a chilling effect on the ability of citizens to talk about issues, which the court correctly noted was hopelessly intertwined with discussions of political candidates.[38] To use an easy example, many pieces of legislation are best known by the names of their sponsors rather than their official title—such as the Taft-Hartley Act, the Hatch Act, or the McCain-Feingold bill. More generally, candidates and issues are typically discussed in tandem. If spending were banned anytime it raised issues "relative to"

34

a candidate, it could become almost impossible to engage in paid political discourse on current affairs. Thus the Court held that such language must be interpreted to apply only to expenditures that used "express terms" of support for or against a candidate, such as "vote for," "vote against," "support," and the like. To the extent individuals might speak under these guidelines, the 1974 FECA amendments would still have limited such expenditures to just $1,000, meaning, in effect, that no citizen could make any significant financial effort to convince the public to support a candidate, even if done anonymously and independently of a candidate. Having held that only express advocacy was subject to regulation, the Court went on to strike down the $1,000 limit on independent expenditures that expressly advocated the election or defeat of a candidate, arguing that if the independent actor were truly acting independently, no danger of quid-pro-quo corruption existed. The court noted, wisely, that such independent expenditures might not even help a candidate, since they could cause a candidate to lose control of his or her campaign and message. The Court did hold that voluntary limits on spending, such as those created for the presidential system, were constitutional.

The 1974 FECA amendments, as modified in *Buckley*, remain the basic framework for federal campaign finance laws at the beginning of the twenty-first century, with one important exception. In 1978, the Federal Election Commission ruled that the national parties could use a mixture of funds raised pursuant to the federal limits, and funds raised pursuant to state law, to pay for such grassroots party-building activities as buttons, bumper stickers, brochures, posters, local offices, yard signs, voter registration, and get-out-the-vote drives. The commission's theory was that these party-building activities affect both state and federal elections, and so could be paid for with a mix of funds raised under both federal and state law, and apportioned to reflect the relative state and federal impact of the activities. In 1979, Congress seemed to endorse this emphasis on grassroots political activity, amending the FECA to allow parties to spend unlimited sums of money raised pursuant to the federal rules for these grassroots activities, without counting such expenditures as "contributions" to federal candidates. These funds, raised for purposes other than the express advocacy of the election or defeat of candidates for federal office, soon became known as "soft money."[39]

Despite the Supreme Court's evisceration of spending limits, the fact is that the Court upheld most of the act, including what many reform advocates considered to be the most crucial part of the law—contribution limits. By the 1976 elections, the United States had entered a period of unprecedented regulation of political speech in federal elections. No individual could contribute more than $1,000 to a single candidate in a federal election, nor more than $25,000 total. No group of individuals, or PAC, no matter how many people it represented, could contribute more than $5,000 to a candidate in any election. Direct corporate and union contributions from the general treasury were barred. An independent government agency was in place to press charges against violators. Presidential races would be publicly funded, with limits on total spending.

As a federal law, FECA did not, of course, regulate contributions for state campaigns, leaving states free to set their own rules for state elections. Several, such as Virginia, had still not moved to regulate their campaign finance systems by the year 2000, with no obviously harmful effects. However, within a few years of the passage of FECA, a majority of states adopted some variation of the federal model of regulation, with disclosure and contribution limits, although only a handful of states have any sort of tax funding for candidates. By the mid-1970s, the great part of the battle for campaign finance "reform" had been won.

Yet, within a few years of the passage of the 1974 FECA amendments, strange things began to happen. Incumbent reelection rates began to rise, reaching record levels in the late 1980s and setting off a nationwide craze for term limits. Incumbents actually increased their fund-raising advantage over challengers after FECA was passed, from approximately 1.5 to one to more than four to one. Total spending on congressional campaigns continued to rise, by nearly 400 percent from 1976 through 1998, and candidates began to spend more time, rather than less, raising money for campaigns. Special interests, instead of declining in influence, actually seemed to grow in influence and importance.[40]

Strange things also began to happen to the way in which campaigns were run in America. Corporate PACs proliferated, institutionalizing corporate giving as never before. A cadre of professional campaign lawyers and consultants sprang up, locking out true grassroots movements. These lawyers and consultants, in addition to handling the legal work of setting

36

up the proliferating PACs, developed new techniques to raise and spend money—techniques that often offered less accountability than anything done before. One such technique was called "bundling," a tactic by which an interest group solicits members and supporters to write campaign checks to candidates but then to send them to the interest group, which delivers them, "bundled," to the candidate. Because the checks came from individuals, disclosure reports no longer revealed that they were collected by the interest group. Thus the interest groups might still receive private credit for large contributions, but the ability of the public quickly and easily to trace those contributions to the interest groups declined. Much like the old convention books, corporate sponsors were solicited to cover various expenses at national conventions.

Moreover, a marked shift began by which candidates became less and less important to the campaign itself. By the mid-1990s, interest groups, which were prohibited by FECA from supporting candidates directly, learned that they could influence voters and operate free from government regulations by running large-scale advertising campaigns that attacked the records of various candidates, without ever urging voters specifically to vote for or against a candidate. By the end of the decade, these "issue ads" were an increasingly important element of American politics. The ads were typically more negative than traditional candidate ads, which added to public concern about "negative" campaigning. Political parties also began to exercise their free-speech rights through issue ads, and raised funds in large contributions for that purpose. Because this "soft money" was not being used to support any particular candidate, it was not subject to the limitations of FECA, as interpreted in *Buckley v. Valeo*. With issue ads expanding left and right, candidates began to complain that they were no longer able to set their own campaign agenda, yet by the late 1990s, most candidates, especially challengers, realized that large issue-advocacy campaigns were very important to their election chances.

Other results affected the public more directly. Public confidence in government, measured in both polling data and voter turnout in elections, continued to decline. The percentage of the public willing to support the public financing of presidential campaigns with even $1 to $3, the amount provided for on the federal tax return check-off, peaked in the early 1980s at less than 30 percent and steadily declined until, by 1999, barely 10 percent of taxpayers made the contribution. It became all but impossible to run a campaign for any state or elective office without first contacting a lawyer. Meanwhile, ordinary citizens found themselves hauled into court for distributing homemade political leaflets and for criticizing local officials for government cost overruns. Retirees with no legal experience found themselves in violation of federal law for writing checks to support the political candidates of their choice. Individuals who joined professional groups in order to get information on political issues found that flow of information blocked by threats of litigation, based on the idea that such communications would constitute an illegal campaign contribution. Indeed, litigation itself became a major campaign tactic.[41]

These consequences, however, did not lead the major "reform" lobbying groups to reevaluate their legislative goals. Instead, these groups stepped up their campaign to control political speech. The Herculean effort of cleaning up campaign finance, they argued, had only begun; if the FECA seemed to have failed, it was only because far more regulation was needed.

And so we arrived at the dawn of the twenty-first century. The first federal effort to reform campaign finance was made in 1907, and the law had been amended to close "loopholes" or add further restrictions in 1910, 1911, 1925, 1939, 1940, 1943, 1947, 1971, 1974, and 1979. After nearly a hundred years of trial and error, it is fair to ask, "will anything work?"

Chapter 3

FAULTY ASSUMPTIONS OF
CAMPAIGN FINANCE REFORM

Perhaps, if past efforts to regulate campaign spending and giving have failed to achieve their objectives,
we have misdiagnosed the problems. Thus the starting point for reform should be to examine the way
in which campaign contributions affect the political
system in practice.

Campaign finance regulation is generally assumed
to be necessary to achieve two important societal objectives: the promotion of political equality, and the
prevention of political corruption. In recent years, a
third objective, that of reducing the time spent on
fund-raising by legislators, has come to the fore. I
have chosen not to devote space to this argument
because the increased time that legislators spend

raising campaign funds seems to be such a direct and obvious consequence of laws that restrict the size of contributions. That is to say, the problem exists primarily, if at all, because of past efforts at regulation. It is one more cost of a heavily regulated system. However, it has not historically been an argument against a deregulated system.[1]

The arguments for both equality and the prevention of corruption rest on a combination of empirical and theoretical assumptions about how money should and actually does work in the political process. This chapter examines the empirical underpinnings of the case for "reform" as that term has historically been used—that is to say, more regulation. Arguments that favor increasing limitations on private contributions to and spending by candidates and political committees rely generally on one of four allegedly factual observations: first, too much money is spent on political activity; second, campaigns funded with large contributions are not representative of public opinion, and tend to drown out campaigns that would otherwise more directly address voter concerns, leaving voters without desirable choices; third, a candidate's spending largely determines electoral results, that is, money "buys" elections, in essence making the right to vote meaningless; and fourth, money exerts a powerful corrupting influence on the legislature. Given these alleged truths, it is argued that the end result of an unregulated system of campaign finance will be a corrupt political process increasingly dominated by wealthy individuals and corporations whose interests are at odds with those of "ordinary" citizens. Not all of these empirical assumptions are shared, of course, by all proponents of greater regulation, and some have more empirical support than others. Each includes certain tacit assumptions about how representative government ought to work. Nevertheless, together they represent the general empirical arguments for reform, as opposed to the more theoretical argument that all citizens ought to have "equal" influence in politics, or that equality requires equal spending—concepts discussed more fully elsewhere in this work. For now, the question to address is whether or not these empirical assumptions are warranted. Do they really represent the reality of money in politics? In this chapter, I argue that each is at best vastly overstated, at worst plainly wrong.

Campaign Spending Is Too High

Is too much money spent on political campaigns? One poll found that a whopping 90 percent of respondents agreed with the proposition that "there's way too much money in politics," and other polls have reported similar results.[2] The language in which campaigns are described in the general press certainly suggests that too much is spent. Candidates "amass war chests" with the help of "special interests" that "pour" their "millions" into campaigns. "Obscene" expenditures "careen" out of control or "skyrocket" upward. But to say that too much money is spent on campaigning is to beg the question of how much ought to be spent.

Within academic circles, even many advocates of regulation scoff at the notion that too much is spent on political campaigns. Marlene Nicholson, for example, writes that the overall level of spending is "a non-battle. . . . No thoughtful student of campaign finance will dispute . . . this point, despite the fact that demagogues may occasionally still argue to the contrary." Nevertheless, Nicholson admits that "reform proposals designed by Democrats in Congress routinely include overall expenditure limitations," and she herself, like many other academic writers, supports spending limits.[3] At a minimum, it may be fair to say that many of those who don't think that "too much" is spent on campaigns nevertheless see little harm in lowering the amounts spent.

In the two-year election cycle that culminated in the elections of November 1998, approximately $740 million were spent by all congressional general election candidates. Although this set a new record for spending in congressional races, the amount is hardly exorbitant, amounting to roughly $4 per eligible voter spent over the two-year period. Total direct campaign spending for all local, state, and federal elections, including those for Congress, over the same period can be reasonably estimated as between $1.5 and $2.0 billion, or somewhere between $7.50 and $10 per eligible voter for all elections over the two-year cycle. Early estimates for the 2000 campaign indicated total spending might reach as much as $3.0 billion, a substantial increase from the prior presidential cycle that ended in 1996.[4] Neverthless, even such a substantial increase would amount to no more than some $15 per eligible voter. When one

41

considers that this is spread over many candidates across a two-year election cycle, it is hard to suggest that office seekers are spending "obscene" sums in the attempt to get their messages through to voters. Indeed, total U.S. political expenditures constitute just .05 percent of gross domestic product. On a per-voter basis, the United States spends less on political activity than several other democracies, including some that are considerably poorer.

We might also compare political spending to amounts spent by Americans on various other products. For example, Americans spent two to three times as much money each year on the purchase of potato chips. Procter & Gamble and Phillip Morris Company, the nation's two largest advertisers, spend roughly the same amount on advertising as is spent by all political candidates and parties. In 1994, California congressman Michael Huffington drew a great deal of criticism for spending over $20 million of his own money on a U.S. Senate race. Shortly after Huffington concluded his campaign, Sony Music International announced plans to spend some $30 million to promote a Michael Jackson CD with the lyrics, "Jew me, sue me, everybody do me, kick me, kyke me, don't you black or white me." In 1995, approximately $100 million was spent to advertise syndicated reruns of the television comedy "Seinfeld."[5] This was substantially more than the 1996 general election budgets of presidential candidates Bill Clinton, Bob Dole, or Ross Perot. The value of such comparisons can be disputed: if one views the problem as the allegedly corrupting effect of campaign money, an issue we take up shortly, then the suggestion that it may take less to buy politicians than to sell soap, tobacco, music, or TV reruns is of little comfort. But such numbers are useful to put spending into perspective where the raw levels of spending are challenged, and to consider the probable effect on political communication of reform measures that would limit spending.

Increased campaign spending does translate into a better-informed electorate. Observers unfamiliar with the data are often shocked by the extreme ignorance of the American electorate. For example, in December 1994, one month after the 1994 congressional campaigns in which Newt Gingrich's campaign strategy and policy stances had received massive coverage in the press, 57 percent of Americans had never heard of Gingrich. Nevertheless, as Professor Gary Jacobson has shown, "the extent and content of information [voters] do have has a decisive effect on how they vote." But how is a candidate to get information to voters? A typical district for the United States House of Representatives has over 300,000 people of voting age. To reach these potential voters directly, without relying on the filter of the press, requires the expenditure of money. One analyst has calculated that a candidate for president who hopes to reach each potential voter with ten short ads on cable, local, and network television; three thirty-minute "fireside chats" on cable television; five radio ads and one newspaper ad in each major metropolitan paper; two pieces of direct mail literature; a videocassette, and the traditional buttons, bumper stickers, and billboards, would need to spend upward of $600 million, or nearly ten times what presidential candidates were given in federal funds for the 2000 general election.[6] Without such spending, candidates are at the mercy of a small group of professional journalists to interpret and inform the public of the candidate's message.

It is hard to take seriously the proposition that too much money is spent on political campaigns in some absolute sense. What then, accounts for the widespread public perception that too much is spent, besides the demagoguery of some journalists and reform advocacy groups? It may be the belief that what is spent is largely ineffective or even destructive. In other words, the perceived problem, on closer examination, may not be that too much is spent but that too little benefit is received in return. Campaigns are viewed as vacuous and empty. In particular, advocates of reduced spending have often managed to link high spending to the disgust that many voters feel over what is perceived as the relentless negativity of modern, televised campaign advertisements. If spending has little social value, there may be little cost to regulating it.

Not all negative advertising is created equal, of course. It may be true that some voters are "turned off" by negative ads, and that excessive negativity can create an unhealthy level of distrust and cynicism.[7] But besides being popular with voters, in the sense that many voters respond to them, negative ads can also serve valuable purposes. As Bruce Felknor, former executive director of the Fair Campaign Practices Committee, has stated, "without attention-grabbing, cogent, memorable, negative campaigning, almost no challenger can hope to win unless the incumbent has just been found guilty of a heinous crime." It is a mistake to assume that the elimination of negative campaigning would necessarily serve the public. Negative advertising that is relevant to the issues can serve the public well. Felknor notes that without negative campaigning aimed at showing up an opponent's bad side, "any knave or mountebank in the land may lie and steal his or her way into the White House or any other elective office." He thus distinguishes between "fair" and "unfair" campaigning, based on truth and relevance. To suggest that candidates should not point to each other's perceived shortcomings, writes Felknor, is "preposterous." Irresponsible negative campaigning may harm political debate, but efforts to expose corruption, unpopular positions, or weak character in an opponent are vital to having an informed electorate.[8]

Efforts to limit spending on campaigns—either directly, through spending limits, or indirectly, through contribution limits—bear no relationship to the negativity of the campaign, and may actually cause an increase in unfair, negative campaigning. Less spending only reduces the amount of communication; it does not mitigate any negative tone of that communication. In fact, the likely consequence of a reduction in spending would be to make well-produced negative advertising more valuable. Negative ads are used because they work. They are memorable, and voters act on the information they contain. If less were spent, candidates would need to maximize the political mileage from each expenditure, and negative ads may be an effective formula for doing so. More perniciously, candidates who have reached a spending limit would be unable to respond to late, false, and unfair negative assaults.

The best response to irrelevant or false and misleading negatives ads is an informed electorate. Spending money helps to create that informed electorate. Studies show that voter understanding of issues does, in fact, increase with the quantity of campaign information received. Most obviously, higher spending allows for more advertisements, especially more television advertisements. Somewhat less recognized is that the repetition inherent in television advertisements is one of the most important factors in voter education. Studies show that campaign spending increases the ability of voters to identify candidates on issues and ideology, and particularly affects the accuracy of the public's perception of incumbent ideology. Moreover, higher spending does not result in higher levels of voter cynicism or distrust, which suggests that efforts to link negative

44

campaigns to high spending are, as theory would suggest, wrong. Spending less on campaigns will, in most cases, result in less public awareness and understanding of issues.[9] A public that is less aware of a candidate's positions on issues and less able accurately to place the candidate on an ideological spectrum is more likely to be fooled by inaccurate or irrelevant negative ads.

Ultimately, there are no objective criteria by which to measure whether "too much" is spent on political campaigns. What is spent on campaigns, we might fairly say, is the amount that individuals feel it is worthwhile to contribute and candidates find it is effective to spend. Considering the importance of elections to any democratic society, it is hard to believe that direct expenditures of approximately $15 per voter for all local, state, and national campaigns over a two-year period requires, on its face, government regulation and limitations on spending. Indeed, the opposite conclusion seems more plausible: given the level of voter ignorance, and the positive effects that candidate spending has been shown to have in overcoming that ignorance, the goal should be to increase spending. The emphasis on reducing spending, whether for its own sake or in the interest of addressing alleged ills such as corruption or the need of legislators to devote time to fund-raising, may add to other problems, such as voter ignorance and false and misleading campaigning.

Campaigns Based on Small Contributions Are More Democratic and Better Represent Public Opinion

Within the reform movement lies a deep-rooted assumption that political campaigns in a democracy, if not financed by the government, should be financed by small contributions. This assumption often flows from the belief that large contributions corrupt either or both the electoral and legislative systems. However, the assumption often exists independently of other interests, on the apparent belief that even if money were not corrupting, small contributions epitomize the American belief in self-government and participatory democracy, and that campaigns funded by small contributions are, therefore, more likely to represent "real" concerns of the public. As Professor Frank Sorauf describes it, "it was the hope of reformers in 1974 that the FECA would replace the big money and big contributors of the Nixon era with a grass-roots, mom-and-pop system of local contributions in small sums."[10] Campaigns funded by large contributions, on the other hand, are routinely described as being indebted to "special interests." In some sense, this notion represents a crude version of more sophisticated equality arguments discussed in later chapters. For now, however, let us consider, in its crude form, whether campaigns funded by small contributors better capture the mood of public opinion, and so are more likely to yield up the type of candidate that voters want, or address the issues of greatest concern to voters.

Today, as many as 18 million Americans make some financial contribution to a political party, candidate, or PAC in an election cycle. Indeed, short of voting itself, monetary contributions are the most common method by which voters formally link themselves to political candidates and campaigns. No other system of campaign funding anywhere in the world even approaches so broad a base of voluntary support. Yet this broad base of support still amounts to less than 10 percent of the voting-age population.[11] And though it represents a far broader base of financial support than existed in the eighteenth and nineteenth centuries, few would argue that this expanded base of donors has made the political system more democratic or more responsive. Indeed, it is an article of faith among campaign finance reform advocates that our democracy is becoming less responsive. Why this contradiction between reality and reformist rhetoric? Once again, the underlying assumption is wrong.

It is simply not true that the ability to raise large campaign sums in small contributions makes a campaign in some way more representative or more attuned to the popular will. In many cases, those candidates who are best able to raise campaign dollars in small contributions are those who are most emphatically out of the mainstream of their time. Barry Goldwater's 1964 presidential campaign, for example, raised $5.8 million from 410,000 small contributors, before going down to a landslide defeat. On his way to an even more crushing defeat in 1972, George McGovern raised almost $15 million from small donors, at an average of approximately $20 per contributor. And if we assume that reliance on numerous small contributions makes a campaign in some way more "democratic," then perhaps the most "democratic" high-profile campaign of the last

46

decade of the twentieth century was the 1994 U.S. Senate campaign of Oliver North. North raised approximately $20 million, almost entirely from small contributors, and actually outspent his nearest rival by nearly four to one. Yet he still lost to an unpopular opponent plagued by personal scandal.[12] Similarly, the most "democratic" campaign of 1996 may have been that of former GOP representative Robert Dornan of California, who also lost his seat in Congress despite outspending his opponent and raising most of his money in small contributions. Dornan was known in Congress as one of the most conservative members of the House. All of these candidates ran among the most "extreme," if we may use that word, and ideological campaigns in recent decades. This suggests that the ability to raise large sums in small contributions is a sign of fervent backing from an ideologically committed minority, rather than a sign of broad political support. With the exception of the occasional candidate who can whip up an ideological fervor on the edges of mainstream politics, such as McGovern in 1972, North in 1994, or presidential candidate Patrick Buchanan in 1996 and 2000, Americans are simply unwilling, individually, to contribute enough money in small amounts to run modern campaigns.

In fact, even most successful ideological movements have historically relied on a relatively small number of large contributors for "seed money," if not for the bulk of their funding. As far back as the turn of the century, antiestablishment candidates such as Robert LaFollette, William Jennings Bryan, and Hiram Johnson (once elected on the slogan "Kick the corporations out of politics") were financed by a small number of wealthy supporters.[13] More recently, candidates such as Eugene McCarthy in 1968 and Ross Perot in 1992 relied on small numbers of wealthy supporters or self-financed campaigns.

Advocates of radical campaign finance reform tend to overlook the significant collective action problems that discourage most voters from contributing financially to candidates. No single contribution, especially a small contribution, is likely to have a significant impact on an election. This would remain true even if large contributions were banned. Voters, therefore, have little rational incentive to make political donations. These collective action problems may be overcome in some instances by a radical campaign in which donors are motivated by strong ideologies rather than rational, utility-maximizing calculations. Such campaigns are likely to have relatively little appeal, however, to the larger mass of voters, who tend to be less ideological in orientation. Thus, in most instances, there will not be sufficient funds available to finance campaigns at a level that adequately informs the electorate about the candidates unless a resort is made to government subsidies. In any case, a system of private campaign finance will almost inevitably come to rely on large individual donors who believe that their more substantial gifts can make a difference, or who are attached to candidates through personal loyalties, and on interests groups (that is, PACs) that overcome voter inertia by organizing voters to address particular concerns.

Efforts to limit large donations, then, may have the effect of both reducing the flow of information to voters and aiding more radical candidacies at the expense of centrist candidacies.

Money Buys Elections

The third assumption of campaign finance reform is that money "buys" elections in some manner incompatible with a functioning democracy. It seems axiomatic that a candidate with little or no money to spend is unlikely to win most races. Furthermore, the candidate who spends more money wins far more often than not. But correlation is not the same as cause and effect, and one must be careful not to make too much of such simple numbers.

The strong correlation between spending and victory may stem simply from the desire of donors to contribute to candidates who are likely to win, in which case the ability to win attracts money, rather than the other way around. A case in point would be the 2000 presidential campaign of George W. Bush, who by early 2000 had raised over $65 million from more than 80,000 contributors. Bush had been dominating Republican polls for months even before he declared his candidacy and began raising money. Bush's fund-raising reflected, rather than created, his popularity, and indeed his popularity dropped as the actual campaign began, despite much lower expenditures by his rivals. High levels of campaign contributions to and spending by a candidate often reflect a level of public support that is later manifested at the polls. Generally speaking, the same attri-

48

butes that attract voters to a candidate will attract donations, and those that attract donations will attract votes. In other words, the candidate who is able to raise more money would usually win even if that candidate did not spend that added money, because the ability to raise money is itself evidence of political prowess and popularity that would normally translate into votes.[14]

This is not to say that money is not important, or that spending more is not preferable, in most races, to spending less. If, as studies suggest, spending informs the public, then the candidate who spends the most has, other things being equal, the best chance to inform the public as to why he or she should be elected. However, higher spending does not necessarily translate into electoral triumph. As one long-time observer puts it: "Having money means having the ability to be heard; it does not mean that voters will like what they hear." One need only look at election results to prove this point. For example, in the 1994 U.S. House elections, which had the highest turnover of any congressional election in the 1990s, many incumbents won although they spent considerably less than their opponents. More pointedly, the thirty-four Republican challengers who defeated Democratic incumbents in that year spent, on average, just two-thirds of the amounts expended by their opponents, and one spent less than one-twentieth as much as his incumbent opponent. Given the inherent advantages of incumbency, this is powerful evidence that a monetary advantage alone does not mean electoral success. Similarly, in 1998 Democrats scored rare House gains for a party controlling the presidency in a nonpresidential election year, despite being heavily outspent in the aggregate by their Republican opponents. Four of the ten most expensive House races of 1998 were won by the candidate spending the least; two of the six won by the higher-spending candidate were the races for the respective party leaders in the House, Newt Gingrich and Richard Gephardt, neither of whom faced serious opposition.[15]

One reason why having the most money does not spell automatic success is that money, like any good, has a declining marginal utility. The more that a candidate has already spent, the less value there is to spending the next dollar. Moreover, some candidates—especially incumbents—will already be well known to voters from past campaigns or free publicity, reducing the value to them of spending. Once voters form an opinion of a candidate, added spending is relatively insignificant. Thus, in a theme that we will explore more fully further on, we find that the higher the rate of total spending, the less benefit there is to having a spending advantage. The problem is not that some candidates "buy" elections by spending "too much," but that other candidates spend too little to reach the mass of voters. The solution is to spend more all around, not less.

But, it is often suggested, the ability of some candidates to amass large sums in advance of the election may also scare off potential challengers entirely. This is sometimes called the "war-chest mentality." The "war-chest" phenomenon is restricted almost entirely to incumbents, for as we will see in the next chapter, existing limits on contributions make it almost impossible for challengers to match incumbents' early fund-raising. In any case, research by economists Philip Hersch and Gerald McDougall has found that a large incumbent "war chest" does indeed correlate with a lower likelihood of a serious challenge in House races.[16]

On closer examination, however, the war-chest theory is merely a variation of the incorrect basic assumption that money is the primary determinant of who wins office. In the war chest version of that assumption, one candidate, usually the incumbent, has simply raised cash early enough that opponents do not try to contest the seat, recognizing that such a quest is unlikely to succeed. But this still does not account for how or why the incumbent is able to raise large sums early in the election cycle. Hersch and McDougall note that a large campaign fund at an early date tends to indicate that the candidate is popular and has the types of political attributes that make reelection likely. This early accumulation of cash also demonstrates a determination by the candidate to run a hard, competitive campaign. Thus the war chest serves as a signal to potential challengers that the incumbent is popular and determined, and that a challenge is unlikely to succeed.

Indeed, a close look at the data shows that it is not the size of the war chest, but rather the popularity and determination that the war chest represents, that diminishes the probability of a serious challenge. The average war chest in the Hersch-McDougall study was just $159,000, rising to just $203,000 in races in which the incumbent eventually ran without serious competition. Yet these amounts barely reach the lower end of the estimated $150,000 to $500,000 needed to run a competitive congressional campaign at the time of the study.[17] Thus, a challenger would normally have expected the incumbent to spend at least the amount of the war chest, and probably quite a bit more, regardless of what the candidate had on hand well before the election. If a rational challenger would have expected the incumbent to spend the amount of the war chest, or substantially more, the mere fact that the incumbent had already accumulated much of that money ought not to scare the challenger off. When challengers are deterred, then, it appears not to be the amount in the war chest but rather the nonmonetary attributes that the early accumulation of resources represents. The war chest per se represents tenacity, political ability, and popularity, and it is these attributes that discourage challengers.

The assumption that money buys elections is based on simple correlation: The candidate who spends the most usually wins. It would be surprising, however, if this were not the case, as contributions naturally flow to those candidates who are popular and are perceived as having a good chance of winning. Despite this correlation, it is clear that many candidates win despite spending considerably less than their opponents, and the correlation between spending in electoral success, though strong, is not as strong as certain other correlations, including incumbency and success.[18]

Money Is a Corrupting Influence on the Legislature

A fundamental tenet of the effort to further regulate campaign finance is that money has corrupted the legislative process. Encouraged by extreme language of the press and reform advocates, large numbers of Americans, according to polling data, have come to view campaign contributions as the dominant influence on policymaking. And experience and human nature tell us that legislators, like most people, are influenced by money, even, we might presume, when it goes into their campaign funds rather than into their pockets for personal use.

Many lawmakers and former lawmakers themselves have complained of the influence of money in the legislature. Former Arkansas senator Dale Bumpers is quoted as saying, "Every Senator knows I speak the truth when I say bill after bill after bill has been defeated in this body because of campaign money." Another senator, West Virginia's Robert Byrd, has been quoted as stating, "Money talks, and the perception is that money will talk here in this Senate. Money will open the door. Money will hold the balance of power."[19]

As we begin to analyze the truth or falsity of this assumption, we must first recognize that in the context of the debate over campaign finance reform, the term "corruption" takes on a special meaning. What is meant by "corruption" in this context is not the common definition of the term, that is to say, personal enrichment of a legislator in exchange for a vote, although some of the more demagogic reformers seem to hope that their audience interprets it in that way. That type of traditional corruption, after all, is prohibited by bribery laws. What reformers mean by "corruption" is that legislators react to the wishes of constituents; or what, in other circumstances, might be called "responsiveness." What makes this particular incidence of responsiveness "corrupt" is that the constituents involved have taken an active role in supporting the candidate's campaign for election. Normally we would expect, and hardly consider it inappropriate, for candidates to take positions that reflect the views of their supporters or, to turn it around, for groups and individuals to support candidates who reflect their views. Thus we would not normally think anything amiss unless, as a starting point, it appeared that candidates adopt positions which they would not otherwise adopt for the primary purpose of obtaining campaign contributions. The starting point for finding corruption, it would seem, is to establish a causal link showing that contributions cause legislators to vote differently from the way they would otherwise.

Nevertheless, many reform advocates seem to consider it "corruption" if a lawmaker merely votes in a manner consistent with the desires of those groups or individuals that have contributed to his or her campaign—unless, of course, the reform-minded advocate thinks that the position is correct, in which case it becomes a vote on principle. Browse the web pages of pro-"reform" groups such as Common Cause, Public Campaign, and the Center for Responsive Politics, and one finds numerous "studies" of campaign giving that simply assume that a correlation between voting and contributions indicates corruption. For example, the September 1999 issue of *Capitol Eye*, the newsletter of the Center for Responsive Politics (CRP), notes that Senator Slade Gorton received a

$1,000 contribution from the National Rifle Association in May of 1999, and then, "emerge[d] as a prominent supporter of the NRA in the [debate over a gun control bill]," as if this indicated the corrupting influence of money. However, even CRP acknowledged elsewhere that Gorton was "a longtime critic of proposed gun curbs." A Common Cause bulletin from November 1999, reports that the "sugar and peanut industries together" gave $14.2 million in political contributions between 1991 and 1997, and that, "in return, these industries have benefited from anti-competitive government policies."[20] No effort is made to show that any congressman or senator, let alone a majority, voted against his conscience or the wishes of his constituency in exchange for votes on the issue. This may be for good reason—the total $14.2 million, given over two presidential elections and three congressional elections, to all candidates (including those who did not win election) and parties, totals substantially less than one-half of 1 percent of spending on federal campaigns in that time period.

A discrepancy occurs here in the way in which political results are described. No group ever argues that it won a public policy debate because it outspent its opponents. It is only when we lose that we claim the other guy had some unfair advantage. For example, Democrats rarely complain that we periodically raise the minimum wage because Capital Hill is swarming with union lobbyists or because unions spend millions of dollars on political activities; and Republicans would never argue that a minimum wage increase was defeated thanks to the influence of business contributions, rather than sound economic considerations. Perhaps we should consider the possibility that the representatives believe what they say.

More serious academic observers require more than mere correlation, of course, before putting forth cries of corruption. They agree that there must be a causal link between contributions and legislative behavior before the issue of corruption gains legitimacy. But how far does this take us? Few could deny that campaign contributions may play a role in a legislator's complex calculations of how to vote and what to say and do. The question is how great a role.

I find it implausible that this is really a major problem in American government. For one thing, the assertion that lawmakers vote to please financial contributors is simply not supported by the bulk of systematic evidence. Serious studies of legislative behavior have overwhelmingly concluded that campaign contributions play little role in floor voting,[21] and these conclusions are no longer seriously disputed by the would-be regulators.[22] Instead, it is now argued that the corruption exists where it is harder to see—in committee activities, in "the speech not given," and in prioritizing. Of course, if corruption cannot be measured or seen, this assertion cannot be disproven, which is something of a handicap for those skeptical of this justification. On the other hand, the assertion of widespread corruption is backed by bits of anecdotal evidence, usually quotes from present and former legislators explaining their support for campaign finance regulation or explaining why they were unable to accomplish certain legislative objectives. Typical, for example, is a quote by former representative Hamilton Fish: "Certainly amendments are influenced by campaign financing."[23] But even this "first-hand" evidence is not terribly persuasive, for there is a human tendency to blame defeat on "unfair" factors, such as corruption, rather than to admit that our ideas were not strong enough, our allies not numerous enough, or our side not organized enough, to gain legislative victory. Moreover, the fact is that the vast majority of current and former legislators do not make such comments, and indeed, there are similar types of anecdotal quotes running in the opposite direction, even from the supposedly unbiased former representatives with nothing left to hide. For example, the former senator and congressman Dan Coates, a twenty-two year Capitol Hill veteran, states, "Never, not once . . . have I witnessed or been informed of the exchange of dollars for political favors. Not by me or my supporters, not for any amount of money, and not by anyone I have known or served with."[24] In addition, there is the inability of regulatory advocates actually to name corrupt legislators or episodes of such corruption. The fact is, it is still shocking when episodes such as Abscam and the Keating Five come to light, precisely because such episodes are rare. Conventional wisdom aside, most people don't do it.

Part of the stubbornness behind the idea of hidden corruption is that experience and human nature warn us that legislators, like other people, are influenced by money, even when it does not go directly into their pockets but into their campaigns. Yet the idea that political donations play a relatively minor role in legislative behavior is also a matter of common sense, really. After all, all that a contribution can do is help a candidate try to persuade people to vote for him or her. Thus, adopting an unpopular position in exchange for a donation will not generally be a wise course of action. It is votes, not dollars, that win elections. A candidate must get more votes. Contrary to the heated rhetoric of some reformers, the "wealthy" do not vote with their dollars. All they can do with their dollars is attempt to persuade others how to vote. That is free speech, and the essence of the First Amendment.

A further bit of reflection tells us why it is unlikely that money "corrupts" the legislature to any great extent. Campaign money is of little value if it cannot be turned into an electoral victory,[25] and it makes little sense to betray one's personal convictions, lose the support of one's party, and offend public opinion in order to obtain a contribution. It should not be surprising, therefore, that empirical studies show that the influence of contributions is dwarfed by that of party agenda, personal ideology, and constituent desires, as the latter is revealed in polls, letters, calls, and conversations with voters.[26] Common sense and experience tell us that money matters, but they also tell us that people who are attracted to public office generally do have strong personal views on issues. This rather obvious observation often seems lost on political observers, even those with an otherwise skeptical eye. For example, one skeptic of "reform" still found it "scandalous" that sixty-four Democrats in the House of Representatives voted for a capital gains tax cut in 1989, writing, "I cannot believe [they] would have voted for this bill . . . were they not so dependent on campaign contributions from the sector of the population most likely to benefit from the bill." This suggestion—that only contributions can explain this vote—seems little short of bizarre. It is hard to think of a contested legislative issue in which the arguments were so one-sided that *only* "corruption" could explain the votes of nearly 15 percent of the entire legislative body. In this case, though the issue was hotly debated, considerable literature suggested that a reduction in capital gains tax rates would actually increase government revenue. Perhaps these Democrats found such studies persuasive and merely wanted to cut the then sizeable federal budget deficit, or raise added revenue to fund social programs?[27]

On a personal level, for many years I have been associated with a variety of public policy think tanks, and until recently sat on the Board of Trustees of one such institution. Never have I known any of these groups to take a position, or to avoid taking a position, in order to please or to avoid offending donors. To the contrary, I have frequently seen them take stands that incur the wrath of donors and cause major declines in donations. In my role as a trustee, the only time I have seen the questions of donors even come up is when discussing either how to inform a donor of the position the organization intends to take, or when discussing how to convince a donor that he or she should continue to contribute to the organization, despite its adoption of a position known to be at odds with the contributor's view. I believe that this is how most of the professors who write on "reform," and most of the staffers and board members of advocacy groups that champion more regulation, conduct their affairs, as well. It strikes me as odd, if not offensive, that these people assume that most members of Congress are feckless suits, easily swayed by a few dollars to their campaign organizations, while they themselves are men and women of principle.

Second, there are institutional and political incentives to support party positions. These include logistical and financial support, appeals to party unity, rewards and punishment through such perks as committee assignments, and promises of support from party leaders on other issues. All of these can be more valuable for pleasing constituents, gaining favorable press coverage, and accomplishing legislative objectives than most campaign contributions could ever be.

Third, large campaign contributors are usually offset in legislative debate by equally well-financed interests who contribute to a different group of candidates. Few candidates, especially incumbents, are particularly reliant on one industry or source for campaign funds, so that a vote that offends any particular interest is rarely, if ever, a potential death knell for future sources of funding. In fact, major contributors frequently suffer enormous losses in the legislative process. For example, tobacco companies, often cited by regulatory advocates as an example of an industry that "buys" votes in the legislature, have been pummeled in recent congressional legislation.

Finally, money is not the only political commodity of value. For example, in April 1999, as Congress was considering gun-control measures opposed by the National Rifle Association (NRA), Common Cause issued a press release noting that from 1989 to 1998, the NRA had contributed nearly $8.4 million to congressional campaigns. During that same ten-year period, however, total spending by congressional candidates and parties easily topped $4 billion, so the NRA's share of the total congressional spending was less than two-tenths of 1 percent of the total. In this light, contributions hardly seem to be a realistic explanation for the NRA's alleged power. A more logical explanation is that, in addition to its PAC, the NRA also has over three million members who focus intently, or even solely, on Second Amendment and gun-ownership issues in their voting. In many congressional districts, the NRA is capable of shifting vote totals by as much as 5 percent. The NRA's power would seem to come more from votes than from dollars. However, to the extent that it comes from dollars, that, too, may be a function of votes. The group's large membership is part of what allows it to raise PAC money. Groups that advocate gun control often complain that the NRA outspends them, but rarely mention that the NRA also outvotes them.[28]

The NRA, with its large, ideological membership, of course, may not be the typical group. How do smaller, less ideological groups such as used-car dealers, sugar-beet growers, and the tobacco industry, to use three examples suggested by one critic, succeed? The answer is in much the same way as the NRA. For example, over 80,000 used-car dealers dot the American landscape, employing tens of thousands of workers. Sugar-beet growers can be found in every state from Ohio to California, and are often supported by a vast network of employees and suppliers. Coupled with the domestic corn syrup industry, sugar-beet growers provide over 420,000 jobs. These employees in turn have family members and friends, and in many small towns in the Midwest, the economy is contingent on the local processing facility. Similarly, the oft-maligned tobacco industry can call on large numbers of voters throughout the upper South, and even in parts of southern Ohio, Indiana, and Maryland, which are home to tobacco growers, processors, pickers, packagers, marketers, and more. Behind them stand millions of Americans who enjoy smoking, and may therefore oppose higher taxes, for example, on the product.[29] And it is certainly worth noting that many very influential groups, such as the American Association of Retired Persons or the American Bar Association, have no political action committee and make no political contributions at all.

57

Thus it is not surprising that personal ideology, party loyalty, and constituent views are far more important than the influence of campaign contributions on the legislature. Moreover, ideology, party, and constituency do not even begin to cover the myriad nonmonetary considerations that determine legislative activity.

Other factors that undoubtedly affect a legislator's actions might include anticipated newspaper endorsements or the slant of reporting, including deciding what qualifies as "news"; the opinions of staffers and personal friends and family, who are themselves likely to have strongly held views; perceptions of whether or not a stand on an issue could be distorted by an opponent into an effective campaign attack; potential endorsements by interest groups; and (I suspect) a host of other factors.

Consider just what it would mean for a legislator to act in a "corrupt" manner. For centuries, philosophers, political scientists, and others have debated how a legislator ought to make decisions; there is no consensus on the issue. However, democratic theorists have suggested a few ways of decision making which, I think, have enough legitimacy that even those who disagree with them would not suggest that they are "corrupt."

First, U.S. congresspersons or senators might choose to act according to the desires of a majority of their constituents, whether or not doing so comports with their own best judgment. Second, they might choose to act according to their own best judgment and ideological principles, whether or not doing so comports with the wishes of their constituents.[30] This would be a legitimate method of acting, whether the legislators are measuring the benefits according simply to what is best for their constituents or whether they are considering what is best for the nation as a whole. These do not exhaust the possibilities for legitimate legislative action. Legislators might also act legitimately (that is, non-"corruptly") in a manner opposed to both their own best judgment *and* the desires of a majority of their constituencies. For example, if a legislator thinks it would be a good idea to allow private discrimination against homosexuals in the rental housing market, and recognizes that a majority of his or her constituents hold a mild preference for allowing such private discrimination against homosexuals, he or she might still act in support of a law barring such discrimination because of the much more intense preference of a minority

58

of constituents who favor such legislation. This, too, is generally regarded as a legitimate mode of legislative action.

Which theory is best is, of course, a question for another day. At this point it is enough to note that a vote cast along any of these three lines cannot really be called "illegitimate" or "corrupt." In practice, I suspect that most legislators are frequently torn between these theories, and will usually vote their best judgment unless it means probable electoral defeat or, conversely, will usually vote with the constituency unless the legislators hold very strong opinions to the contrary.

In any case, to find "corruption," we must assume that the representative is acting against his or her own best judgment and principles, against the wishes of a majority of his or her constituents, and against the intense preferences of a minority, and that this is being done in order to gain a campaign contribution (as opposed to a media or other endorsement, favorable press coverage, or some other electoral advantage). How likely is any legislator to do such a thing for a mere contribution? Yet people express surprise that empirical studies fail to show that monetary contributions exert much influence.

So what, if anything, is the role of money? Why do donors give? The simple answer is that donors give primarily to elect candidates with whom they agree on issues important to the donor or, sometimes, simply because they are asked. And, we might add, it is hardly inappropriate for a legislator to vote in ways that please his or her constituents and that may, therefore, help the legislator to accumulate future campaign donations. Voters who do not like the legislator's record can record their votes at the next election.

Another reason that many donors themselves give for making political contributions is to assure access to legislators. Once again, regulatory advocates are quick to suggest that contributions play a dominant role in determing "access." Says former Representative Romano Mazzoli, "People who contribute get the ear of the member and the ear of the staff. They have the access." But like the "corruption" story, the "access" turns out not to be entirely true. The fact is, the vast majority of campaign contributors never seek access, and legislators meet regularly with people who have never made contributions. Nor does every contributor who seeks access get it.[31]

To the extent that the access theory is true, however, it is hardly shocking. For one thing, such contributors are often well informed on public issues and provide valuable information to representatives. Whether or not such minor influence is good or bad will depend on one's views of the legislation. But certainly the exclusion of knowledgeable interests from the legislative process can just as easily lead to poor legislation with bad, unintended consequences, as can the inclusion of such interests. Those donors who expect their contributions to gain them particular legislative results not otherwise compatible with the lawmaker's ideology and constituency views are almost always disappointed. For example, after the 1996 presidential campaign, much was made of an arms dealer named Roger Tamraz, who made contributions to the Clinton campaign and confessed quite openly that he hoped to gain federal subsidies for a Caspian Sea oil pipeline. Less noted is that Tamraz's project was rejected by the president. As former Senator Coates says, "a contribution is by no means necessary to obtain a meeting, and a meeting by no means guarantees results."

The access question seems to rely on a romantic and highly implausible view of political life. There seems to be a notion that but for monetary contributions, the typical congressional representative would . . . well, would what? Randomly call citizens in his or her district to get their opinions? Or spend more time golfing? And if the added time was used to call constituents, would it be time well spent? Imagine the probable results of such phone calls: a large number of hang-ups, many more "I don't knows," and a great deal of off-the-cuff advice by persons with little knowledge of the issues the representative may be dealing with. But of course, legislators do meet regularly with concerned constituents. What evidence is there that legislators refuse access to constituents in order to meet only with donors? If meetings with contributors were eliminated, the most likely result, I think, is that the typical representative would spend more time with the people who already surround him or her most of the day, and who make up the single largest occupational group of witnesses in congressional committee hearings: other government employees and officials. If private contributions were banned we can be sure that the overwhelming majority of citizens would still never, ever, get to spend even two minutes discussing public affairs with their congressional representatives; and we could make a reasonable guess that the number of private citizens with whom that representative does discuss public affairs would almost certainly decline.

In recent years, the popular arguments of reform advocates have grown more and more specious. For example, one popular tactic has been to lump together dozens, or even hundreds, of contributions, made over several years and several campaigns, by numerous donors who share one or more characteristic, which may or may not be their dominant characteristic.

A recent Common Cause report on the influence of the broadcast industry, for example, tells us in breathless prose that all broadcast interests, over a ten-year period ending in November 1996, gave about $9 million in total PAC contributions to candidates and soft-money contributions to parties. The report then suggests that this influence resulted in passage of legislation which, in Common Cause's eyes at least, was detrimental to the national interest. Of course, these contributions were made over five campaigns, with changing issues and candidates, and there are any number of reasons why contributions may have been made. The total includes contributions by interests frequently hostile to one another, such as Time-Warner and Turner Broadcasting, and by interests allied on some issues but opposed on others, such as networks and their affiliates, or in other instances, franchisers and franchisees. Further, Common Cause fails to point out that during this same decade, the recipient candidates and parties spent about $9 billion on political activity. So even assuming a unity of interest on the part of all "broadcast interests," broadcast contributions total about one-tenth of 1 percent of total national spending over this time. From this—one-tenth of 1 percent of total spending, over five campaigns, including contributions to persons no longer in Congress, contributions for state campaigns, including donations made for any reason whatsoever, we are to believe that a majority of Congress—more than 218 United States representatives and 51 senators—voted for a bill that they would otherwise have opposed and that they believed was against the interest of a majority of the voters they have to face in the next election. Meanwhile, more obvious reasons for any industry influence—that broadcasters own most of the broadcast outlets and so control reporting on campaigns—was ignored. Oddly enough, efforts to limit how much can be spent on political activity would only serve to strengthen the disproportionate influence of the broadcast and print media, as the overwhelming source of influence for these groups—broadcast time—would be untouched by reform. The Common Cause argument is not intended to be taken seriously. But Common Cause is hardly alone. In one report, typical of many on its web site, the Center for Responsive Politics casually lumps together all contributions by the insurance, securities, and banking industries, even while admitting, further on in the story, the substantially different interests among these industries. A variation of this tactic was done by Charles Lewis in his book, *The Buying of the President 2000*. Lewis lumped together all contributions from donors over a politician's career, to create a list of "career patrons" for each candidate, and suggested that the candidates are totally controlled by these donors.[32]

Indeed, unable to demonstrate "corruption" in any serious manner, reform groups have resorted to what might be called "guilt by innuendo." That is, they never say who is actually corrupt but simply hint they everyone is, or that the "system" is corrupt. But this is demonstrably not true. During the 1996 campaign, for example, the president's fund-raising tactics drew considerable public criticism—in particular a practice of allowing large campaign contributors to sleep in the Lincoln Bedroom at the White House. But it should be obvious that not every president does what the Clinton campaign did to raise funds in 1996. Furthermore, in November 1996, that same public ratified Clinton's substantive policies with a lopsided electoral victory, and his approval numbers continued to climb in 1997, even as the fund-raising "scandals" grew. Similarly, in the late 1980s, Senator John McCain was one of five senators caught up in what became known as the Keating Five scandal. The senators were accused of improperly interfering in regulatory decisions in order to assist campaign contributor Charles Keating. But what brought the Keating Five scandal to the public's attention and made it a scandal is that it was not typical. It was out of the ordinary. After the Keating Five scandal broke, the voters of Arizona twice returned Senator McCain to office by substantial margins—thanks, I am sure, to his many other virtues and his generally sound representation of the people of Arizona. And Senator McCain, far from being castigated by campaign reform advocates as "corrupt," was, by the mid-1990s, their single most prominent legislative hero, running a competitive campaign for the Republican presidential nomination in 2000. When challenged to name individuals corrupted by campaign contributions, reform advocates fall silent. Instead, they assert only that it is the "system" which is corrupt. But if we cannot name individuals corrupted by the system, on what basis should we conclude that the system is corrupt?

Ultimately, the claims of corruption seem to rest on the idea that legislators should respond to some notion of the "public good" that exists apart from the views of any particular group of voters. But legislators respond disproportionately to the interests of select constituents all the time, depending, among other things, upon the intensity, the degree of organization, and the willingness of those constituents to vote on those interests, and those interests alone. To the extent that it is argued that a legislator might use Burkean judgment to resist the blandishments of powerful groups, or even the majority, in favor of what the legislator, with his or her added knowledge, believes to be good public policy, I support that notion. I am a Burkean. But to the extent that Common Cause or some other group not accountable at the polls claims to know what that good public policy is, and therefore to know when legislators are violating their trust—and to the extent that they then seek to justify limits on the political advocacy of others—such actions are very dangerous to First Amendment rights.

Conclusion

The pressure for campaign finance regulation has been based on assumptions that are, at best, seriously flawed. The fact is that campaigns are not particularly costly, with the total spending every two years on congressional campaigning amounting to roughly the cost of one home video rental per eligible voter. Studies indicate that higher spending is beneficial for public knowledge of candidates and issues, without eroding public faith in government. The reality is that the public is unwilling to fund campaigns through small contributions at a level adequate to provide voters with basic information. Now, as throughout our history, the burden of campaign finance falls on relatively few. The truth is that expenditures do not "buy" elections; large campaign expenditures are subject to diminishing returns, especially for incumbents, which strongly suggests that heavy spending cannot "buy" a seat if the voters do not like the message the campaign puts out. And finally, the fact is that the causal link between campaign contributions and the voting patterns of elected representatives appears to be significantly overestimated by reformers, and has not been supported by empirical research.

This is not to suggest that money is not without its problematic aspects. But the greater threat to the democratic nature of our system comes less from the growth of campaign expenditures than from the ill-conceived regulation that has been based on these faulty assumptions. In fact, our efforts to regulate the system have had a number of consequences that might be termed broadly "undemocratic."

Chapter 4

THE FOLLY OF REFORM:
CONSEQUENCES OF CAMPAIGN
FINANCE REGULATION

Reforms that are based on poor assumptions about the empirical effects of money on political campaigns and legislative activity are not likely to accomplish their stated goals. But the problem with campaign finance regulation has been greater than just that. By failing to recognize and understand the actual effect that money has in the political system, the reforms of the past have actually exacerbated many of the problems they were intended to solve, and created new problems along the way. This chapter discusses some of these problems.

Campaign finance reform has generally focused on three specific tactics for promoting change: limiting contributions, whether by individuals, unions and corporations, or PACs; limiting campaign spending; and, ultimately, using taxpayer funds to pay for campaigns. This chapter discusses some of the effects of limits on contributions and spending in the context of privately funded campaigns. Chapter 5 discusses issues pertinent to taxpayer-funded campaigns.

The reform tactics of imposing limits on contributions and spending have had several consequences for American political life that can be broadly labeled "undemocratic." Specifically, campaign finance reform efforts, based on ever-increasing regulation of the political process, have entrenched the status quo; reduced the choices of both candidates and issues available to the electorate, while contributing to the negativity of campaigns; made the electoral system less responsive to popular opinion, while favoring special interests; strengthened the power of select elites; and limited opportunities for grassroots political activity.

Campaign Finance Regulation Has Entrenched the Status Quo

Campaign finance regulation, in particular limits on contributions and overall spending, has insulated the political system from challenge by outsiders, and hindered the ability of challengers to compete on equal terms with those already in power.

Contribution limits tend to favor incumbents by making it relatively harder for challengers to raise money and thereby make credible runs for office. The lower the contribution limit, the more difficult it becomes for a candidate to raise money quickly from a small number of dedicated supporters. The consequent need to raise campaign cash from a large number of small contributors benefits those candidates who have in place a database of past contributors, an intact campaign organization, and the ability to raise funds on an ongoing basis from PACs.[1] This latter group is heavily skewed toward current officeholders. Candidates with low name recognition—a group that is heavily skewed toward challengers—have difficulty in raising substantial sums of money from small contributors. Being less well known, these candidates find relatively few potential donors for their campaigns. Not surprisingly, donors tend not to give to candidates with whom they are unfamiliar. Thus, challengers generally, and political newcomers in particular, have traditionally been more reliant on a small number of large donors, both individuals and groups, to back them with "seed money" in the form of large contributions. The donors who make these large "seed money" contributions tend to do so because of political or other affinities with the candidate. The end result is that contribution limits hit political newcomers especially hard.

In fact, even well-known public figures who challenge the status quo have traditionally relied on a small number of wealthy patrons to fund their campaigns. For example, Theodore Roosevelt's 1912 Bull Moose campaign was funded almost entirely by a handful of wealthy supporters. Senator Eugene McCarthy's 1968 antiwar campaign relied for seed money on a handful of six-figure donors, including Stewart Mott, who gave approximately $210,000, and Wall Street banker Jack Dreyfus, Jr., who may have contributed as much as $500,000. John Anderson would probably have had more success in his independent campaign for the presidency in 1980 had his wealthy patron, the same Mr. Mott who had supported McCarthy, been able to contribute unlimited amounts to his campaign.[2]

Beyond making it harder for challengers to raise cash, contribution limits also tend to decrease overall spending. This is because a candidate's spending is limited to available funds. Contribution limits reduce available funds by reducing how much donors can give, and so indirectly lower overall spending levels. Low spending also works against challengers generally, and political newcomers in particular.

In most races, incumbents begin the campaign with significant advantages in name recognition. They are able to attract press coverage because of their office, and they often receive assistance from their staffs and send constituents postage-free mailings, using their franking privilege. Through patronage and constituent favors, they can further add to their support. The value of incumbency has been estimated at up to several hundred thousand, or even millions, of dollars.[3] To offset these advantages, challengers need to make their names and positions known, and the most effective way to do that is usually to spend money on paid advertising. Incumbents spend money, too, of course, and even before contribution limits were put in place in the 1970s, incumbents usually outspent challengers. But the built-in edge that incumbents possess in name recognition and free media attention also makes it hard for incumbents to improve their general standing with the public through added expenditures. In simple economic terms, incumbents hit the point of declining marginal utility for each dollar spent much sooner than most challengers, and better-known challengers hit that point sooner than lesser-known challengers.

Studies that have attempted to isolate and quantify the effect of campaign spending on votes have found that once a candidate spends the minimal amount needed to penetrate the public consciousness, additional spending affects a very limited number of votes.[4] Candidates would rather spend more than less, of course, and as a result may continue to raise funds. But it is clear that the positive effect of added spending is, in most cases, significantly greater for challengers than for incumbents, if only because incumbents are better known to their constituencies at the start of the campaign.[5] The advantages they gain from holding office can be viewed as money already spent in a campaign, and indeed often reflect past campaign spending. As such, incumbents reach a point of diminishing marginal returns sooner than challengers; better-known and longer-serving incumbents reach that point sooner than lesser-known and short-term incumbents. In fact, so strong is the decline in marginal utility that some studies have shown an inverse relationship between very high levels of incumbent spending and incumbent success. The most likely explanation for this phenomenon is not that the spending actually hurts the incumbent but simply that it doesn't help much. Such heavy spending by an incumbent indicates that the incumbent is in electoral trouble and faces a well-financed challenger, who, likely as not, is gaining greater benefits than the incumbent from each dollar spent.[6] Anecdotal evidence supports this point. For example, in the 1994 U.S. House elections, three incumbents lost despite spending at least $1 million more than their challengers. The three were among the best-known, longest-serving incumbents in Congress: Dan Rostenkowski, Thomas Foley, and Jack Brooks.[7]

Because an incumbent's added spending is likely to have less of an effect on vote totals than the additional spending of a challenger, limits on total campaign spending will hurt challengers more than incumbents. By lowering overall campaign spending, therefore, contribution limits further lock into place the advantages of incumbency and disproportionately harm challengers. Absolute spending ceilings have the potential to exacerbate this problem considerably. In *Buckley v. Valeo*, recall, the Supreme Court banned compulsory limits on campaign spending. But *Buckley* left open the door for legislatures to enact "voluntary" spending limits, in which a candidate agrees to limit his or her spending in return for a government benefit. The best-known example is the system of funding in presidential elections. Under the system, if a candidate agrees to limit his spending, the federal government provides matching funds in the primaries and a sizable amount—about $66 million for the 2000 election—in the general election. In recent years, several states have made efforts to ratchet up the "incentives" to make it all but impossible for a candidate to opt out of the system. For example, Kentucky's system provides that if a candidate agrees to a spending cap, he receives two dollars in government funds for each dollar raised in voluntary contributions. However, it then goes further and allows the candidate to exceed the spending cap, and continue receiving government funds, if his or her opponent chooses not to accept the cap.[8] The anticipated result is that few candidates would ever decide not to accept the "voluntary" spending cap. Set low enough, however, such spending caps may make it impossible for challengers to attain the critical threshold at which they can reach enough voters to run a credible race. Yet the only alternative is to ignore the cap and thus face an incumbent who, in addition to the other perks of incumbency, now gains the added benefit of a substantial government cash subsidy.

Incumbent lawmakers will always have powerful personal incentives to set spending caps at a level that puts their challengers at a disadvantage.[9] For example, in 1994, 1996, and 1998, not a single Senate challenger won who spent less than the "voluntary" spending cap included in the most popular "reform" bill proposed in the 104th and 105th Congress, the McCain-Feingold bill, while not a single incumbent spending less than that amount lost. Similarly, House challengers who exceeded the "voluntary" cap under those sessions' versions of the Shays-Meehan bill, the primary "reform" bill in the House, were approximately ten times more likely to win than challengers who spent less than the proposed cap, regardless of the level of incumbent spending.

Overall spending caps also prevent challengers from ever spending more than incumbents. Although spending more than one's opponent is not necessary to win an election, a challenger's ability to outspend an incumbent can help to offset the advantages of incumbency.[10] Spending caps hit hardest at precisely those challengers who would otherwise be best positioned seriously to challenge incumbents. Because spending benefits challengers far more than it does incumbents, spending limits destroy one of the few advantages that might be available to a challenger.

Thus efforts to limit spending, whether mandatory or through incentive-based "voluntary" caps, should therefore not be viewed as benign or neutral. Like contribution limits, they work directly to reduce electoral competition and entrench the status quo.

Campaign Finance Regulation Has Reduced the Number of Candidates and Favored Wealthy Candidates

Although campaign finance restrictions aim to reduce the role of money in politics, they have helped to renew the phenomenon of the "millionaire candidate"—Donald Trump, John Corzine, Ross Perot, and Steve Forbes are just a few of the most celebrated examples.

Contribution limits force candidates to raise all of their funds in small amounts. In the *Buckley* decision, however, the Supreme Court held that Congress could not limit the amount that a candidate could spend on his or her own campaign. This ability of a candidate to spend unlimited amounts of his or her own money, coupled with restrictions on raising outside money, favors those candidates who can contribute large sums to their own campaigns from personal assets. A Michael Huffington, Herb Kohl, or Jay Rockefeller becomes a particularly viable candidate precisely because personal wealth provides a direct campaign advantage that cannot be offset by a large contributor to the opposing candidate.[11]

But the problem is not simply that contribution limits favor rich candidates. More important, the system works to reduce the potential field of candidates. For example, Ross Perot's 1992 presidential campaign was possible because Perot was able to spend millions to advance his own candidacy. However, the contribution limits upheld in *Buckley* made it illegal for Perot to bankroll the campaign of a more plausible challenger, such as General Colin Powell. This problem became a concrete reality in 1996, when millionaire publisher Malcolm S. "Steve" Forbes, Jr., a political neophyte, declared his intention to seek the Republican presidential nomination. Forbes indicated that he would not have sought the nomination had former congressman and secretary of housing and urban development Jack Kemp decided to run. Kemp chose not to run in large part because he did not want to engage in fund-raising. Had Forbes been able to donate to Kemp the $25 million he planned to spend on his own campaign, Kemp might have run and would quite likely have been a front-runner for the Republican nomination.[12]

This problem must play itself out for thousands of candidates at lower levels of politics every year. Those who would heavily regulate campaign spending often suggest that large numbers of potential candidates are discouraged from running by their inability to raise funds. This is almost certainly not true. Perhaps this can best be shown through a simple thought experiment. Imagine that all campaign expenditures were banned. Who would surface as viable candidates for Congress? Most likely, it would be a small coterie of local celebrities (such as athletes, television personalities, and car dealers whose names are well-known from their business ads); current office holders; a handful of successful business persons, lawyers, and physicians who have been extremely active in their professions or the community; and perhaps a few other well-known community leaders, such as the head of the local police or teachers' union, some community activists, or pastors of large churches. Overall, it is a group not too different from those who run now, although probably a bit smaller in number and a bit less diverse. In an unregulated system of private finance, virtually all of these people could raise the money needed to run a serious campaign—in some cases from a large number of small contributions, in others from a small number of large contributions.[13] The important thing is that some people not in this group can also raise the funds to become viable candidates.

As it is, candidates work frantically and spend their money in desperate attempts just to get the typical voter to know their names.[14] Name recognition is central to candidate success. Spending money allows a candidate without that initial name recognition to have a fighting chance.[15] What makes us think that the ability of some candidates to spend money to gain name recognition somehow decreases the pool of viable candidates? Did Steve Forbes decrease the pool of viable Republican presidential nominees? Of course not. If anything, in both 1996 and 2000 his presence as a candidate seems to have increased interest in alternatives to the front runners, Bob Dole in 1996 and George W. Bush in 2000.

Reduced spending by candidates merely helps a very small group who already have high name recognition, a group dominated by those already in power—incumbent office holders—and a handful of others. Contribution limits do not help other potential candidates raise the funds that must be raised if they are to introduce themselves and their ideas to the public. The trick, then, is not to limit spending but to make it easier for political newcomers to raise money. An unknown candidate will find it a daunting task to raise a half million dollars for a congressional race, or even $50,000 for a campaign for the state legislature, from small donors. By allowing friends, family, and others to contribute relatively large amounts, it becomes possible for such potential candidates to enter a race. Such "seed" money can be used to place one's message before a segment of the public, and if the message is attractive, the candidate ought then be able to attract still more potential contributors and compete effectively.

Once we recognize that speech is not free—that it costs money for a candidate to communicate with potential voters—we can compare the situation of the would-be candidate to that of a would-be entrepreneur. Let us assume that this would-be entrepreneur needs $100,000 to start his or her business. Like candidates for political office, there are undoubtedly large numbers of individuals with ideas for a business, invention, or product, who are discouraged by their inability to raise the necessary funds from the bank. But what is important is that the entrepreneur need only convince one bank to lend the start-up cash. Imagine how much more difficult, and discouraging, the task would be if no one bank could loan over $5,000. The entrepreneur would have to convince not one but twenty banks before his or her business could get under way. This is akin to the daunting task that contribution limits place before newcomers to politics.[16]

This fund-raising burden of contribution limits is, paradoxically, most likely to harm candidates who represent the political interests of the poor and working class. Historically, candidates with large constituencies among the poor and the working class have obtained their campaign funds from a small base of wealthy donors. This is to be expected, as

72

these constituencies, by definition, have fewer individuals with the economic means to contribute. Thus these candidates rely on wealthy patrons to get their message out. But contribution limits destroy the ability of wealthy sympathizers such as Stewart Mott to finance these efforts. Meanwhile, candidates with many supporters who can afford to give the legal limit—since 1974 $1,000 at the federal level—will tend to be relatively unscathed by "reform" legislation. As a consequence, campaign regulation has probably served to strengthen the political power of the wealthy and upper middle class at the expense of the working class.[17]

Campaign Finance Regulation Has Inhibited the Robust Discussion of Public Issues

To many campaign observers, it may seem counterintuitive that restrictions on campaign giving and spending have closed off much meaningful discussion of political issues and made it more difficult for candidates to propose creative solutions to policy matters. After all, aren't candidates afraid to discuss issues because of the fear of offending some financial contributor? But this is only counterintuitive, perhaps, until we recall that we are, today, in the most heavily regulated era of political speech in American history.

Contribution limits do not reduce the need for candidates to spend money in order to communicate with voters. All that they do is make it more difficult for candidates to raise that money. A candidate's efforts often have two phases: first, the candidate must persuade political activists and other potential supporters that he or she is a potentially successful candidate, one that the activists and supporters would want to elect. These activists and supporters will then form the core of the campaign staff and provide the campaign with the resources, financial and otherwise, to take the candidate's message to the public. At each phase, the candidate has two thresholds to cross: convincing the activist audience that he or she can be victorious, so that resources and votes are not "wasted" on the candidacy; and convincing the larger, voting audience that it would benefit from his or her election. The candidate has two options for convincing the second audience. The first is to convince that audience that he or she believes what they believe. The second is to convince that audience that the candidate's ideas, if new to or previously unheard by the audience, are actually good ones. In other words, a substantial number of voters have to be convinced that they ought to believe what the candidate believes. The second approach, of course, is most valuable to the candidate who is proposing new or creative solutions as, by definition, such ideas are less likely to be already on the public agenda or supported by large numbers of potential voters. Contribution limits work against that second type of candidate.

For example, assume that a candidate needs $600,000 to run a competitive race for the U.S. House. The candidate is typically indifferent as to whether the $600,000 is raised from one contribution of $600,000, six contributions of $100,000, six hundred contributions of $1,000, or six thousand contributions of $100. Let us further suppose that, without any restrictions on the size of contributions, the average contribution from those who will make a political contribution is $4,000, with the size of particular donations determined by both financial resources of the contributor and the intensity of the contributor's support for the candidate. Without limits, the candidate would need approximately 150 average donations to reach his target. However, the fund-raising goal could be reached with even fewer truly dedicated supporters willing to give more. With a $1,000 contribution limit, on the other hand, the candidate now needs a minimum of 600 contributions. In fact, he or she almost certainly needs more, since some donors will give less than the maximum and this cannot be made up by others contributing more than the maximum. As one can readily see, contribution limits force the candidate to try to attract a broad base of donors. Yet these contributions must come from a relatively small group of individuals—only about 10 percent of Americans ever give to political campaigns, and the same individuals tend to give from one election to the next.[18]

To succeed in this environment, the candidate is wise to stress platitudes and milquetoast solutions that will offend as few potential contributors as possible. Any proposed change to the status quo will offend at least some people who benefit from that status quo. The candidate cannot rely on the intensity of other contributors to give more in order to make up for any "lost" potential contributor, because all potential contributors are subject to the contribution limits. This dynamic helps to explain not only why campaigns seem to be becoming void of debate but also why they seem to be becoming, according to many, more negative in tone. For if the candidate risks losing contributions by discussing issues, the most obvious available option is to focus on the negatives in one's opponent. By attacking, one might reduce the number of contributors willing to give to one's opponent, and such a reduction cannot be offset by added contributions from prior donors—even though those contributors, upset by the attacks, may be more fervent in their support than ever. More important, by stressing the opposing candidate's negatives and creating an image that election of the opponent would be an unmitigated disaster for all, the candidate gives contributors a reason to support him or her, without losing any potential contributors by proposing an actual policy that may gore particular political oxen.

In contrast, in an unregulated system, a candidate might be able to propose bolder solutions and rely on a handful of donors to provide "seed capital" for the campaign. The candidate could then use this seed money to try to persuade voters that his or her approach to issues is a good one. Contribution limits cut off this option, driving all candidates away from bold solutions; campaigns become efforts to pander to what the largest number of voters think, rather than to debate issues on the merits, and create support for new ideas.

It is no surprise, then, that in both the 1992 and 1996 presidential campaigns, the candidates who seemed most determined to discuss substantive issues, and whose proposed solutions most challenged status-quo thinking, were Ross Perot and Steve Forbes, self-funded multimillionaires not reliant on large numbers of contributors. Perot helped to force the issue of the federal budget deficit onto center stage. The influence of his candidacy should not be ignored today, with the federal government looking at projected surpluses far into the future. Similarly, Steve Forbes made discussion of a flat-rate income tax part of the national policy debate. In each case, the messenger was perceived by many to be seriously flawed. But in each case, the message could be heard only because the multimillionaire himself agreed to become the candidate. The money could not be given to a better messenger or to someone better prepared to fill the office of president. Such is the working of campaign finance regulation. And it is worth noting that but for *Buckley v. Valeo*, even the option exercised by Perot and Forbes would not exist, and the 1992 and 1996 campaigns would probably not have included discussion of the issues they brought to the fore.

By forcing campaigns to rely on large numbers of donors at the outset of the campaign, contribution restrictions have penalized candidates who would seek to educate or bring new issues forward. It has simultaneously rewarded candidates who base their appeal on the lowest common denominator. In both ways, it helped to impoverish political discussion over the last decades of the twentieth century.

Campaign Finance Reform Has Promoted Influence Peddling, Reduced Legislative Accountability, and Caused Dereliction of Duty

Contributors to political campaigns can choose between two strategies. The first is an electoral strategy in which the contributor aims to influence electoral outcomes so that the candidate preferred by the contributor wins. The contributor following such a strategy hopes that such contributions will be used to persuade voters to support the candidate, secure in the knowledge that if the candidate wins, he or she shares the ideology of the contributor and will vote in ways that the contributor generally agrees with. This is core First Amendment speech by almost any definition. Indeed, it is exactly what civics textbooks tell us campaigns are all about: attempting to persuade other voters of the merits of a particular candidate. Using this strategy, the contributor will normally seek to donate to candidates involved in close races.

The second approach is a legislative strategy, in which the contributor, rather than being concerned with who wins the race, hopes to influence the voting pattern of whichever candidate wins. The contributor using this strategy has little concern with close races. Rather, he or she will attempt to donate to races in which the likely winner can be determined in advance, thus assuring an audience with the legislator after election. It is this latter strategy that generally creates the greatest public concern about the potential for corruption. Yet strangely enough, contribution limits, the most popular reform measure, encourage PACs and other monied interests to adopt legislative strategies, which results in greater threats of "corruption" and a representative system that is less responsive to public opinion.

Campaign contributors must weigh the costs and benefits of pursuing an electoral strategy versus a legislative strategy. Even in close races, so long as a contributor is limited to a maximum contribution of $5,000 (the current limit for PACs) or some other relatively low amount, the contributor's campaign donation is unlikely to increase significantly the odds of a victory for the challenger. This makes an electoral strategy an unattractive option, because giving is unlikely to affect the outcome of any particular race significantly. The alternative is to contribute to incumbents in the hope that a legislative strategy might succeed, at least by helping the contributor gain access to plead a case to the office holder. Thus, by reducing the odds of a carrying out a successful electoral strategy, contribution limits can tend to lock the rational contributor into a legislative strategy.[19] To the extent, then, that campaign contributions might influence legislative behavior, campaign finance regulation in the form of contribution limits is likely to make the problem worse.

One possible solution to this problem would be to set the contribution threshold at a level so low that a legislative strategy would have no real chance of success. The amount could be $100, or even $5. At these levels, it is hard to see a legislator being swayed by any single contribution. However, this would make bundling of contributions, independent spending, and issue ads—three other villains in the reformist literature—more valuable, and because these tactics take more political organization and skill than straightforward giving to a candidate, such a measure might further increase the power of organized special interests. Moreover, at such low contribution levels candidates for federal office would lack the necessary resources to communicate with the public effectively. Leaving aside the fact that this might make such limits unconstitutional, it would have the effect of protecting incumbents from effective challenge, thus reducing accountability rather than promoting it.

Limits on contributions make the system less responsive in other ways, as well. For example, a favorite target of regulatory advocates for many years has been political action committees. Many proposals have been made to ban PACs, including some versions of the McCain-Feingold bill. However, political action committees perform a valuable monitoring function in the current campaign regime, a function that would be largely lost if contributions were set at such a low level. It has been suggested that the real issue that the campaign reform movement attempts to address is "shirking," or the tendency of elected officials to betray the public trust in favor of their own or other interests. One difficulty voters face is monitoring the performance of elected officials. By banding together with others having similar concerns, individuals can perform the monitoring function at a reasonable cost. Interest groups, and the PACs they spawn, thus play an important role in monitoring officeholders' performances so as to prevent shirking. Therefore, measures that would limit or eliminate the role of PACs are likely to reduce legislative monitoring, and lead to a legislature ever more isolated from the people.

Low contribution limits promote shirking in two other ways. First, they divert the legislative attention away from official duties and toward fundraising. The current federal contribution limit of $1,000 for individual contributions has not been adjusted for inflation since it was first enacted in 1974. Since then, the cost of campaigning has been affected by inflation and other factors. Imagine an hourly worker attempting to pay year 2001 bills on a 1974 hourly wage. The worker would labor long hours indeed! Much the same has happened to political candidates. With costs rising and each contributor limited to the amount given over a quarter of a century ago, raising the money necessary to run an effective campaign requires an ever-growing number of donors. This correspondingly requires that more time be devoted to fund-raising. This in turn makes campaigns longer, which is a complaint of many voters in and of itself. It benefits incumbents, who usually know earlier than challengers of their intention to run. But it also provides an incentive for legislators seeking reelection to shirk their legislative duties so as to devote time to fundraising.[20] This effect is most extreme at the presidential level, where millions are needed to run a competitive race. Raising money for a presidential campaign has been likened to trying to fill a swimming pool with a teaspoon. Lower limits, such as those proposed in many "reform" bills and passed by referendum in some states, simply make the problem worse.

Second, contribution limits promote shirking by increasing the pressure on legislators not to offend contributors. Simply put, contribution limits dry up the supply of campaign funds. This has the effect of creating a

78

"shortage" of funds. With funds in short supply, a candidate pays a higher cost for offending any potential contributor—if the donor is lost, the candidate will have more difficulty replacing the lost contribution by, for example, getting larger contributions from those supportive of the proposed action. Thus, to the extent that campaign contributions play a role in legislative behavior, contribution limits make that problem worse by increasing the value of any particular contribution.

Finally, there is always the possibility that limiting private contributions will simply increase the value of a more corrupting alternative: outright bribery. It is naive to think that when the government is heavily involved in virtually every aspect of economic life in the country (and quite a few noneconomic spheres as well), people affected by government actions will accept whatever comes without some kind of counterstrategy. In this way, too, low contribution limits may ultimately make the electoral system less responsive to public opinion and, therefore, less democratic.

Campaign Finance Regulation Has Favored Select Elites

Campaign finance regulation is usually sold as a populist means to strengthen the power of "ordinary" citizens against dominant, big-money interests. In fact, campaign finance reform has favored select elites and further isolated individuals from the political process.

There are a great many sources of political influence. These include direct personal attributes, such as speaking and writing ability, good looks, personality, time and energy, and organizational skills, as well as acquired attributes, such as wealth, celebrity, and access to or control of the popular press. In any society, numerous individuals will rise to the top of their professions to become part of an elite. Both as a prerequisite to their success and as a reward for it, such individuals will have certain financial and nonfinancial assets that they can often use for political ends. For example, Hollywood celebrities, by virtue of their fame, may gain audiences for their political views that they would not otherwise obtain. They may be invited to testify before Congress, despite their lack of any particular expertise, as when, in the mid-1980s actress Meryl Streep was invited to appear before Congress to discuss environmental issues, even though she later admitted to no particular expertise. Similarly, in 1988,

Congress heard testimony on agriculture from a trio of actresses—Sally Field, Jessica Lange, and Sissy Spacek—whose only qualification was having played farmers or farm wives in movies. Celebrities may also use their notoriety to assist campaigns through appearances at rallies.[21] Successful academics may write powerful articles that change the way people think about issues. Labor organizers may have at their disposal a vast supply of human resources that they can use to support favored candidates. Media editors, reporters, and anchors can shape not only the manner but also the content of news reporting. Those with marketing skills can apply their abilities to raise funds or to produce advertising for a candidate or cause. Successful entrepreneurs (and, indeed, most others on this list, especially celebrities) may amass large sums of money that can be used for political purposes.

The regulation of campaign contributions and spending restricts the political employment of immediately available wealth but not any of these other attributes. This begs the question of why the successful entrepreneur should be denied the ability to transfer his or her talents at creating wealth to the political arena, while the successful marketer or political organizer is permitted to do so. There is no a priori reason why a person with a flair for political organizing should be allowed political influence that is denied to the person with a flair for manufacturing.

The common response to this argument is that money can buy other sources of political power: It can purchase labor, marketing know-how, media access, even speaking coaches and improved physical appearance.[22] This argument is simply incorrect, however, insofar as it sees this as a unique feature of money. A winning personality, the ability to forge political alliances, and the time to devote to politics can, like money, be used to gain access to the media, labor, and other prerequisites to political success. Moreover, these skills, like the ability to produce effective television ads or to write persuasive campaign literature and speeches, are themselves convertible into money. For example, money can be raised through slick direct-mail pitches, operation of phone banks, advertisements, speeches at rallies, booths at county fairs, and countless other means. The trick to effective electoral politics is to take the assets with which one begins and to use them to obtain additional assets that one lacks. Money is no different. Many candidates who are able to raise substantial amounts of campaign cash are unable to convert that cash into other political assets. Conversely, many candidates who begin with relatively little cash are able to use their other political talents to raise the money necessary to take their message to the voters.

Once we accept the fact that different individuals control different sources of political power, it becomes apparent that attempts to exclude a particular form of power—money—from politics only strengthen the position of those whose power comes from other, nonmonetary, sources, such as time or media access. For example, although the Supreme Court has allowed states to limit even independent expenditures by nonmedia corporations in candidate races,[23] newspapers, magazines, and TV and radio corporations can spend unlimited sums to promote the election of favored candidates. Thus Donald Graham, the publisher of the *Washington Post*, has at his disposal the resources of a media empire to promote his views, free from the campaign finance restrictions to which others are subjected. ABC News anchor Peter Jennings is given a nightly forum on national television in which to express his views. Interestingly, surveys have indicated that the views of journalists often differ sharply from those of the public at large, with members of general public nearly eight times more likely to describe themselves as "conservative" than are journalists.[24]

Media elites are not the only group whose influence is increased by campaign spending and contribution limits. Restricting the flow of money into campaigns also increases the relative importance of in-kind contributions and so favors those who are able to control large blocks of human resources. Limiting contributions and expenditures does not particularly democratize the process but merely shifts power from those whose primary contribution is money to those whose primary contribution is time, organization, or some other resource. For example, limits on monetary contributions may merely shift influence from working individuals to retirees and students, who may have more time to devote to political activities. Others who benefit from campaign finance limitations, such as political middlemen, public relations firms conducting "voter education" programs, lobbyists, PACs such as Emily's List, that "bundle" large numbers of $1,000 contributions, and full-time political activists, may or may not be more representative of public opinion than the wealthy philanthropists and industrialists who financed so many past campaigns. I suspect that they are not.

In theory, it may be possible to limit in-kind contributions in the same manner as monetary contributions.[25] In fact, campaign regulators choose almost exclusively to target the influence of money. In practice, efforts to limit in-kind contributions create almost insurmountable administrative difficulties and, in the end, would not solve the unequal treatment created by the prejudice against money. Consider, for example, a politically talented, twenty-five-year-old Harvard law student from a privileged background who chooses to volunteer on a presidential campaign during summer break, passing up a law firm clerkship that pays $15,000 for the summer. Consider, at the same time, a West Virginia high-school dropout who goes to work in a body shop at age seventeen, scrapes together some money to launch his own shop at age twenty-two, opens a second shop two years later, and then at age twenty-five, angered over government policies affecting his business, seeks to promote political change by contributing $15,000 to a political campaign. Each individual seeks to forego $15,000 in consumption to promote his political beliefs, but only the activities of the Harvard law student are legal.[26] As this simple illustration shows, truly limiting the comparative advantages of in-kind contributions is simply not possible. How, for example, would we limit the ability of Arnold Schwarzenegger to turn his celebrity into Republican votes in any manner compatible with the First Amendment? Could we order Democratic campaign guru James Carville to divide his time evenly between Democratic and Republican candidates? Prohibit Meryl Streep from giving congressional testimony? Order Jesse Jackson to cease his voter registration campaigns, which are clearly aimed at registering more probable Democratic than Republican voters? The question is not money versus no money. The question is whether all people will be allowed to convert their varied talents into political influence to the best of their ability. For most Americans, the best way to convert their talents to influence is through cash contributions. Efforts to limit the flow of cash exclude from the process those whose talents do not directly lend themselves to political purposes, thereby increasing the relative power of those whose talents are directly applicable to the political arena.

82

Efforts to limit the influence of money simply favor nonmonetary elites. This targeting of a single source of political power—money—does not necessarily make the system more responsive to the interests of the "common person," however defined. It merely increases the relative power of other elites.

Those who are not in a position to exert political power are best served by allowing for the interplay among those elites, rather than attempting to exclude a single elite. For this interplay keeps any one group from gaining power, and provides more openings for newcomers to affect events. Efforts to ensure "equality" of inputs to the campaign process are less likely to guarantee popular control than is the presence of multiple sources of political power.[27] By decreasing the number of voices in the political debate, a strategy of excluding one source of influence increases the power of groups whose types of contributions remain unregulated. By creating added instability and a decentralization of power, the interplay of numerous elites may increase opportunities for traditionally less empowered groups to obtain influence. It allows those less powerful groups more opportunities to join alliances and assert a balance-of-power influence when more powerful groups are deadlocked.

Campaign Finance Regulation Has Favored Institutionalized Special Interests Over Grassroots Political Activity

Campaign finance regulation is also undemocratic in that it favors well-organized special interests over grassroots political activity. Of course, one person's "special interest" is another's "grassroots lobby," and vice versa. By "special interest," I mean a person or group that seeks to influence legislation and government policy, usually in pursuit of a narrowly defined economic interest, typically employing professional staff, and usually having a strong, top-down leadership structure. Such a group is usually more concerned with influencing legislative than public opinion. By a "grassroots lobby," I mean a group that tends to operate outside of traditional centers of political leadership, that typically relies more heavily on volunteer help and a decentralized structure, and that is more likely to be ideologically motivated, even if focused on a narrow issue.

83

Such a group would be somewhat more populist and would usually aim not to influence legislative opinion directly so much as to influence public opinion and awareness and make public opinion known to legislators. I recognize that these definitions are far from precise, and that many groups will have characteristics from both categories. Nevertheless, this seems a workable definition of each. The point is that campaign finance regulation leads to a professionalization of politics that may alienate more typical voters and hinder local, volunteer, and unorganized or less organized activity.

Limitations on contributions and spending work against grassroots groups. By definition, limits require significant regulation of the campaign process, including substantial reporting requirements as to the amounts spent and the sources of funds. Typically, regulation favors those already familiar with the regulatory machinery and those with the money and sophistication to hire the lawyers, accountants, and lobbyists needed to comply with complex filing requirements.[28] Such regulation will naturally disadvantage newcomers to the political arena, especially those who are themselves less educated or less able to pay for professional services. Although the necessary legal expertise can be bought, the cost will often be higher for candidates and groups with no prior political experience. In local races, funds may not be available to counter the expertise gained by incumbents through experience. And, of course, it would seem to cut against the grain of the entire reformist effort to increase the importance of specialized legal skills, not to mention the availability of funds to pay for those skills, in determining who wins a campaign. Efforts to regulate campaigns in favor of small contributors thus have the perverse effect of professionalizing politics and distancing the system from "ordinary" citizens.

Regulation also creates opportunities to gain an advantage over an opponent through use of the regulatory process, and litigation has now become a major campaign tactic. The mere act of filing a campaign finance complaint against an opponent can, in some cases, intimidate that opponent into silence. At a minimum, it can tie up valuable resources. Again, one can expect such tactics to be used most often by those already familiar with the rules. Indeed, there is some evidence that campaign enforcement actions have been disproportionately directed at challengers, who are less likely to have staff familiar with the intricacies of campaign finance regulation.[29]

Perhaps those most likely to run afoul of campaign finance laws, and thus to be vulnerable to legal manipulations aimed at driving them from the political debate, are unaffiliated individuals engaged in true grassroots activities. For example, in 1991, the *Los Angeles Times* found that sixty-two individuals had violated FECA contribution limits by making total contributions of more than $25,000 to candidates in the 1990 elections. As the *Times* noted, although many of these sixty-two were "successful business people" who "usually have the benefit of expert legal advice on the intricacies of federal election laws," the next largest group of violators consisted of "elderly persons . . . with little grasp of the federal campaign laws.[30] Threats of prosecution have, in fact, been used in efforts to silence dissent from those without "the benefit of expert legal advice on the intricacies of federal election laws," such as Margaret McIntyre, the Ohio housewife, or Leonard Smith, the Connecticut web site operator, whose cases were discussed in chapter 1.

Even sophisticated interest groups have found campaign finance laws to be a substantial hindrance to grassroots campaign activity and voter education efforts. In 1994, for example, both the U.S. Chamber of Commerce and the American Medical Association (AMA) decided not to publish and distribute candidate endorsements to thousands of their dues-paying members, in response to threats of litigation from the Federal Election Commission (FEC). Under the effective FEC regulations, only sixty-three of the chamber's 220,000 dues-paying members qualified as "members" for the purposes of receiving the organization's political communications. Similarly, the FEC had held that it would be unlawful for the AMA to distribute endorsements to some 44,500 of its dues-paying members. One AMA lawyer noted that, under the circumstances, communicating endorsements to its dues-paying members was not "worth the legal risk."[31] Yet presumably many of these members joined, at least in part, to get exactly this type of information. Thus the law closed off sources of information to voters. Oddly, such restrictions work against groups that rely on a large, mobilized memberships to be effective, while doing little to regulate groups that rely more heavily on professional lobbyists for their political involvement.

Conclusion

Campaign finance regulation has been packaged as a means of returning power to "ordinary people." In truth, however, such regulation has had the effect of excluding ordinary people from the political process in a variety of ways: It has insulated incumbents from the voting public, in both the electoral and legislative spheres; it has increased the incentives for legislative "shirking"; it has increased the ability of certain elites to dominate the debate by eliminating competing voices; it has placed a renewed premium on personal wealth in political candidates, and limited the number of candidates and the types of issues they discuss; and it has hampered grassroots political activity. These problems are not the result of a poorly designed regulatory structure but rather the inevitable result of a regulatory structure built on faulty assumptions. All of these costs are very real. And yet, at least in theory if not in practice, all of these problems with campaign finance regulation might be resolved. There is always the hope that if we just tinker with the rules long enough, and somehow close enough "loopholes," the lawmakers will outsmart the candidates, contributors, consultants, and campaign managers, and regulation might work.

Yet all of these costs, significant as they are, are dwarfed by yet another cost of campaign regulation. Throughout the history of American constitutional debate, discussion of the First Amendment has tended to center on whether or not the amendment was intended to cover obscenity and pornography, commercial speech, "fighting words," and treasonous statements. It was always taken for granted that the First Amendment applied to political speech—indeed, that political speech was the core of the First Amendment. Yet in January 1997, the minority leader in the U.S. House of Representatives, Richard Gephardt, spoke for many when he argued that "What we have here is two important values in conflict: freedom of speech and our desire for healthy campaigns in a healthy democracy. You can't have both."[32] And Gephardt made clear where he stood: in order to allow for greater regulation of campaign finance, he cosponsored an amendment to the U.S. Constitution that would have, in effect, repealed the freedom of speech clauses of the First Amendment, at least insofar as they might protect political speech from congressional regulation. The amendment failed, but more than a third of both the House and Senate voted for it.

Gephardt's statement lays bare the ultimate price of campaign finance regulation: such regulation is not compatible with the free speech guarantees of the First Amendment. It is not exaggeration to say that campaign finance "reform" poses the greatest threat to free speech in America since the Alien and Sedition Acts two hundred years ago. Ultimately, campaign finance regulation is based on premises that are at odds with the traditional notions of equality and free speech embedded in the Constitution.

Chapter 5

SOME PROBLEMS WITH THE SOLUTION
OF GOVERNMENT FINANCING

Frustration with the failure of regulation to cure the alleged evils of a private finance system has contributed to intellectual support for financing all campaigns with tax dollars. Though this is usually called "public" funding, that term is a misnomer. Campaigns are funded by the public now—by hundreds of thousands, even millions of citizens who make voluntary contributions to various candidates and organizations. What is euphemistically called public funding actually means government-funded campaigns, or tax funding of campaigns, and should be addressed as such. Government-funded campaigns are attractive because they can potentially take monetary inequality out of the equation, and because, by eliminating the need for candidates to rely on private donors, they can free officeholders to ignore the wishes of these donors, presumably to act in accordance with the individual officeholder's own conception of the public good.

Because the United States has limited experience with government-funded campaigns, it is difficult to analyze the empirical results of government funding in the same manner as we can analyze the effects of regulation on the private campaign finance system. The most notable ongoing experiments are the government-financed elections for president that date from the 1976 campaign, and state funding of legislative campaigns in Minnesota and Wisconsin, which also date from the 1970s. Most other systems, including that of New York City, are far too new for us to make more than the most preliminary assessments of their effects.

Complicating the matter further is the almost endless array of potential government-financing systems. To say that one favors government financing of campaigns is a bit like saying that one enjoys sports. Are we talking football? Kayaking? Downhill skiing? Ballroom dancing? Chess? The options are endless. Many people may favor government financing in principle, but oppose many, or even most, particular plans for government financing. Say, for example, one proposed a government-financing plan that provided that incumbents would receive twenty times the amount of money as challengers; it would have little support, even among those who generally favor government financing.[1] At the same time, there must be many people generally opposed to government financing who would, nonetheless, support the right plan for government financing. I suspect that this group is much smaller, however, because so much of the opposition to government financing is ideologically based. There are many who have a blanket objection to any government financing of campaigns as inherently beyond the scope of either good government or the Constitution, or both.

In any case, when analyzing government-financed campaigns, it makes more sense to focus on broad principles than to attempt to analyze in detail the incredibly diverse mix of proposed and potential schemes. We begin, then, by considering a few criteria by which any campaign finance system ought to be measured, and comparing how well government-financed plans generally fulfill these criteria relative to private finance systems.

Five Criteria and Some Difficult Issues for Government Financing

The criteria proposed here are, I think, relatively noncontroversial; they are quite similar to those proposed, for example, by Professor Richard Briffault, an advocate of government financing.[2] They are:

- *Administrability.* First, a system of campaign finance should be easy to administer.
- *Flexibility.* Second, it should be flexible, and able to adapt quickly to changing political environments and to new technologies and techniques for campaigning.
- *Opportunity.* Third, it should, if not necessarily foster more candidacies and entry into politics by political newcomers, at least not overly discourage such challenges.
- *Competitiveness.* Fourth, it should, if not necessarily promote more competitive races, at least not overly insulate incumbents from challenge.
- *Communication.* Finally, it should provide candidates with adequate funds to communicate with and educate voters.

Left off of this list for now are what are arguably the two most important criteria: the system should promote equality, and the system should insulate legislators from the influence, or "corruption," of money. These topics I explore elsewhere in this book. As for the five criteria listed above, they may not constitute an exhaustive list but they are certainly enough to get us started. Although there are potential advantages for government-financed systems in meeting some of these criteria, in none of them is it clear that government financing systems are preferable to private ones.

Ease of Administration

Campaign finance regulation creates compliance costs for both government and private political actors. Many systems will require that substantial government resources be devoted to monitoring and enforcement. A system that is too complex can create significant administrative, compliance, and funding difficulties for candidates, and this burden is likely to weigh most heavily on those candidates and groups that are new to political wars.[3]

When it comes to ease of administration, no system can beat that of a private, unregulated system of funding, such as existed in all parts of the United States until very late in the nineteenth century, when laws regulating campaign finance first appeared. A completely unregulated system of campaign finance requires no government monitoring, auditing, or enforcement. There need be no federal agency of any kind entrusted with regulating the system. (This is not to say that there would not be routine law enforcement agencies engaged in prevention of bribery, blackmail, and other crimes that may take place in the context of political campaigns.) Similarly, on the candidate's side there is no need to devote resources to compliance, and record keeping can be done with the needs of the candidate, rather than government monitors, foremost in mind. Against a baseline of unregulated private finance, government financing loses the test on ease of administration every time.

We do not, however, have an unregulated system of private finance but rather one that, at the federal level, is quite heavily regulated. It is unlikely that all regulation will end anytime soon; at a minimum, disclosure of private campaign contributions seems here to stay for the foreseeable future.[4] Thus a system of government financing of congressional campaigns may actually reduce administrative costs from their current levels, though probably not to the level they would be at in a deregulated system. From a government perspective, for example, the Federal Election Commission devotes far fewer resources to administration of the federal presidential campaign fund than to enforcement, audits, and disclosure.[5] At the congressional level, the lion's share of those enforcement, auditing, and disclosure costs are incurred because the system relies on regulated private financing. If a government financing system were established that succeeded in gaining participation of most congressional candidates, and were sufficiently simple to administer, it might lower government administrative costs. Moreover, it might actually lower costs for candidates, as well, particularly if it succeeded in getting candidates out of the time-consuming and expensive fund-raising business altogether.

Coming up with such a simple system is not so easy. For one thing, the Constitution, as interpreted in *Buckley v. Valeo*, prevents the government from simply requiring all candidates to take public funds and limiting candidates' private spending.[6] Thus government financing proposals must draw candidates into optional schemes of public financing, which usually include "voluntary" spending limits.

This could probably be done with ease if we were willing to fund campaigns adequately from the government till. We could provide, for example, a major party Senate nominee in California with $30 million for the general election, a Senate nominee in Ohio with $8 million, or a House nominee in any district with $2 million or more. If we did, and such amounts were indexed for inflation, most candidates would probably accept the government subsidy and the accompanying spending limit. Indeed, relatively few candidates raise such amounts—only eleven House candidates took in more than $2 million in the 1997–1998 election cycle, for example, and only thirty-nine topped $1.5 million.[7] Furthermore, money does have, after all, diminishing returns, and beyond the type of spending levels suggested above, additional spending would not be expected to translate into many votes, if any. Candidates would probably find it worthwhile to take the money, accept the spending cap, and devote time to activities other than fund-raising.

The problem is that we are not inclined to provide government financing at such lavish levels. For example, Annelise Anderson of the Hoover Institute has estimated the cost of a reasonable communications program for a presidential campaign to be at least $600 million. The figure is based on a campaign that includes enough thirty-second ads on network, cable, and local television in major media markets to reach most adults ten times each; three to four thirty-minute cable "fireside chats"; radio ads that attempt to reach listeners in major radio markets five times each, one or two full-page ads in every major newspaper in the country, two pieces of direct mail sent to each potential voter, a videocassette on the candidate sent to each household, and traditional billboards, buttons, and bumper stickers.[8] We presently provide major party presidential nominees with less than $75 million for the general election campaign, yet virtually all reform measures suggest that we should lower, rather than increase, spending.

When subsidies are set too low, many candidates will be reluctant to join voluntary government-financing schemes, figuring that they can raise more money and run a more effective campaign on private contributions. To provide incentives for candidates to opt in despite low funding levels, many proposals for government funding include complicated provisions that increase administrative costs and can hamper grassroots candidacies.[9] Until state funding advocates are willing to do away with such complicated and generally punitive trigger mechanisms and provide true incentives to take the government funds, it is likely that most proposals for government funding will increase administrative costs beyond those involved in the present system of regulated private financing, and far beyond those that would exist in an unregulated, or at least substantially deregulated, system of campaign finance.

Flexibility

A finance system should be flexible. Politics—in terms of issues, personalities, technologies, and tactics—is a rapidly changing field. Magazines such as *Campaigns and Elections* now exist for the purpose of keeping campaign managers and tacticians up to date on the latest developments in campaigning. A system that is geared to regulate or subsidize the last campaign may "distort" politics, and in particular runs the danger of "locking in" certain parties or candidates.[10]

Unfortunately, government is notoriously slow at adjusting to changing realities. For example, not until 1999 did the FEC allow campaign contributions made on-line by credit card to count toward federal matching funds in the presidential race, or allow electronic mail to be used to obtain payroll deductions for employee contributions to company political action committees.[11] Yet in this area the FEC has actually acted with relative speed—much faster than Congress, for example, which has passed no legislation to clarify whether or not it believes that the Federal Election Campaign Act applies to certain Internet communications. Similarly, Congress's 1974 enactment of a $1,000 contribution limit has never been adjusted, even though that limit has been substantially eroded by inflation.

Political practices often evolve specifically in response to, and to avoid the reach of, federal regulation. Long before passage of FECA, unions created "political action committees" to avoid the ban on union contributions and gain an advantage for Democrats over Republicans.[12] Since 1980, we have witnessed the rise of independent expenditures and bundling, followed by the rise in the importance of "soft money" and "issue advocacy." These and other tactics exist in an effort to affect the outcome of elections in favor of the groups using them. For example, trial lawyers use "bundling" very effectively; many trial lawyers have incomes that allow them to donate $1,000 to a campaign, so the Association of Trial Lawyers of America is able to collect substantial checks and deliver them, "bundled," to favored candidates. This technique is less effective for a group such as National Right to Life, whose members and sympathizers generally have lower incomes than trial lawyers. However, right-to-life groups have been very effective at using candidate "scorecards," which play to the groups' strength—a broad membership base and a ready distribution network through churches and home school groups. Both bundling and the use of issue advocacy candidate scorecards are the result of efforts to limit direct contributions and in-kind donations to candidates. What is of added interest, however, is that regulation will often favor some groups and harm others. It is often not possible for opposing interests to take advantage of the same technique as their adversaries. Different groups find different types of fund-raising techniques and political action most effective. Thus, a system that successfully limits scorecards, but not bundling, benefits trial lawyers and harms right-to-life groups. Limit bundling, but not scorecards, and you get the opposite result. Limit both, and some other group will gain a relative benefit. Government simply cannot keep up with the fluid world of political campaigning, and this means that government-dominated systems will tend to favor some groups over others.

Similarly, it has long been noted that one major difficulty in reforming campaign finance laws is that most changes will be perceived as benefiting either Republicans or Democrats. As both sides will fight tooth and nail to block reform perceived as detrimental to their political prospects, reform efforts are prone to gridlock.[13] If we add to this the noted propensity of campaign finance regulation to be particularly prone to the law of unintended consequences, we have a recipe for a system that creates more problems than it solves.[14]

The alternative, we might note, is hardly more inviting—if gridlock does not set in, we might see constant tinkering with the law in an effort to gain partisan advantage. In short, campaign finance is an area in which we cannot afford to have the law in constant flux, due to the propensity of temporal majorities to aim for partisan advantage. Nor can we afford a static, heavily regulated system, due to its distorting effects on political life. Campaign finance, we must glumly come to realize, is a theater in which the law is particularly ill equipped to act.

Opportunity

A third problem is to design a system that does not discourage meaningful candidates from running. In this regard, the alleged shortcomings of an unregulated private system are well documented.[15] Potential candidates might be prevented from running for office by their inability to raise the necessary funds, or discouraged from running by the difficulty of raising funds. This is more true in a regulated private system than in an unregulated one, of course. A system that limits the size of private contributions makes it harder for all candidates to raise funds and almost always works against political outsiders and newcomers by making it harder for them than for incumbents and well-known figures to raise money.

There is little reason to believe that there are a large number of viable candidates for office who cannot raise the necessary funds in a deregulated system, as opposed to one that limits private contributions and spending. As discussed in chapter 4, most people who would have any chance of running a serious campaign for office can attract the necessary funds, and the freedom to raise and spend money increases the pool of viable candidates.

Nevertheless, a government-financed system could potentially increase the pool of candidates beyond that of a deregulated private system by assuring that adequate financing is available to more candidates. But it could decrease that pool of candidates as well, if the incentives created to encourage acceptance of public financing make it extremely unlikely that a privately financed candidate can win, while at the same time setting the bar for government financing higher than most candidates can reach.

The problem here is in deciding who ought to receive government funds. Most observers seem to reject the notion that funds should be available to every potential candidate, seeing such a loose standard as a giveaway of public money. Funds need to be available on a broad enough basis to encourage "legitimate" candidates, but should not be so broadly available that the very availability of tax dollars for campaigning promotes frivolous candidacies. For this reason, most proposals for government financing require candidates to show a measure of "popular support."

The current presidential financing system, for example, provides "matching" funds to a candidate seeking his party's nomination who raises at least $5,000 in each of twenty states in amounts of $250 or less. Contributions are then matched, up to $250 per contribution, from the federal till. In the general election, party nominees receive public funds to run their campaigns in an amount determined by their showing in the last election. The system is structured to make certain that the Republicans and Democrats will have the same amount of money in the general election, and more than any other party's nominee.[16]

This system appears to be both overinclusive and underinclusive in terms of financing candidates. It is overinclusive in that, under the system, a number of fringe candidates have qualified for federal matching funds, most notably convicted felon Lyndon LaRouche, John Hagelin of the Natural Law Party (which advocates greater use of transcendental meditation as the key government policy), and Lenora Fulani of the New Alliance Party (a socialist party that has been accused of engaging in cult-type brainwashing).[17] This problem has grown in recent years, because the qualifying thresholds have not been adjusted upward for inflation, illustrating again the inflexibility of government systems. Yet the system is also overinclusive in that a party may be eligible for general election funds, based on past performance, even though it is unlikely to contest the future election. At the same time, it is underinclusive because any new major third-party nominee would not be eligible for funds prior to the general election. Such a nominee is only eligible to receive funds after the election, provided that he gets at least 5 percent of the vote. This is of little use to the candidate during the critical campaign before the election, as candidate John Anderson discovered in 1980, when he was unable to borrow campaign funds before the election on the basis of anticipated federal funds after the election. Thus, Anderson's campaign floundered for lack of funds when they were most needed.[18]

Other plans use other devices to cut down the potential number of candidates who might make a claim on the government purse. For example, so-called "Clean Money Campaign Reform" bills that the lobbying group Public Campaign began to promote in the states in the late 1990s require candidates to garner a substantial number of $5 contributions in order to qualify for government funds. As introduced in the United States Senate, a "Clean Money" bill requires the larger of either one thousand $5 contributions or a number of $5 contributions equal to one-quarter of 1 percent of a state's voting-age population.[19] I have no way of knowing whether or not such a figure is too high or too low, and the truth is that the promoters of these bills do not either. As Public Campaign itself has written, the threshold, "must be high enough to screen out frivolous candidates who are unable to demonstrate a threshold level of support. At the same time, it must be low enough so as not to present a barrier to serious challengers. . . . It should also be noted that the required number will need to be reviewed and, probably, revised once the new law has been in effect." The sponsors recognize that this threshold is likely to be manipulated by incumbents who seek to protect their seats, adding that "it will be easier to revise the numbers upwards than downwards . . . (incumbents being unlikely to encourage more challengers)."[20]

In any case, the "Clean Money" plans are also both under- and overinclusive. They are underinclusive in that they will exclude late-starting candidates who might otherwise gain substantial support but who do not have time to gather the necessary small contributions, and they will exclude serious candidates who have available substantial funds with which to campaign and raise name recognition, but who, prior to using those funds to campaign, lack the necessary organization, public support, and name recognition to gather large numbers of small contributions. This illustrates a typical "reform" trap of mistaking the purpose of campaigns with the purpose of voting. The "Clean Money" acts are based on the premise that spending should reflect a preexisting level of public support. In fact, it usually will, but there is no particular reason why it should: the purpose of spending money is to gain public support, not merely to reflect preexisting popularity.

These "Clean Money" acts are overinclusive in that candidates who are not viable candidates will still qualify. As the lobbyists for these "Clean Money" bills admit, getting signatures on a petition is not truly representative of any level of popular support.[21] Getting $5 contributions is more difficult, of course, and the theory is that few people will usually give money to a cause with which they are not in agreement. However, I will speak simply from personal experience: In my neighborhood a variety of political groups, such as Greenpeace and Public Interest Research Groups (PIRGs), regularly send young student volunteers or low-paid workers through the neighborhood to collect $5 contributions for various causes. These volunteers appear at the door, describe a horrible problem facing the neighborhood, city, or state, and ask for a small contribution. I assume by their regular appearance that they find this to be a successful way to raise money. I doubt that most of the donors have any real idea about the issues involved, and my conversations with neighbors who have contributed confirm this. I doubt, therefore, that any real depth of public support will be found in collecting $5 contributions on simplistic, one-sided presentations of issues to voters who otherwise know little or nothing about the candidate.

Government-financed campaigns might therefore be better or worse than a deregulated private system in promoting worthwhile candidates. It will depend largely on where the threshold is set for qualifying for funds. Given the uncertainties involved, the tendency for incumbents to protect themselves, and the fact that even a rule that at one point works well may periodically need revamping—which may come slowly or not at all due to the lack of flexibility in the system—we should be skeptical that there is much to be gained from tax funding.

Competitiveness

Very similar problems arise when it comes to fostering competitive races. Government-funding advocates, such as Richard Briffault, argue that "public funding clearly outdoes private funding" when it comes to competitiveness, but the comparison they make tends to be between a tax-funded system with adequate campaign funds and a heavily regulated private system.[22] In fact, since the era of heavy federal campaign finance regulation began in 1974, incumbent reelection rates have continued to rise and the number of competitive, or marginal, districts to decrease.[23] It is not clear, of course, that this trend is not a mere statistical blip, or perhaps caused by political background factors.[24] It is certainly not true that this trend as a whole can be laid at the feet of campaign finance regulation. Sophisticated, computer-driven gerrymandering, to give just one example, may share more of the blame. As discussed in chapter 4, however, there are reasons why limits on contributions and spending within a privately financed contribution system distort political campaigns in favor of incumbents. For instance, prior to the passage of FECA, challengers in U.S. House races tended to raise about sixty-seven cents for every one dollar raised by incumbents. After FECA, that number dropped to about twenty-five cents by a challenger for every one dollar raised by incumbents, before rebounding somewhat to its 1996 level of forty-two cents per incumbent-raised dollar.[25]

Whether or not government financing will improve the situation of challengers relative to that in a deregulated private system is open for debate. In those two states that have meaningful experience with tax financing for their state legislatures, studies of government-financing systems have yielded mixed results. A 1995 study of Minnesota's system by Patrick Donnay and Graham Ramsden concluded that Minnesota's system "promises more competitive campaigns, but does not go far toward creating them." The authors attribute this failure to the program's design, which—not surprisingly—gives more benefits to incumbents than to challengers.[26] A study of Wisconsin's system by Kenneth Mayer and John Wood seemed to yield a similar result. They concluded that "public financing has had no effect at all on the level of electoral competition," and "public financing of congressional elections, by itself, will not eliminate the problem of uncompetitive elections."[27] In a later study, however, Mayer argues that "a well-designed and adequately funded public finance program can dramatically increase competition levels."[28]

So, will government financing foster competitive elections? Again, it depends on the type of financing system that might be adopted. For example, to the extent that government financing with a spending cap equalizes expenditures, it might help challengers, who are usually outspent even in a deregulated system. Public financing, however, also prevents challengers from ever spending more than incumbents. Given the tremendous value of incumbency, many believe that challengers are only on equal footing with incumbents when they can spend more. Challengers in a position to spend more than an incumbent are usually the strongest challengers. Thus, a flat spending cap may harm those challengers most likely actually to defeat an incumbent.

Complicating the question further, strong evidence suggests that the key variable is not really who outspends whom but whether challengers spend enough to make their names and positions known to the public.[29] Thus, a government financing system with an expenditure cap that sets the limits high enough may make races more competitive, whereas a system that sets the spending level too low may make races less competitive. The presence of adequate funding is a key element to Mayer's 1998 findings that public financing can "dramatically increase" competition.[30]

But can we expect government to set funding at adequate levels? As Mayer notes, Wisconsin has failed to do so.[31] One reason that it is difficult to assure that government funding is both enacted and maintained at adequate levels is that it is easily criticized as "welfare for politicians," and as an unnecessary state expense in any period of budget cutbacks or austerity. There is, quite simply, "no hint of a political will to dramatically expand the levels of [tax] financing."[32] A partial solution to the problem of the public's miserly attitude toward government financing of campaigns can be found in a creative proposal by Daniel Hays Lowenstein. He proposes that government funds go not to candidates but to political parties, which could then distribute the funds.[33] The advantage to this system is that party leaders should tend to spend their funds on competitive races, but will not provide substantial funds for races that appear to be lopsided. This should support competitive races while keeping overall costs lower than if equal funding were given to each candidate. Not only would this be a more efficient use of campaign funds but it could keep "safe" incumbents from further entrenching themselves through large spending in noncompetitive races—thus making competitive races more likely in the future. This is, at best, only a partial solution; there will still be pressure to lower the amounts provided to uncompetitive levels. Indeed, since many Americans distrust political parties, Lowenstein's proposal, if enacted, may actually increase the antipathy to providing adequate funds.[34]

A second reason, however, why spending caps will probably be set too low is simply that incumbents, who want to be reelected, will set the levels of the caps. For example, when Congress debated spending caps in 1997, the bills establishing those caps set the spending limit at a level at which challengers could not be competitive.[35] Every challenger spending less than the proposed limit in Senate campaigns had lost in each of the 1994 and 1996 elections, whereas every incumbent spending less than the limit had won. Similarly, only 3 percent of challengers spending less than the proposed limit for House races had won in 1996, whereas 40 percent of challengers spending more than that limit had won.[36] It is not necessary to attribute pernicious intentions to legislators to realize the danger that limits will constantly be set too low. Incumbents, who already have substantial name recognition and know how much they need to run an effective campaign, may simply have forgotten how much challengers need to spend to do the same.

Worse, even if the original cap seems adequate, it may not remain so. For example, in the federal system, it appears that the amounts allotted to the major parties for the general election of the president, even though adjusted for inflation, are no longer adequate. This deficiency has prompted increased spending on "issue advocacy" and increased amounts of "soft-money" contributions.[37] In Wisconsin, spending limits have not been raised since 1986, becoming, in the process, woefully inadequate.[38] Thus, we see that the lack of flexibility within a government-financing campaign, coupled with political pressures to reduce spending, makes it difficult to keep government limits adequate, even if they were when first enacted.

Of course, the argument that the spending cap may be set too low is easily rebutted by proposing a program—such as Minnesota's, perhaps—in which the cap is set at an appropriate level and indexed for inflation (although, in fact, cost for campaign staples such as paper and broadcast advertising has increased faster than general inflation). But it is legitimate to question whether the incentives and dynamics of the issue make it more likely than not that a government-financing system will come to favor incumbents. It is true that a tax-financed system can assure that all candidates, especially challengers, have the critical mass of funds necessary to make them competitive. It seems at least equally likely, however, that such a system will be used to lock in incumbents and deter serious challengers. Considering the limited experience at the state and federal level and what we know about political behavior, a government-financing system could increase competitiveness, but probably will not.

Communication

While addressing the difficulty of providing for funds adequate to foster commpetition, we have already considered the electoral advantages of incumbency. One reason that incumbents do well when spending caps are set too low is that voters are deprived of both information about challengers and information that challengers would provide about incumbents. Because voters start with more information on incumbents, but rarely with any concerted effort to find potential flaws with the incumbent, low spending favors incumbents. Also, because challengers are less well known, and usually receive less free coverage than incumbents (by virtue of not holding office or engaging in the public acts and discussion that go with holding office), low spending tends to penalize challengers. Again, it is certainly possible to devise a government system that provides for adequate funds, but there is little reason to think that such a result is likely or, even if temporarily achieved, that funding levels will remain adequate. Without campaign spending, voters' information is limited to what they can get through the media.

A deregulated private system may not always provide adequate funds to challengers, but given that the general thrust of political reform efforts is to reduce the amount spent on political campaigns, we should not be optimistic that government financing will increase voter education levels.

Overall, there are no guarantees that a tax-financed system will perform better than a deregulated private system judged by any of these criteria of administrability, flexibility, opportunity, competitiveness, or communication. Tax financing does offer potential improvements in some areas, but what we know about politics and government regulation suggests that such benefits are unlikely to be realized. In fact, negative consequences are perhaps the more likely result.

The Futility of Government Financing

Even if one holds an optimistic view of government financing, there is one more issue to address. The fact is that, without a major change in constitutional jurisprudence (probably requiring a constitutional amendment), government financing will not solve either the equality or the corruption problems that beleaguer the system.

We have 100 percent government financing, with voluntary spending limits, of the presidential general election campaigns now. No major party nominee has ever opted out of the system. Yet those who demand more regulation, in this case those who favor extending some type of tax financing to congressional and senatorial campaigns, do not generally consider the presidential system to have even remotely resolved the problems of equality or corruption. The reason is simple: the primary result of public funding of presidential campaigns has been to distort political campaigns and cause monetary participation to take new forms. In particular, the successful effort to chop off the head of "evil" in presidential campaigns—private donations to candidates—has caused the Hydra-like growth of the twin "evils" of "soft" money and "issue advocacy," which would-be regulators now denounce. Thus, candidates' campaigns don't spend money, yet money is spent on independent expenditures, issue ads, convention sponsorship, party-building activities financed with soft money, and more. Soft money and issue advocacy, to focus only on the two most disparaged evils, cannot be successfully regulated, for both practical and constitutional reasons.[39]

Even if proposals to regulate "soft" money and "issue advocacy" were to be upheld against constitutional challenge in the courts—or perhaps implemented after constitutional amendment—this would not solve the regulators' dilemma. There are simply too many ways for those who want to influence public policy to do so. For example, in 1996 the Republican and Democratic parties spent nearly $41 million on their national conventions, although only $8 million was provided in federal funds for the conventions. The extra money came in the form of corporate sponsorship for "civic and commercial" purposes.[40] In fact, such sponsorship both helps the conventions work as part of the campaign (by firing up activists and

103

drawing added paid and free media attention) and provides a method for donors interested in supporting candidates and parties to do so.

Convention sponsorship is an obvious way of rerouting political spending in a world of spending caps. Even if soft money and issue ads could be constitutionally regulated, many other approaches would spring up, perhaps including the purchase of partisan media outlets. There are numerous other ways to sidestep even these draconian types of regulation. With a federal government that currently spends over $1.5 trillion per year and that claims the right to regulate local education, virtually every phase of the employer-employee relationship, prices, wages, gun ownership, birth control, tobacco use, drug use, foreign trade, health care, and much, much more, there is no reason to think that those who seek to influence who holds power in this monumental government will not be creative enough to circumvent the regulations.

To the extent that government financing aims to prevent potential corruption or equalize voices, it presupposes that other expenditures will be stopped, either by law or "voluntarily," through incentives to limit spending. But simply mandating an end to private expenditures is, as we shall see in succeeding chapters, unconstitutional, and with good reason. And the only real voluntary spending limit comes when those who care about politics decide not to spend any more. Everything else is a coercive limit on political speech, or else it need not be included in the law. Because the limit is not voluntary, and because we have a First Amendment that allows free discussion of political issues, a way will be found around that limit. So long as this is the case, the goal of reducing the political influence of "special interests," whether we define that influence as creating an "equality" problem or a "corruption" problem, is not going to be met merely through government financing.

Conclusion

In theory, government subsidies of political campaigns, if not tied to bans on private contributions and spending limits, may indeed have certain benefits for political life.[41] A well-designed system might increase competitiveness, and therefore accountability, and it might also increase the flow of information to voters as well as the availability of well-qualified candidates. But we must consider government financing not in a purely academic sense but in the context of what the political system is likely to yield. For reasons discussed above, we should be skeptical that such a well-designed system could be enacted or maintained. In any case, such a system is probably off the charts politically: none of the major "reform" groups seems willing even to consider a government funding proposal that does not include limits on contributions and spending.[42]

Government financing plans that include limits on contributions and spending, whether deemed "voluntary" or mandatory, may well be doomed to failure, as with the current system for financing presidential campaigns. At a minimum, it would be naive to put too much faith into government financing as a means to solve the alleged corruption and equality problems of campaign finance while avoiding the undemocratic consequences of regulation of private contributions and spending.

Perhaps it is time not to rethink our historic opposition to government-financed campaigns but for self-styled reformers to rethink their opposition to deregulated campaigns.

Part II

Constitutional Matters

Chapter 6

MONEY AND SPEECH

Passage of the Federal Elections Campaign Act in 1971, and more so the 1974 amendments to the act, ushered in a period of unprecedented regulation of politics. Already we have seen that campaign finance regulation has had broadly "undemocratic" consequences for American political life, and that these consequences flow naturally from the enterprise. Nevertheless, the regulations were not so strict as they might have been. Even before the 1974 amendments, the Second Circuit Court of Appeals decision in *United States v. National Committee for Impeachment* had prohibited, on First Amendment grounds, enforcement of the FECA against groups engaged in nonpartisan speech about political issues. Though the National Committee for Impeachment's ad mentioned a "clearly identified candidate" (President Nixon, who was seeking reelection) and had the potential to "affect" a federal election, the court held that the First Amendment prohibited such regulation of political speech. Further, as we have seen, the 1974 amendments were almost immediately challenged in federal court. In *Buckley v. Valeo*, the Supreme Court upheld portions of the Federal Elections Campaign Act that imposed limits on the size of political campaign contributions, but struck down limits on independent expenditures made in support of a political candidate, on total campaign spending by a candidate or the candidate's committee, and on campaign spending by the candidate from personal or family resources. All such restrictions, the Court held, violated the First Amendment right to free speech.

Buckley has since become one of the most widely scorned decisions in the recent history of the Court. Although it has detractors who argue that it does not go far enough in protecting speech and the right to participate in politics, most commentary proceeds from the conviction that *Buckley* erred in failing to allow more legislative leeway.

Attacks come from three directions: the first argues that *Buckley* erred in protecting monetary contributions on First Amendment grounds; the second avers that although the *Buckley* Court correctly found a compelling state interest in preventing corruption, it adopted too narrow a definition of corruption to be useful to the state; the third attacks the Supreme Court's refusal to accept political equality as a compelling state interest sufficient to overcome burdens on free speech.

In fact, the weakest part of the constitutional analysis in the *Buckley* decision is not, as so many assume, the portion that strikes down aspects of congressional regulation. Rather, *Buckley's* constitutional Achilles heel is its holding that the alleged anticorruption interest of the government justifies the burdens that certain campaign finance regulation places on First Amendment rights. Political speech is not free when it is burdened by regulation. In this and the following two chapters, we consider the constitutionality of campaign regulatory schemes.

The threshold constitutional question, covered in this chapter, is whether campaign contributions and expenditures are even protected by the First Amendment. In answering this and the other constitutional questions surrounding campaign finance regulation, we must first be cognizant of the legal standard under which courts will evaluate the competing claims of regulatory and antiregulatory forces.

Standard of Judicial Review

In considering the constitutionality of laws passed by the legislature, the Supreme Court has established for itself different standards of review. Generally, government laws and programs that do not discriminate on the basis of race, sex, or national origin, and that do not burden "fundamental" rights, are reviewed by the courts only to determine if the government has a "rational basis" for enacting the law. Most laws reviewed under this standard pass the constitutional test. Laws that burden "fundamental rights" are subjected to a much more searching review, known to the court as "strict scrutiny." Under this test, a government law that burdens a "fundamental" right must be justified by a "compelling" government interest of the highest order. Furthermore, the government solution must be "narrowly tailored" to address the problem, with every effort made to avoid incidental effects not relevant to solving the problem that justifies the regulation. The court's jurisprudence, and academic and political commentary, as to what does or ought to constitute a "fundamental right" is extraordinarily long and complex. For our purposes, we can accept that no one in the last half century has ever seriously challenged the fact that laws regulating freedom of speech burden "fundamental rights." Thus, this most exacting level of judicial review, strict scrutiny, is applied to regulations burdening First Amendment rights. If spending or contributing money for political purposes is a form of free speech, or, more properly put, if limiting such expenditures and contributions burdens free speech, then strict scrutiny ought to apply to efforts to regulate campaign finance, and supporters of such regulation must face a very heavy burden before regulating political giving and spending.[1]

Speech and Action

Most of the time, recognizing speech is easy. Few would argue against the proposition that a speech is speech; that a newspaper editor's decision on the publication of articles in a newspaper is speech; or that the very publication of pamphlets and newspapers is speech. Similarly, most agree that protest, in the form of marching, carrying placards, singing, and the like, is speech.[2] The difficulty in defining the contours of speech has gener-

111

ally come when the speech in question is nonpolitical speech, such as commercial speech, pornography, and so-called "fighting words" or "hate speech."[3] Even those with the narrowest view of the First Amendment, however, have always assumed that it applies to political speech. Since campaign contributions and expenditures are clearly political, the threshold question for evaluating campaign finance regulation under the Constitution is whether or not, in the most simplistic terms, money is speech. More precisely, the question is whether or not gifts and expenditures of money for political purposes constitute a form of protected speech. If so, they are entitled to First Amendment protection, and laws regulating them will be subject to strict scrutiny.

In the mainstream media, it is popular to ridicule the idea that a campaign contribution or expenditure could be "speech" entitled to First Amendment protection. This largely accounts for the overwhelming bias of the institutional press in favor of efforts to regulate campaign finance, and it is certainly a view held by much of the general public. Nevertheless, most observers are ready to recognize that an action or activity can be, and often is, a form of protected speech, and despite its symbolic nature, relatively few have argued that a gift of money is not protected by the First Amendment, at least when given for political purposes. Perhaps the most notable exception is J. Skelly Wright, who as a judge on the U.S. court of appeals for the D.C. Circuit voted with the court of appeals majority to uphold almost all of the Federal Elections Campaign Act,[4] only to be reversed by the Supreme Court in *Buckley*.

Judge Wright argued, in two prominent law review pieces published shortly after the *Buckley* decision, that "nothing in the First Amendment commits us to the dogma that money is speech."[5] Rather, Wright argued that limits on contributions and spending were not limits on speech, but only limits on property having an incidental effect on speech. Abandonment of the "dogma" that "money is speech," however, is far more risky than many advocates of campaign finance regulation seem to recognize, for *Buckley* is not the only case to hinge on that theory.

In *New York Times v. Sullivan*, one of the Supreme Court's most widely applauded decisions, the Court upheld the First Amendment as a defense to a libel suit against the *New York Times*. At the height of the civil rights movement, the *Times* was charged with libel after publishing a paid ad critical of racist conduct by public officials in Alabama. The *Times* itself was not the originator of the ideas expressed, in the sense that it did not write the ad. Thus, the case relied in part on whether or not the fact that the *Times* was engaging in paid speech on behalf of others somehow stripped the speech of its First Amendment protection. The Supreme Court found that the speech was entitled to First Amendment protection. However, if the expenditure of money were not also given that First Amendment protection, *New York Times v. Sullivan* would lose much of its value. For had the Court not assumed that the advertisers were protected in spending money to speak, it would be easy to silence all such future speakers not by suing the newspaper but by suing the advertiser, or by simply prohibiting newspapers from accepting paid ads—at least ones critical of government officials!

If spending money were not a form of speech, the First Amendment would become hollow for all but newspapers and other press outlets, since any effort to spread one's message, through advertising or pamphleteering, could be stripped of First Amendment protections simply by attacking the expenditure of money. Thus, although a natural first reaction of many Americans to constitutional limits on campaign finance reform is to complain that spending money is not speech, on closer reflection statements such as Judge Wright's cannot be accepted at face value. Limiting monetary expenditures certainly does limit speech, as Judge Wright recognized when he added, "there *are* delicate links between political giving and spending . . . and political speech," and, "no one disputes that the money regulated by the campaign reform legislation is closely related to political expression."[6] Nonetheless, Wright pushed the argument that a contribution of money was "action," rather than speech, and so open to greater regulation.

In fact, the Supreme Court has for decades been generally consistent, and correct, in offering strong First Amendment protection to actions or conduct that constitute "symbolic speech." Such actions have included the refusal to salute the U.S. flag or say the Pledge of Allegiance, the wearing of an armband to protest a war, displaying a flag, and burning the United States flag.[7] This First Amendment protection has accrued to both the right to speak through symbolic action, such as by wearing an armband, and to the right not to speak through symbolic action, such as refusing to say the Pledge of Allegiance.[8] To be protected, this symbolic speech need not convey a "narrow, succinctly articularly message," nor even any "particularized message" in order to merit protection. This strong First Amendment protection given to symbolic actions in visible in one of the Court's most recent decisions in the field, *Hurley v. Irish-American Gay, Lesbian, and Bisexual Group of Boston*. In *Hurley*, a group of parade organizers refused to allow a gay and lesbian organization to enter a float in its St. Patrick's Day parade. The parade organizers had no particularized message, only a broad desire not to be perceived as endorsing the message—whatever that might be—of the Irish-American Gay, Lesbian, and Bisexual Group. The absence of the gay float would not send any particular message to the assembled parade watchers, most of whom would have no idea that the float was even excluded. Nevertheless, the Court sided with parade organizers on First Amendment grounds. The organizers' rights to free speech meant that they could not be forced to include any particular float in the parade, regardless of how vague a message exclusion might be. *Hurley* epitomizes the sweeping protection given to symbolic speech actions even when they convey only the most general message.

Given this case history over many years, it is too late, really, to argue that a gift of money is not a form of protected symbolic speech, at least when made to a political candidate. Such a gift is an action intended to convey support for a candidate and, it is generally presumed, his or her views.

Some who are not satisfied with this analysis point out that, rather obviously, money is not itself speech, but a form of wealth or property.[9] However, this becomes a distinction without a difference, for the ability to spend money can be, and is, instrumental to protecting the right to free speech. If monetary expenditures or contributions are not protected, the right to speech could be easily overridden by aggressive governments. For example, rather than attempt to require the parade organizers in *Hurley* to include gay floats in the parade, the government could refuse to allow any expenditure of money to organize and host a parade that excluded gay groups. Rather than attempt to ban the display of a particular flag, the government could prohibit any expenditure of money to produce, import, or display the flag. Movies could be censored by banning private expenditures to make movies, or at least the wrong type of movies; television and newspapers could face the same fate. The expenditure of money is inextricably linked to free speech. A contribution of money to a political candidate is a speech act.

It is not really necessary to expand upon or interpret the thousands of pages of United States Supreme Court and appellate court decisions that form the legal basis for this view. Rather, a few more examples might better illustrate the connection. For example, the Supreme Court has recognized a right to interstate travel, and this right is widely accepted and utilized by the public. Suppose, however, that the government, in an effort to reduce the costs of road and airport maintenance and the emulsion of engine pollutants, banned all corporate travel and limited the amount that individuals could be spend on interstate travel to $1,000 per trip or $25,000 per year. The ban would extend to all expenses involved in travel, including fuel, equipment purchase and maintenance, automotive and travel accident insurance, lodging, meals, entertainment, and so forth. This would assuredly infringe on the right to travel. Yet this is essentially what the campaign finance laws do when they ban corporate contributions and limit individual contributions to political campaigns to $1,000 per candidate and $25,000 per year.

Alternatively, consider another right protected by the First Amendment, freedom of religion. Suppose that in an effort to conserve building resources and urban space, the government limited the amount that could be spent to construct and maintain church buildings. Would this not obviously violate the First Amendment's right to the free exercise of religion? Or suppose that the government limited the amount that a publishing house could spend to publish a book, or that a newspaper could spend to publish its paper, or that a broadcast station could spend to be on the air? Although each such restriction would only restrict the spending of money, not the actual speech itself, each would rather clearly violate the First Amendment by constricting the overall flow of information.

However, the mere fact that an action or a use of property can have communicative significance, and therefore be entitled to the protections of the First Amendment, does not exempt it from all regulation. In certain circumstances, speech can still be regulated. One cannot, in the classic example, shout "fire" in a crowded theater, without facing potential legal consequences. One can be forced to pay damages for libel or slander. The next question, then, is whether or not campaign contributions and spending are the type of speech that can be regulated. Judge Wright, once again a prominent and well-articulated spokesman for his point of view, argued that it could.

According to Wright, campaign finance laws regulate conduct, with only an incidental effect on speech. FECA, he suggested, only regulates the use of money, not speech.[10] Judge Wright argued that because campaign giving is basically action with an incidental speech element, it can and should be regulated under the principles announced by the Supreme Court in *United States v. O'Brien*.

The question that the Supreme Court faced in *O'Brien* was whether an individual could be prosecuted for burning his draft card as a protest against the Vietnam War, or whether such an act was protected under the First Amendment as symbolic speech. In what is perhaps the most controversial of the symbolic speech cases, the Court agreed with O'Brien's contention that burning his draft card was symbolic speech. Nevertheless, the Court upheld O'Brien's conviction for destroying his draft card by holding that symbolic speech could be restricted where such restrictions furthered a significant government interest, provided that that interest was unrelated to the suppression of free expression, and that the "incidental" restriction on First Amendment freedoms was "no greater than is essential." The court noted that the punishment for draft card burning did not limit the amount of speech at all.

Those who favor a high level of judicial deference to campaign finance regulation have zeroed in on *O'Brien* as justification for judicial deference to legislative limits on political spending and contributions. They have argued that, like O'Brien's draft card, the money at stake in political giving is merely a vehicle for political expression, not political expression itself. Thus, such speech may be regulated under legislation that serves an important governmental interest. A law that targets money, rather than speech directly, should therefore be subjected to a less rigorous level of judicial scrutiny.[11] However, this view is ultimately unsatisfactory.

This is because the dichotomy between "speech" and "conduct" is ultimately a false one.[12] The reason for this is that many actions are intended to communicate truthful messages or opinion, and some speech—such as libel, or intentionally making a false cry of "fire" in a crowded theater—is not.[13] The real issue is not the distinction between speech and conduct but whether or not the governmental interest in regulating the particular form of symbolic speech is one "that . . . would arise even if the defendant's conduct had no communicative significance whatsoever."[14] In other words, does the harm arise from an effort to present an opinion or fact to the public?

This understanding of speech versus conduct is reflected in later Supreme Court decisions, such as *Hurley*, which recognized that even the act of a parade, with no particularized theme, is protected speech entitled to the highest level of judicial protection. In *Hurley*, the alleged harm to the dignity of the excluded gay community came about precisely because some believed that their exclusion had communicative significance.[15] In other words, the harm that the government attempted to prevent by prohibiting the exclusion of gay organizations from the parade was directly tied to the communicative significance of their exclusion. Therefore, the parade organizer's speech was protected.

Conversely, in *O'Brien*, the government did not seek to prevent the expression of antiwar views. The government did not seek to prohibit O'Brien's expression, or to prevent O'Brien from burning, for example, a copy of his draft card. The government expressed no concern over why the card was burned—had it been burned simply because O'Brien was cold and wanted to start a fire, the action would still have been illegal. Nor did the government try to limit the amount of speech. O'Brien was free to speak as much as possible.

In *Buckley*, on the other hand, the government sought specifically to limit the amount of speech, and to do so because of its political content. The Federal Election Campaign Act sought to limit both expenditures and contributions of money because they were to be used for political expression. When the government seeks to limit the expression itself, then the highest level of judicial review, "strict scrutiny," is the appropriate standard of review.[16]

In the realm of campaign finance, legislatures have sought to regulate campaign giving precisely because such giving is believed to have communicative significance.[17] The justification for regulation is the perceived communicative significance of campaign giving, either in communicating a message to lawmakers to support or oppose legislation, or in convincing other citizens to vote for or against a candidate. If there were no perception that campaign contributions convinced legislators to support certain views, or voters to vote in certain ways, there would be no concern over spending in campaigns. Thus, strict scrutiny is the appropriate level of judicial review for campaign finance regulation, and the presumption ought to exist that most regulation will be unconstitutional.

Content Neutrality

Nevertheless, Judge Wright and others who favor greater deference to the legislature in campaign finance issues have also argued that, despite the burdens placed on free speech, limitations on campaign contributions and spending can withstand judicial scrutiny because they are "content neutral."[18] Under the doctrine of content neutrality, speech regulations that are not motivated by the content of the speech may be subjected to a lesser standard of judicial scrutiny.[19] Judge Wright and others have argued that campaign finance laws are "uniquely" content neutral, and therefore subject to this lower standard of review.[20]

However, even if we assume that campaign finance laws are "content neutral," mere content neutrality is not enough to assure constitutionality. A regulation that unduly constricts the flow of information and ideas is not normally constitutional, even if it is content neutral.[21] For example, even Judge Wright conceded that a statute "banning all political advertisements in newspapers during the week preceding an election . . . should be struck down."[22] Yet this type of law is clearly "content neutral," as it applies to all political speech regardless of the views expressed therein. Nevertheless, Judge Wright apparently felt that the unconstitutionality of such a law was so obvious that he offered no rationale for this view, other than a quick cite to *Mills v. Alabama*. In *Mills*, the Supreme Court invalidated a law that prohibited newspapers from running election-day editorials in support or opposition to a candidate. Such a law, Wright correctly noted, "targets the communication itself."[23] Judge Wright's hypothetical statute barring all newspaper ads, like the law at issue in *Mills*, is content neutral. Moreover, and again like the statute at issue in *Mills*, it does not even limit the total amount of speech in the campaign, only

118

the timing of the speech. Campaign expenditure limits, on the other hand, though content neutral, directly restrict the total amount of speech. No speech is allowed beyond a certain point. Thus expenditure limits can be more restrictive of speech than a statute that Wright himself admitted "should be struck down." Campaign contribution limits also limit the total amount of speech by candidates indirectly, by limiting the money available to speak, and they directly limit speech by the contributors, acting as an absolute barrier to particular speech by the contributors.[24]

Unlike Judge Wright's hypothetical statute banning newspaper ads one week before an election, campaign contribution and spending limits effectively eliminate serious alternatives for donors and campaigns to communicate their messages. As the Court noted in *Buckley*, all communication in modern society requires at least some expenditure of money.[25] Wright recognized that an attorney general who sought to defend a statute that banned all political newspaper ads in the week before an election "would of course lose."[26] Yet Judge Wright failed to offer any reason why such a statute would be more burdensome to First Amendment rights than a statute, such as that at issue in *Buckley*, which limits not only the timing of ads but, by restricting total advertising expenditures, also limits all ads after a certain quantity. Presumably, Wright would recognize that a law banning all political speech, though content neutral, would violate the First Amendment. Spending ceilings, such as those struck down in *Buckley*, ban all political speech above the spending limit. Contribution limits restrict the contributor beyond that limit, and also indirectly restrain total spending on campaigns.

Furthermore, even where a statute uses content-neutral language, it does not automatically escape strict scrutiny. The Supreme Court has a duty to look behind the language of the statute lest the apparent neutrality be, in fact, aimed at a particular point of view.[27]

Judge Wright argued that "It is, to say the least, not immediately apparent how [campaign spending and contribution] ceilings—so long as they apply evenly across the board—could be designed so as to cast a disproportionate burden on minority or disfavored points of view."[28] Contrary to this assertion, however, there is substantial reason to believe that campaign finance reform proposals have been designed precisely to place a disproportionate burden on certain points of view.[29] Even supporters of campaign finance regulation have noted that a key difficulty in passing legislation is that both major parties will attempt to disadvantage their opposition and its allies through superficially neutral reform.[30] Simply by knowing the political views generally taken by groups, it is relatively easy to target "content-neutral" legislation in such a manner as to limit the influence of one's political enemies and increase the influence of one's friends. For example, a ban on contributions may benefit groups such as the liberal lobbying/activist group ACORN, which sends low-paid workers and volunteer student activists out into the community to promote its issues, but may hurt groups composed of elderly individuals or entrepreneurs who may have financial capability but lack the good health or the time to engage in ACORN-type lobbying activity.

To take a more concrete example, in July of 1996, House Republican leaders introduced a reform package that limited the practice of bundling donations and required both corporate and union political action committees to renew automatic check-off provisions each year. Though facially neutral, the bill would have hampered Democrat constituencies more than Republican, because the most effective practitioners of bundling had been the liberal women's PAC Emily's List, and the Association of Trial Lawyers of America (a prime Democratic constituency), and because unions, more than corporations, rely on automatic deductions for PAC contributions.[31] Similarly, Democrats have expressed far more concern than Republicans about banning "soft money," which consists mainly of corporate contributions and is an area of fund-raising in which the GOP has traditionally had the upper hand.

If we may once again use Judge Wright as a typical spokesperson for the pro-regulatory point of view, we see that his own writings give him away on the question of content neutrality. As examples of the need for campaign finance limitations, Wright cited resistance to "the windfall profits tax on oil companies, hospital cost containment, efforts to create a superfund for victims of toxic chemicals, or any other legislation that affects powerful interests," as well as opposition to Federal Trade Commission regulations of used-car dealers, and support for investment credits for certain industries[32]—a grab bag of "liberal" causes from the late 1970s and early 1980s, during which time he wrote. At no point did Wright cite what was commonly viewed as a "conservative" position sty-

120

mied by campaign spending. Proregulation lobbyists demonstrate similarly strong political views in their efforts to show that campaign finance reform is necessary. For example, a March 2000 visit to the web page of Public Campaign, a group devoted to promoting government-financed campaigns at all levels of politics, found articles arguing that private political contributions needed to be restricted because they were responsible for foiling greater regulation of guns, HMOs, and chemical companies, for allowing deregulation of telecommunications, pharmaceuticals, and banking, and for promoting procreditor bankruptcy reform and tax cuts for small business. A 1998 editorial by the president of the proregulatory group Common Cause complains about "corporate welfare," the need for heavier regulation of the tobacco industry, and reduced minimum taxes on corporations.[33] All of these are views generally associated with the political left. Campaign finance is inherently political, because it regulates political speech. To suggest that any scheme could be content neutral is to misunderstand the purpose of the enterprise: people who favor campaign finance reform do so because they feel that the present system of finance gives some individuals too much influence, and leads to disfavored electoral and legislative results.

Gifts of money, and the expenditure of money, are forms of speech. Across-the-board regulation of monetary gifts and spending is not content neutral, and if it were, one suspects that many of the most ardent campaign finance regulation proponents would lose interest in the subject. Campaign finance regulation attempts to limit speech precisely for its communicative value, and does so in ways that are not content neutral. Furthermore, it significantly interrupts the flow of information by silencing certain voices and limiting the total amount of communication between candidates and the public. Thus strict scrutiny, as provided for in *Buckley*, is entirely appropriate.[34]

The question remains then, whether or not there are substantial enough government interests involved to justify regulation against the strictures of the First Amendment that "Congress shall make no law" regulating speech. Two primary interests have been proposed: the prevention of corruption and the promotion of equality. The next two chapters consider these interests.

Chapter 7

MONEY AND CORRUPTION

The Supreme Court held in *Buckley v. Valeo* that the government interest in preventing "corruption" or the "appearance of corruption" was sufficiently compelling to uphold some campaign finance regulation against First Amendment challenge. Specifically, the Court upheld requirements for the disclosure of contributions, and for limits on contributions, though it struck down mandatory limits on spending of all kinds.[1] As we have seen in chapters 3 and 4, the idea that money is uniquely or particularly "corrupting" in the political process is open to both theoretical and empirical attack, the Court's ruling notwithstanding. In this chapter, we shall see that the Court's decision to uphold limits on political contributions in order to prevent "corruption" or the "appearance of corruption" is also vulnerable on constitutional grounds.

We begin by reminding ourselves that "corruption," as the term is used in *Buckley* and in the world of campaign finance, does not mean the misuse of funds for personal gain, or bribery, or other acts that are illegal apart from campaign finance laws. Rather, "corruption" in the lexicon of campaign finance reform means the overt or implicit exchange of legislative votes in return for campaign contributions; or, more subtly, the determination of a legislative agenda on the basis of contributions; or, in some cases, even the mere "appearance of corruption."[2] In its most refined form, it has come to mean little more than actual or apparent conflict of interest.

Buckley allowed that "corruption" and the "appearance of corruption" were sufficient governmental interests to justify some restraints on political contributions, but not on expenditures. In doing so, the *Buckley* Court appeared to define corruption narrowly to mean quid-pro-quo exchanges in which large contributions are given to assure a political vote or favor. In the Court's language, "To the extent that large contributions are given to secure a political *quid pro quo* from current and potential office holders, the integrity of our system of representative democracy is undermined."[3]

The Court's vague definition of corruption is not altogether satisfactory, because any contributor obviously hopes that election of a favored candidate will lead to favorable political results. Nevertheless, it would seem that the general contours of the Court's definition are at least reasonably clear: the Court believes that the government has a legitimate interest in preventing officeholders from voting on the basis of their contributor list, and without regard to the merits of the issue. By adopting this type of quid-pro-quo corruption as the standard, the Court rejected a broader definition in which corruption is defined as any factor that limits a representative's ability to exercise independent judgment on an issue. This decision was correct, for as we have seen, numerous factors can limit a representative's independent judgment including, among other things, endorsements, party support, newspaper coverage, opinions of family and friends, and even the wishes of his constituency.

In and of itself, the Court quite logically noted, candidate spending could not result in quid-pro-quo corruption of the candidate. After all, although quids might be given for quos when raising money, spending money involves no quid-pro-quo. If a candidate can raise money without trading favors, he certainly can spend it without doing so. Thus, limits on candidate spending were struck down as unjustifiable violations of the First Amendment. These included limits on total spending by a candidate's campaign, limits on spending by the candidate from personal or family resources, and limits on spending by individuals acting independently of a campaign.[4]

However, the Court took a different tack on contribution limits. The Court argued that contribution limits placed only a marginal burden on First Amendment rights, because a contribution only communicated general support for a candidate. Since the "speech" involved was vague, the Court felt that the message communicated did not increase with the size of the contribution. Given this, the Court held that the size of contributions could be limited on the basis of the state's interest in preventing the quid-pro-quo corruption of large contributions made in exchange for specific legislative acts.[5] On each point, the Court's reasoning is suspect.

The Court's finding that contribution limits only "marginally" burden First Amendment rights is suspect on its own and at odds with the traditional First Amendment right of association. As an initial matter, it is not at all clear that the size of a contribution has little communicative impact. Is not a substantially different message communicated when a local merchant pledges $10,000 to one charity (or political campaign) and just $25 to another? In such an example, is it not the size of the donation, rather than the act of donating, that sends the strongest message to the community? It is true that the basis of support for the cause (or candidate) remains vague, yet the message in each gift is substantially different.

More important, although the message may be vague, the alleged vagueness of a message, outside of *Buckley*, has never been a sufficient justification for burdening speech. Much speech is vague, and this is particularly true of symbolic speech. In *West Virginia Board of Education v. Barnette*, the Court held that public school students could not be forced to salute the flag and say the Pledge of Allegiance. The particulars were unimportant to the Court: what precise message the students might be trying to send by their refusal was irrelevant. Similarly, in *Texas v. Johnson*, the Court upheld the right of the defendant to burn an American flag, although the policy or policies that defendant Gregory Johnson was protesting remained vague and unarticulated. Indeed, perhaps Johnson merely sought to demonstrate his broad outrage against living in the United States, a very vague message indeed. Even more vague was the message of parade organizers who sought to exclude a gay group from a St. Patrick's Day parade in Boston, and whose right to do so was upheld by the Court in *Hurley v. Irish-American Gay, Lesbian, and Bisexual Group of Boston*. Given the inherent vagaries of much speech, a standard that allowed the suppression of overly "vague" speech would allow the suppression of most all speech.

If the lack of precision in a message was not the real concern at issue in *Buckley*, what was? It appears it was not the vagueness of the message but rather a concern over whether or not "proxy" speech is protected. The Court seemed to overlook completely the direct communicative significance of a gift of money, incorrectly concluding that the only communicative value was in the ultimate expenditure of the money by a candidate's campaign to convey the candidate's message. In other words, political donors are not speaking at all, but merely relying on the candidate to speak for them: hence the term "proxy speech."

Yet even if one accepts the idea of "proxy speech" as being a legitimate distinction, it does not hold that proxy speech is not entitled to the full protection of the First Amendment.[6] Virtually all political campaign speech is "proxy" speech at some level—that is to say, virtually all campaign advertisements and pronouncements are actually produced by someone other than the candidate. As Professor L. A. Powe points out, "An individual's choice to have a message with which he agrees prepared by professionals is no less speech. Proxy speech is simply a pejorative name for a political commercial. It is still speech."[7] Were proxy speech the problem, indeed, it would be possible to limit candidate spending, since most such spending is used not for candidates to speak directly but to speak by proxy, through professionally prepared advertisements. Indeed, failure to protect "proxy" speech would shake the First Amendment to its roots. It would mean, for example, that a newspaper editorial writer could be prohibited from writing the editorial that the paper would be, theoretically, free to publish. It would make it possible for the government to limit the hiring of speechwriters, layout artists, television and radio directors, or any one else who might assist in preparing a professional presentation of ideas. Yet the notion that an individual is protected when spending $3,000 to argue political views directly, but not when contributing the same amount to the candidate to promote those views, is based on the notion that "proxy" speech is entitled to less protection than direct speech.

Individuals often join with or give their money to others to speak for them precisely because it enhances the impact and value of their desired message.[8] Individuals can certainly enhance the effectiveness of their desired communications by pooling resources with like-minded individuals to hire top advertising talent or a better messenger. Put simply, one cannot make much of a commercial for $100 or even $2,000. Combining financial resources with others allows for far more effective communication. The candidate or the candidate's committee is a logical entity to whom to entrust delivery of the message. Nor is free speech the only issue here. The right of association, also protected by the First Amendment, would lose much of its meaning if the act of association stripped away the rights of free speech.[9] Yet this is the effect of regulation aimed at limiting proxy speech funded by multiple contributors who pool their resources.

If neither vagueness nor the fact that a particular communication is made through "proxy" speech should lower the level of First Amendment protection, then the burden on the government to justify campaign finance regulation that burdens speech is very high. And, indeed, this second part of the Court's analysis, which holds that the state has a compelling interest in limiting contributions to prevent corruption, is also suspect. For even if one accepts the Court's description of contribution limits as only "marginally" burdening free speech, there are, as we have seen in chapter 3, serious empirical questions as to the validity of this alleged state interest in preventing corruption.

The alleged corrupting effect of money is supported by bits and pieces of anecdotal evidence. Reform advocates are particularly fond of quoting legislators as proof, and there assuredly is evidence in those quotes. For example, former Representative Mel Levine (D-California) informs us, "decisions are clearly weighted and influenced . . . by who has contributed to the candidates." Former Representative Tim Penny (D-Minnesota) states, "whether the groups will withhold campaign funds is a consideration that does come into play."[10] Former Senator Barry Goldwater (R-

Arizona), in a fit of pique, once complained "it is not 'We the People,' but political action committees and monied interests who are setting the nation's political agenda and are influencing the position of candidates on the important issues of the day."[11] Of course, anecdotal evidence is only that—anecdotal evidence. The fact is, the vast majority of current and former representatives do not make such statements, and one can easily drum up quotes running the other way from knowledgeable insiders. For example, Dick Morris, former advisor to President Clinton and various other officeholders, argues that money is not terribly important and points out that candidates can raise money in a number of ways: "egomaniacs—people that agree with you ideologically, people that side with your party, people that knew you in high school, and people that hate your opponent—those are five virtuous ways to take money. And if you maximize them, you don't have to do the sixth, which is to sell your soul."[12] Former Republican Congressman and Senator Dan Coates, a Capitol Hill veteran for twenty-two years, states:

> The notion that members of the House or Senate sell access is, in my experience, unfounded. Many political supporters who contribute to officeholders never request a personal meeting, but some do request and receive meetings with legislators or their staffs. But political supporters who do not contribute are also granted meetings, as are constituents having problems with their social security, Veterans, or Medicare benefits, and experts on issues pending before the member's committees. . . . A contribution is by no means necessary to obtain a meeting, and a meeting by no means guarantees results. I reject unequivocally the notion that access is sold, or that access is corrupting.[13]

Former Senator Eugene McCarthy has added, "I don't accept that the ultimate corruption is money."[14]

So we need to go beyond anecdotal quotes before accepting "corruption" as a "compelling" interest. And, in fact, claims of widespread corruption simply have not been supported by any systematic studies of legislative activity. Rather, such studies have consistently found little or no connection between campaign contributions and legislative action.[15] These studies have, instead, found that the dominant forces in legislative voting are personal ideology, party affiliation and agenda, and constituency views.[16] Some "reform" advocates complain that such studies fail to capture the essence of corruption. They argue that the corruption does not show up in such studies because it is hidden in the speech not given, the issue not pressed. Such claims are hard to refute—any claim that requires its opponents to prove a negative is problematic—but as we have seen in chapter 3, there are strong reasons to doubt that contributions have a major impact on legislative behavior. Party, ideology, constituency, press, advisors, and friendships all cut against the thesis that money has "undue" influence in the legislature. It is simply improbable that legislators frequently take actions against the wishes of their constituents and their own ideology or best judgment in return for mere campaign contributions.

This is, once again, not to say that money never plays a role, or that monetary contributions may not weigh on the representative's mind.[17] And, indeed, this simple observation defines a more subtle corruption thesis advanced by, among others, UCLA professor of law Daniel Lowenstein. Professor Lowenstein argues that the fact that donor's wishes will be just one factor among many in a legislator's decision-making process is the problem, and is what makes the role of money so insidious. It is not necessary for money to "corrupt" legislators in any outright way. Rather, the mere fact that it is there, influencing the "chemistry" or "mix" of the legislator's actions, "taints" the legislative process. As former senator Paul Douglas once put it, "Moreover, the whole process may be so subtle as not to be detected by the official himself."[18] To Lowenstein, this inability to pinpoint the corruption is the clinching argument for doing away with private financing. The system cannot be policed because none of us—not even the legislators—can know the exact influence of contributors.

But if the wishes of contributors are just one factor among many, why do they taint the process any more than the fact that the legislator might consider the opinions of family, friends, or staffers; endorsements by newspapers, colleagues, and key constitutents; the information provided by lobbyists or groups that have not made contributions; and any of the other factors that might come into play?

128

One answer, which is apparently not Lowenstein's, is that money is "completely unrelated to the value of the idea it propels" and that other factors "attract the candidate's attention because they are in a position to persuade voters or to deliver blocks of votes."[19] But this is not really the case. The spouse's position in the bedroom and ability to gain a legislator's ear may also be "unrelated to the value of the idea it propels." Staffers and friends are not in positions to "persuade voters or deliver blocks of votes" any more than most contributors. Newspaper and other endorsements are typically decided by a small group of individuals, who then try to persuade voters of the candidate's merit through their editorial endorsements, and are in that respect little different from contributions, which are given to the candidate by a voter or voters so that the candidate can directly try to persuade other voters of the candidate's merit. Clearly the problem is not that money is any more tainting than are many of the other factors that go into decision making, and that, in any event, tend to come into play only after the dominant, "untainted" considerations of ideology and constituency desires.

Lowenstein's answer is that this low-level monetary influence is inappropriate simply because our culture regards it as inappropriate.[20] The potential influence of money is a problem because, among forms of political influence, we consider money a unique problem. Lowenstein argues that proponents of deregulation, "would not be at such great pains to characterize the influence of campaign contributions as minimal if they did not believe that it would be wrong if the contributions were influential, or at least that the overwhelming majority of their fellow citizens believe that it would be wrong."[21] I respectfully disagree. We are at pains to show that the influence of contributions is minimal precisely because we believe that if contributions do not lead to rampant quid-pro-quo corruption, the majority of our fellow citizens will not be any more concerned about the alleged tainting effects of contributions than they are about the role of the press, political parties, or congressional staff, and will cease being supportive of misguided regulation. And the placidity with which citizens react to reform proposals, so-called scandals, and proposals for government financing is evidence of that fact.[22] The fact is, the American people have proven time and time again that they are not particularly disturbed by the way in which campaign funds are raised and the minor role that they might play in legislative behavior.

Lowenstein adds that our culture regards the role of private money as inappropriate because "it constitutes bribery, as that crime is defined in most American jurisdictions."[23] It is doubtful, however, that any state enacted its bribery statutes with campaign contributions in mind, and, as Lowenstein notes, campaign contributions are rarely prosecuted under such laws. He attributes this to the pervasiveness of the practice, rather than to approval of the process. An equally likely explanation for the lack of prosecutions, however, is that no more than a very small minority of Americans really consider private contributions to be bribery. Lowenstein asserts that "It is a fact of our political culture that although a great variety of the pressures brought to bear on politicians embody forces that are regarded as more or less democratic and therefore legitimate, this is not true of pressure imposed by payments of money to politicians, either for their personal benefit or for campaign use."[24]

The truth is that there appears to be no more a cultural norm against private campaign contributions than there is a cultural norm against driving 68 miles per hour in a 65-mile-per-hour zone. This helps to explain why polls consistently show that reform of the campaign system is an extremely low political priority for voters, and why voters continue to reject government financing as a popular alternative. Our political culture does not consider a contribution for campaign use to be particularly corrupt, and millions of American citizens make campaign contributions and never feel the least tainted by the process. Indeed, my own observation is that politicians often find it easier to tell a constituent that his vote was dictated by campaign contributions than to admit that it was dictated by disagreement with the constituent. That strongly suggests that there is not a strong cultural norm against the influence of contributors, even when that influence is described in terms that indicate "corruption" far more than Lowenstein's idea of a "tainted" system.

It is probably true that it is rare for a legislator to admit that contributors influenced his activity, but it is, I believe, equally rare for a legislator to admit that the possibility of a newspaper endorsement, or even the endorsement of a powerful group that represents large numbers of members, influenced his activity. How often does one hear a Democrat say

130

that he thinks minimum wage increases are a bad idea, but votes for them anyway just to keep labor unions happy? Or even that the prospect of getting labor's vote influenced his decision? So the opinions of donors go into the mix, along with the opinions of numerous other individuals whose influence sometimes does and sometimes doesn't have anything to do with their numbers, their talents, or some third party's view of the merit of their opinions.

Most Americans are sophisticated enough to recognize that these donors usually represent large numbers of persons with similar views, and when they do not, it is perhaps even more important that they be heard. Indeed, in some cases it will be a good thing for the representative overtly to consider donations, as monetary contributions can be an indicator of the intense preferences of a minority, or of the preferences of the majority. Given all this, I am simply not persuaded that this influence—and this type of influence alone—is so corrupting that it constitutes a sufficiently compelling interest to allow the government to infringe on First Amendment rights and to limit a primary mechanism, and in many cases the only real mechanism, for millions of Americans to participate in the political system.

Nevertheless, despite the shaky empirical basis for this alleged corruption—not much more than a few stray comments from legislators who had recently lost political battles—the Supreme Court in *Buckley* found that such alleged corruption, or the appearance of such corruption, could justify the First Amendment burdens of contribution limits because "the integrity of our system of representative democracy is undermined," and regulation is "critical . . . if confidence in the system of representative Government is not to be eroded to a disastrous extent." In the fall of 1975, the *Buckley* Court was unwilling to second-guess congressional judgment on the question of the corrupting effects of campaign contributions. But suppose that with empirical studies now in hand, showing little actual impact from contributions, we recognize that private financing, problematic as it may be at times, is not in any actual sense "undermining" our system of representative government—what then? It may be difficult to continue to argue that a compelling government interest exists sufficient to justify the burden that such contribution limits place on First Amendment rights. *Buckley* recognized that restrictions on First Amend-

131

ment speech rights must be "subject to the closest scrutiny," and that remedies must be "closely drawn to avoid unnecessary abridgment of associational freedoms."[25] Perhaps the time has come to review *Buckley's* holding in this area.

The Supreme Court has not always been so deferential to legislative judgments intended to justify impositions on First Amendment rights as it was in *Buckley*.[26] For example, in *Cox v. Louisiana*, the Court conducted an independent review of the record to determine that the behavior of demonstrators did not rise to the level of a breach of the peace, and that therefore the government could not prohibit their activity. Similarly, in *Edwards v. South Carolina*, the Court reached an independent judgment that a peaceful march around the statehouse by students protesting discrimination did not constitute disorderly conduct, despite government assertions to the contrary. The Court has also undertaken an independent review of the facts in the context of libel and obscenity actions.[27] And in *Landmark Communications, Inc. v. Virginia*, the Court rejected the state of Virginia's claim that a blackout of news coverage of proceedings of the state's Judicial Inquiry and Review Commission was necessary to avoid undermining public confidence in the judiciary.[28] Having seen the effects of FECA and having greater knowledge of the effects of money on votes, it would now be entirely appropriate, under traditional First Amendment jurisprudence, for the Court to conclude that in *Buckley* it erred in tolerating contribution limits. "Congress," wrote Chief Justice Burger in his *Buckley* dissent, "[may not] enact its conclusions in the First Amendment area into laws immune from the most searching review by [the Supreme] Court."[29] The claims of corruption being used to justify substantial burdens on the First Amendment remain, at this time, little more than conjecture. Whether that meets the high standard necessary to justify limitations on political speech is doubtful.

Unfortunately, in January 2000, in *Nixon v. Shrink Missouri Government PAC*, the Supreme Court abandoned this long line of jurisprudence insofar as it might apply to campaign finance. The Court of Appeals for the 8th Circuit had struck down Missouri law that limited contributions, noting that Missouri had produced no evidence of corruption or the appearance of corruption save for the unsupported allegations of state lawmakers. The Supreme Court, however, reversed, arguing that the mere fact that such harms might be plausible—even though unsupported by evidence—was enough to justify suppression of speech.

In doing so, the Court again provided core political speech with less protection than other forms of speech. For example, in *Greater New Orleans Broadcast Association v. United States* and *Edenfield v. Fane*, the Court had held that a state could not regulate commercial speech unless it first demostrated that "the harms it recites are real." In *Rubin v. Coors Brewing Company*, the Court had noted that this proof of actual harm was "critical" to government efforts to regulate speech. The end result of *Shrink PAC*, then, was to place political speech a notch below commercial advertising in the First Amendment hierarchy.

Beyond applying a lax standard of review to the state's claims of corruption, both the *Buckley* and *Shrink PAC* courts failed to limit the legislature to a narrowly tailored means of preventing the presumed harm. In a long line of cases, stretching back to the early part of this century, the Court has made increasingly clear that where a government regulation burdens First Amendment rights not only is it subject to strict scrutiny but the government must "narrowly tailor" its solution to the least restrictive means available.[30] By this, the Court means that the state must place no greater burden on First Amendment rights than is absolutely necessary to achieve its legitimate "compelling" interest.

As Chief Justice Burger noted in his *Buckley* dissent, Congress had less restrictive means to assure the absence of quid-pro-quo corruption in the legislature, and in fact included them in the FECA: disclosure. If it is feared that certain citizens will obtain "undue" influence through campaign gifts, disclosure allows the citizenry to manage the problem through informed voting, by refusing to vote for a candidate who accepts large contributions, or who seems to cast legislative votes in return for contributions.[31] Disclosure had been required before FECA, of course, but until 1971 there had been no serious enforcement mechanism. However, the experience with disclosure in the brief interlude between 1971 and 1974 had been positive. In particular, the disclosure of large corporate contributions to the Republican campaign probably contributed to the GOP's debacle in the 1974 congressional elections.

In *Buckley*, unfortunately, the Court seemed to forget about its requirement that solutions infringing on First Amendment rights must be narrowly drawn. In departing from the usual requirement that the legislative solution be the "narrowly tailored" remedy of disclosure, the Court has left the speech rights guaranteed by the First Amendment subject to a relentless attack over many years. This has, in turn, forced the court into a series of narrow, often inconsistent distinctions.

Over the past two decades, the Court has attempted with mixed success to distinguish the right of an individual to spend unlimited sums on his or her own campaign from the right to contribute unlimited amounts to assist the campaigns of others. The former is protected, the latter is not. The Court has tried to distinguish between the right of a candidate to spend money campaigning versus the right of a contributor to give money to a campaign, with the former being unlimited and the latter subject to limits. The Court has distinguished between candidate expenditures and noncandidate expenditures aimed at electing that same candidate. The Court has tried to draw a legal line between spending by "ideological" corporations, which is protected by the First Amendment, and spending by nonideological corporations, which can be limited. In doing so, the Court has been further forced into trying to distinguish between ideological and nonideological corporations, coming to the strange conclusion that Massachusetts Right to Life is ideological, but that the Michigan Chamber of Commerce is not. The Court has distinguished between political spending on ballot issues, which may not be limited, and political spending on candidate races, which are subject to some regulation. It has differentiated between expenditures by media corporations, which may not be limited, and expenditures by nonmedia corporations, which may be limited. And it has made distinctions between expenditures by corporations and expenditures by labor unions.[32] These fine distinctions have created no meaningful pattern, leaving many groups uncertain as to their legal rights in the area. This uncertainty has helped to make litigation a major part of campaign strategy, as candidates, parties, and groups seek to silence, embarrass, or use up the resources of their political adversaries. Winning such litigation is often a concern secondary to embarrassing the opposition and limiting its campaigning.

Despite these problems, and the failure of past regulatory efforts to meet their goals, reformers have called for an ever-expanding web of regulation that will entail even more fine distinctions. Thus political action committees, part of the 1974 reforms, are now assailed as part of the problem.[33] Allowing political parties to use large donations, now dubbed "soft money," to offset certain party expenses, was considered a reform measure, but now threatens to "destroy the system." Similarly, allowing political parties to spend unlimited sums on polling, get-out-the-vote drives, and certain generic advertising for party candidates were added as "reform" measures aimed at strengthening the parties in 1979, but today are considered more "loopholes" in the law. Other popular proposals, as the 1990s drew to a close, included a ban on the practice of bundling, and banning or sharply limiting contributions from persons outside a representative's district.[34] In the states, efforts to limit "issue ads" have become increasingly complex. In short, having abandoned the requirement that any solution be narrowly tailored, the Court has forced itself to become a perpetual policeman as campaign finance reform advocates call for ever-increasing restrictions on political speech. This is the problem that strict scrutiny and least-restrictive-means analysis is intended, in large part, to avoid.

Thus, although proponents of reform have been relentlessly attacking *Buckley* over the years for striking down limits on total expenditures, candidate personal expenditures, and independent expenditures, in fact the most doctrinally suspect portion of the decision is that upholding contribution limits. The idea that serious quid-pro-quo corruption exists is simply not supported by the empirical evidence available to us, and in any case measures that restrict contributions and expenditures do not appear to be the least restrictive means available to address the alleged problem of conflict of interest. By failing to draw a clear line protecting contributions, the Court has drawn itself into making the types of narrow, hair-splitting decisions that much of the rest of the *Buckley* opinion seems aimed at making unnecessary.

The constitutional problem, then, for those who insist that the anti-corruption rationale can justify government restrictions on speech is that anything beyond disclosure is not narrowly tailored to the problem. To the extent that reformers view the "sunlight" of disclosure as insufficient, they bear a very heavy burden under the strict scrutiny analysis. Additional regulations, while significantly burdening First Amendment rights, seem unlikely to achieve the desired result, and have probably made the situation worse when and where enacted into law. Yet the regulators' only real solution is to propose still more regulation, imposing still greater burdens on First Amendment speech rights.

Because it is unproven empirically and relies and a dubious theory of democratic politics, the anticorruption rationale fails to justify existing, let alone additional, regulation of campaign speech and contributions. Indeed, one must conclude that the weakest portion of the *Buckley* decision and its progeny, from a standpoint of constitutional doctrine, is not that portion which struck down spending limits but rather that portion which relies on the anticorruption rationale to justify limits on contributions.

Chapter 8

MONEY AND EQUALITY

Given the doctrinal weakness of the anticorruption rationale and the vigorous dissent it drew from Chief Justice Burger, one might think that that aspect of *Buckley v. Valeo* would have become the focal point of post-*Buckley* commentary. Instead, academic scholarship has been devoted primarily to criticizing the decision on other grounds. Although concern about corruption was the only compelling state interest accepted by the Supreme Court in *Buckley* to justify the First Amendment infringements of campaign regulation, it was not the only interest put forth by the defendants in that case. They also argued that political equality demanded, or at least permitted, government action that restricted the free speech of some through contribution and spending limits.

The *Buckley* Court rejected this equality argument in what may be the most famous line in the entire opinion. Wrote the Court, "the concept that government may restrict the speech of some elements of our society in order to enhance the relative voices of others is wholly foreign to the First Amendment."[1] Yet despite this emphatic rejection of the equality argument, it continues to be heavily promoted in the academic literature and is a persistent theme in popular writing, as well. In this chapter, we examine the constitutional theories behind the alleged equality interest justifying campaign finance regulation.

Constitutional arguments for campaign regulation based on an equality principle have taken two parallel, but distinct, tracks. The first argument is based on a reinterpretation of the First Amendment right to free speech, and is perhaps best exemplified in the work of University of Chicago law professor Cass Sunstein, Yale Law School's Owen Fiss, and Burt Neuborne of NYU School of Law.[2] These scholars argue that intelligent public debate requires that speakers and points of view should be heard with some degree of equality, and that government may, or even must, act affirmatively to limit some voices or enhance others in order to assure such equality. The second argument is based not on a redefinition of free speech under the First Amendment but rather on a redefinition of equality under the Fifth and Fourteenth amendments, which guarantee equal protection under the law. This argument is trumpeted most loudly in academic circles by Jamin Raskin of American University, Richard Hasen of Loyola Law School in Los Angeles, and Edward Foley, a professor at the Ohio State University Law School and later the state solicitor of Ohio, a position from which he continued to argue for sweeping state restrictions on political speech.[3] The theory has also been aggressively, but with a marked lack of success, litigated in federal courts by a foundation-funded, Boston-based group calling itself the National Voting Rights Institute. Their argument is that the Fourteenth Amendment guarantee of equality overpowers First Amendment claims of free speech in order to guarantee equal political influence prior to voting. Like the First Amendment arguments typified by Fiss, Sunstein, and Newborne, this argument demands a radical restructuring of the traditional understanding of equal protection.

The First Amendment and the
"Enhancement" Concept

The text of the First Amendment consists of what would appear to be a bold prohibition on government regulation of speech: "Congress shall make no law . . . abridging the freedom of speech, or of the press." Supporters of extensive campaign finance regulation, however tend to reject the actual text of the First Amendment and instead focus on what they discern as the purpose of the amendment: to foster enlightened, democratic self-government. They argue that private actors, as surely as government, may prevent individuals from speaking.[4] For example, a mall owner may deny protestors the right to picket or distribute leaflets on the mall, or a media outlet may refuse to run an advertisement or editorial of a person or group.[5] If private actors behave in such a manner as to curtail a large amount of speech, certain views necessary for intelligent public discourse may not be heard, or at least may not be voiced in an effective manner. Moreover, it is not necessary that these private actors intend to suppress the speech of others. In certain cases, or so the theory goes, excessive speech by a private actor will have the effect of assuring that others do not have an adequate opportunity to express views. For example, a political candidate who can blanket the airwaves with advertising may make it impossible for others to get ideas into the market.[6]

These advocates go on to argue that just as private action will not guarantee that more voices are heard, not all government action restricts speech. For example, compulsory "public service" television programming, or government "guidelines" regarding the presentation of diverse viewpoints on television may even promote debate. Such laws can promote speech by assuring that certain views not adequately represented in a market system are presented. As the purpose of the First Amendment is to assure the widest possible debate about public matters, they reason, the Constitution may allow infringements on speech, and in some cases even command them, if it assures that more voices are heard. From here, it is only a short leap to the conclusion that in the realm of political campaigning, the Constitution allows the silencing of certain voices through limitations on speech, in order to assure that other viewpoints be heard.[7]

139

This formulation of the First Amendment's role in campaign finance suffers from a series of intellectual and doctrinal errors. First and foremost, it mistakes an effect of the First Amendment—uninhibited, robust debate of political matters[8]—for the substance and principle of the First Amendment, which is liberty of expression.[9] It may be true that one of many goals and consequences of the First Amendment was to ensure vibrant public discussion, but the amendment's very language, which states that government "shall not" act, makes clear that this goal was to be achieved by protecting individual liberty interests against government interference, not through an activist government role in political debate. This reflects a logical decision by the framers to limit government power in this area. For once it has been decided that the government may silence certain speakers in order to assure that others are heard (exactly whom, and on what grounds, remains unclear), it is, in the words of former Massachusetts Supreme Court justice and Harvard law professor Charles Fried, "but a short step to suppression pure and simple."[10]

To this it might be responded that the Fourteenth Amendment to the Constitution, which guarantees equal protection under the law, requires the federal government to promote equality in some way, thereby modifying the First Amendment. After all, the Fourteenth Amendment provides for the federal government to enforce equal protection with appropriate legislation. But like the First Amendment, the substantive clauses at issue in the Fourteenth Amendment are worded in the negative: "No state shall make or enforce any law which shall abridge the privileges or immunities of citizens of the United States; nor shall any state deprive any person of life, liberty, or property . . . ; nor deny to any person within its jurisdiction the equal protection of the laws." The Fourteenth Amendment, in this respect, reinforces the First Amendment as a limit on government power, not a grant of power. It clarifies what state governments shall not do, and authorizes the federal government to enforce those limits against state governments. It does not grant affirmative power to the government to regulate speech.

Quite appropriately, then, the Supreme Court has allowed the government to favor a class of individuals only for the purpose of redressing previous unequal, affirmative treatment by the government. For example, affirmative action to benefit racial minorities is constitutional for the purpose of redressing specific past discrimination. However, even here, the Supreme Court has strictly limited such affirmative action to groups able to show specific evidence of past governmental discrimination, and has required that solutions be narrowly tailored to address only this specific past discrimination.[11] The idea that the Fourteenth Amendment somehow converts the First Amendment's limit on governmental power into a grant of governmental power simply is not tenable.

Advocates of regulation, however, such as Cass Sunstein, attempt to justify the First Amendment as a grant of power on the basis of "negative" rather than "positive" rights, and in doing so commit a second error. The long-accepted reading of the Constitution, and particularly the First Amendment, is that it protects "negative" rights—that is, rights to be free from government action—and does not create "positive rights"—that is, requirements that the government act. Sunstein's solution is to redefine these concepts to assert that negative liberty is at stake when the government acts to assure that certain voices are heard. According to Sunstein, if someone with a particular view is denied the right to state his view on network television, that is only because civil and criminal law may be invoked to prevent him from doing so. The actor is unable to state his or her view only because government will act to restrain him. Without government, Sunstein seems to think, there is no limit on the actor's ability to seize the station for broadcast purposes. Therefore, "negative liberty is indeed involved."[12]

This formulation, however, mistakes the government enforcement of a right against a nonright as the infringement of a right. That is to say, if the speaker seeking to force his way onto a network has no right to do so, no right has been abridged when he is denied access, whether he is denied that access by a private actor or by a public actor. Under a theory of negative liberty, private actors have a right to utilize their justly acquired property, free from arbitrary appropriations under a claim of government authority. This includes the right to exclude physically the would-be speaker from the station. The network has a right to operate its property. To paraphrase the Declaration of Independence, government is instituted to preserve such rights. Thus, to continue with Sunstein's hypothesis, government actions to secure the network's private rights do not infringe the would-be speaker's rights unless the would-be speaker has some prior right to appear on the television station. But Sunstein has failed to identify any basis, either positive or normative, for such a right of access, a right that is crucial to his thesis. As no such right has ever been recognized at common law, such a right could only come into play through a positive act of the legislature. At that point we are, by definition, dealing not with negative liberty but with positive liberty—an affirmative claim created by government statute. As a philosophical matter, such a statute may be well and good. As a Constitutional matter, it is exactly what the First Amendment prohibits when free speech is at stake.[13]

Sunstein's error here is demonstrated in another example he uses. He claims that the First Amendment recognizes that the government has an obligation to protect a speaker from a hostile crowd. The First Amendment, he argues, means that the crowd has no right to physically silence a speaker who is within her rights to speak. But this is clearly not true. For if this speaker attempted to speak at a private gathering, she could be lawfully silenced. What the speaker has is not a positive right to speak without interference from any source, but a negative right not to be silenced by *government*, and a right not to be *unlawfully* restrained or beaten by private actors acting beyond the scope of their rights. This would be true whether the individual were speaking or doing something entirely noncommunicative. Thus, the government that acts to protect the speaker from harm does not violate the rights of others. It is merely acting to secure a legitimate right not to be assaulted. But similarly, when government acts to protect the rights of property owners from having their property confiscated, in effect, by the would-be speaker, it violates no rights, but secures a legitimate right.

Sunstein's response is that the existing distribution of wealth and property—in his first hypothetical, the ownership of the television station—ought not be viewed as a given, but is itself a product of government action. To continue with his example of a broadcast station owner, he argues that there is no "natural" right for the station owners to exclude others.[14] In point of fact, most natural rights theorists would recognize a right of exclusion in these circumstances.[15] But even ignoring any controversy over the scope of "natural rights," here Sunstein commits two errors simultaneously.

First, although it is true that reliance on markets is a system of allocating resources, that is not the same as saying that the existing allocation is

142

the result of government action. The very idea of a market system of allocation is that government does not do the allocating. A change in the background rules against which markets operate does not amount to a government "allocation" of resources. Though it may lead to some change in
private allocations that result, such changes are made without government
interference. Wealth and income statistics in the United States are strong
proof of the fallacy of Sunstein's arguments, for they reveal that in America's private markets, wealth and property allocations are constantly changing. Most Americans move up and down the income and wealth scale over
time, many with stunning rapidity.[16] To suggest that the government's decision to leave matters in the hands of private actors amounts to government
action is effectively to abolish the entire idea of state action, which lies at
the root of the First and Fourteenth amendments.

Second, even if we accept Sunstein's formulation that we may use language to obliterate the distinction between market allocation and government allocation of resources, Sunstein's position pays too little attention
to the fact that the Constitution was enacted against certain well-estab-
lished background rules. Two such background rules were the ownership
of private property and market allocation of most resources. Although
these background rules are not part of the text, history and original intent
should serve to illuminate the meaning of the text where the plain language is otherwise unclear.[17] Given the reliance on market allocation at
the time of the ratification of both the Constitution and the Fourteenth
Amendment, the refusal of the government to reorder economic relation-
ships would not appear to qualify as the type of "action" that the framers
intended when they proscribed certain government actions. Laid against
a text that proclaims that the legislature shall "make no law," any interpretation that would convert the First Amendment into a grant of government power to silence some voices in order to enhance others is highly
implausible. In short, text, history, and intent all argue against the efforts
of Sunstein, Fiss, and others to find a basis for state regulation of political
speech. It may be that some would like to change or amend the Constitution to allow such affirmative government action in the name of enhancement, but one should recognize that that is what one is proposing, and
that such action may only be done in the manner provided for in the
Constitution itself.

143

Burt Neuborne's twist to all this is to call for a "democracy-centered" reading of the First Amendment. Neuborne would move away from what he sees as an excessive concern with a rights/autonomy-based analysis of the First Amendment, to consider the First Amendment as a "structural guarantor of a fair democratic process." This he considers as a "third" way between traditional autonomy analysis and a communitarian analysis that threatens to totally "submerg[e] the desires of the individual in the needs of the group."[18]

This seems at first to break the positive/negative rights quagmire that pulls down Sunstein's argument. But Neuborne's theory merely begs the question: what is a "democracy-centered" reading of the First Amendment? One could certainly argue that, given the importance of speech and property to a functioning democracy, the demands of democratic pluralism, and the crucial role that equality before the law plays in liberal democracy, a "democracy-centered" reading of the Constitution demands the abolition of all restraints on political contributions and spending. Neuborne would not argue this, of course; he believes that "unregulated wealth disparities pose a unique threat to political equality," and so must be regulated. But not too much: regulation may not "depriv[e] the system of the money it takes to run a robust democracy." Just how much "robustness" is needed to satisfy the Constitution is not clear. "*Buckley*," writes Neuborne, "was correct on its facts," but presumably would have been incorrect had it done less to "privilege incumbents."[19]

All of this is fine, of course, and echoes the confused writings of Judge Skelly Wright, who thought campaign contributions and expenditures were "closely related to political expression" but not entitled to Constitutional protection as political expression; or that one could limit total expenditures but not limit expenditures in the week before an election. Neuborne believes we can limit speech within ninety days of an election if it is "calculated to support or oppose [the] election [of a candidate]," but it is hardly clear why ninety days is a magic number, rather than sixty days, or the one week rejected by Wright. Assuming that we all agree to a "democracy-centered" reading, all Neuborne has done is suggest a number of debatable issues. Asking the courts to make such distinctions is to ask them to engage in an exercise in legislative policy, not constitutional law. And as he notes, "policy preferences are not the same as constitutional imperatives."[20] Indeed.

The reason that Neuborne's theory collapses into a mosh-pit of personal policy preferences and contradictory wishes is that he repeats the mistake of trying to interpret the Constitution through its "values" rather than through its actual language, structure, and content. Neuborne sees three ways to read the Constitution, each of which relies less on the Constitution itself than on the "values" that the reader would read into the Constitution. There is an "autonomy" reading, a "communitarian" reading, or his new "democracy-centered" reading.[21] Well, the Constitution certainly reflects values, and it was certainly intended to help implement a society based on certain values. But the Constitution is not simply a declaration of values. Indeed, it is doubtful that the framers would have agreed on the exact values it aims to achieve. The founders did not agree on any one set of values, nor did they have to. What they did agree on was a blueprint for the government of the United States that would sufficiently help Americans achieve their various values, so that it was able to muster the substantial majorities needed for ratification. The Constitution is itself the document that defines how values are to be achieved in the government of the United States. The Constitution establishes a government, and sets out, in some detail, the powers both granted to and denied to that government. One power that the Constitution, through the First Amendment, specifically denies to the government is the power to regulate political speech. This is not to say that the Constitution has no room for interpretation—any written document must be interpreted, and we may, when faced with vague or contradictory language, look to known values in an effort to shed light on the document. But no "democracy-centered" reading can overcome the rather simple, obvious fact that the language of the First Amendment prohibits regulation of political speech. Once Neuborne has admitted that political speech is at stake, his argument has no place to go.[22]

Thus Neuborne's argument ultimately falls back, as Judge Wright's did two decades earlier, on the notion that "content neutrality" is sufficient to save regulation of political speech. Indeed, suggests Neuborne, it must be "relentlessly content-neutral."[23] Like Sunstein and Wright, he is quite

145

correct. In those rare cases in which a "compelling" state interest grants government the power to regulate speech, government must still act in a content-neutral manner. But even if we allow that some types of speech limitation based on equality interests might be Constitutional, it is not at all clear how Congress could act to enhance the right voices in a "content-neutral" manner that would comport with the First Amendment.

The first problem would be to determine what views we are not hearing that we ought to hear. Campaign finance regulators rarely identify with any specificity those views that they feel are not heard enough. A careful dissection of reformist literature, however, suggests that those views generally are left-of-center political views that have failed to gain popular electoral support. Judge J. Skelly Wright, for example, fumed over the legislative defeats of gun control, a windfall profits tax on oil, hospital cost-containment measures, and environmental legislation, and argued that speech could be limited when it concerned "any other legislation that affects powerful, organized interests," whatever that means. Other academic commentators express similar views. For example, Jamin Raskin of American University and John Bonifaz of the National Voting Rights Institute argue that it is the views of the "non-affluent" that are not heard, although what these views might be is not revealed; Edward Foley talks about "rich" citizens biasing elections against the "poor," without defining either group or suggesting any particular policy views held uniformly by the "poor" that are not being discussed; Professor Richard Hasen also keeps the debate limited to "wealthy" versus "poor," although at one point he does suggest that perhaps the "mining industry" is heard too much and "some racial minorities" not enough. A more recent Hasen article expresses concern over the influence of conservative publisher Rupert Murdoch, by name. The self-described "relentlessly content-neutral" Burt Neuborne makes very clear that the problem is that the political views of the "haves," who "tend to possess a set of political beliefs and policies that are dramatically different from the political beliefs generally held by the 'have nots,' " are heard too much. Owen Fiss is also quiet about specific issues, but he is unabashed in his general theory of judicial review: he wants courts to use his new First Amendment theory to reduce the amount of speech by "the right," and to promote the ideas of an "activist state."[24] Fiss has even suggested that unappreciated art

146

such as Robert Mapplethorpe's photography of gay men involved in sex acts may not have received enough attention in public debate, thus *requiring* that it be subsidized by the state, if necessary through court order. On the more practical side, a quick visit to the web sites of proregulatory groups such as Common Cause and the Center for Responsive Politics shows great concern that groups such as the National Rifle Association, banks, tobacco companies, and corporations generally have too much power.

In fact, it is hard to believe that opposing views on any of these issues have not been adequately represented in political debate. Even the vague references to views of the "poor" being underrepresented (assuming such uniform views exist at all) are probably off base. Some commentators, in fact, have argued that a cottage industry exists for representing the "poor."[25]

When we look at the literature of campaign finance reform, and the public policy decisions that upset those who favor greater regulation to "enhance" free speech, it seems doubtful that any reform measure would pass a content-neutrality test. Indeed, those who argue that campaign finance regulation is constitutional if it is content-neutral fail to understand the point of the entire exercise: regulations are proposed precisely because certain observers believe that some views, which they do not like, are heard too much, and others, which they prefer, are heard too little. The persistent theme of proregulatory groups is to cite to specific issues on which the "wrong" side prevailed, allegedly due to their "buying" of representatives, as proof of the need for reform. Certain industries or groups, such as "Big Tobacco" and the National Rifle Association, become particularly favorite whipping boys. Never is an allowance made for the notion that millions of Americans own guns, or that millions smoke, or that millions more see such regulation as none of government's business. Politically active individuals hate to lose legislative battles, and it is always easier to blame defeat on the other side's money rather than the failure of one's own message. This problem is not merely one of the political left; political conservatives who favor campaign finance regulation, such as columnist and three-time presidential candidate Pat Buchanan, express similar views, but simply substitute a different set of policy issues on which the "favored" view has failed. For Buchanan, the favored views are economic protectionism and limits on immigration. If these supporters of regulation did not want to silence certain views, there would be little debate, at least not on the question of whether or not all voices are heard "equally."

The biased intent of reform appears with appealing frankness in Owen Fiss's writing. Fiss is quite open about wanting to reduce speech associated with the political "right" and promote views favoring a larger, more activist role for government. Thus Fiss would not have courts defer to the legislature on these matters. Instead, he has suggested that courts should order legislative bodies to fund certain views if such views are not, in the court's opinion, adequately represented.[26]

In calling for government to take sides in the debate, Fiss argues that the average citizen is excluded from public debate. He bases his argument on what he considers to be the paradigm of First Amendment speech, the street-corner speaker. Fiss argues that whereas a century ago, such a person might have some meaningful say in events, in a modern society of television networks, free speech is abridged unless that person can command television air time, or has other means of access to the modern forms of mass communication.[27] Even assuming the validity of this example, Fiss's analysis fails: the street-corner orator never had the influence of those who could publish or write for newspapers, write law review articles, organize political campaigns, and the like. But if Fiss's argument ever had any validity, technology has already passed it by. In today's society, the argument that certain voices are being "drowned out" by better-financed interests is patently absurd. As one commentator has stated; "It is simply not the case that no one will publish unpopular views. Information technology is so far advanced that it takes relatively small capital—capital that almost anyone can assemble—to put out one's message in print form. One need only listen to the news and information programming of public broadcasting to hear the broadest array of opinions—with opinions on the left generously represented.[28] Yet even this passage understates the level of influence available to an average person. With minimal capital and training, one can sit at a computer and, within minutes of an event taking place or a bill being introduced, download text from a legislative speech or bill, add comments, and fax or e-mail the material off to thousands of individuals with a few strokes of the keyboard.[29] In light of these new technologies, the current effort to "enhance" certain voices seems less concerned with seeing that certain ideas are heard than with seeing that other ideas are not heard.

To ask Congress and the courts to determine which views need to be "enhanced" is an almost absurd task. To determine whether a view has been insufficiently represented, the state would have to make several distinctions that it is not equipped to make. For example, would the view of a traditional conservative require the response of a libertarian as well as a liberal? What about a socialist? Such assessments would immediately be caught up in contests for political advantage, since the assessors would themselves be active in the political arena.[30]

But even if we could trust Congress and the courts somehow to identify which views are not "adequately" represented, there remains no reason to believe that restrictions on political campaigning will succeed in "enhancing" those views. When certain points of view are not heard, the problem is usually that those viewpoints are not being communicated effectively, not that other views are being communicated. In terms of political campaigning, it has been shown that the most important funding issue is neither the total level of spending nor the difference in incumbent/challenger spending but rather that the challenger spend enough to deliver his or her message to the public. A more appropriate answer to the equality question, then, would be a state subsidy, not restrictions on the speech of others. The other obvious answer would be to remove restrictions on campaign contributions and spending that limit the ability of individuals to make themselves heard.

As a practical matter, campaign contribution and spending limits often work most strongly against the type of groups that those who favor enhancement theories seem to believe are underrepresented, including "the poor" and "grassroots" movements. This is partly due to the nature of government regulation, which favors those with the lawyers and the technical know-how to comply with and take advantage of the system. Another, related reason is the tendency of less educated and less wealthy voters to be less politically active and less familiar with the machinery of government and public policy debate. These groups are therefore more likely to require a "champion" with the resources and articulate vision to promote their interest. There are also collective-action problems that work against

149

interests without a strong institutional base. Put simply, groups without a permanent presence and the contacts and organization that go with it will find political activity more difficult than other groups. This lack of organization can be overcome, once again, if a single individual or small group can spend the resources needed to get an organization moving.[31]

The reality is that limits on campaign contributions and spending aimed at enhancing some voices tend only to silence others. For example, in *Austin v. Michigan State Chamber of Commerce*, the Supreme Court upheld a Michigan law that restricted corporate expenditures in candidate races. What is interesting about the case is that the advertisement placed by the Michigan State Chamber of Commerce, in violation of the law, was a model of intelligent, informative campaign advertising. It explained the makeup of the Chamber's membership and the organization's goals; discussed the high cost of workers' compensation and high personal income tax rates in Michigan, and how those may have been affecting economic development in the state; and concluded by explaining why the Chamber thought candidate Richard Bandstra was the best choice to address such issues. The ad offered no hyperbole, no negativity, and no images, only text.[32] Moreover, the Chamber offered a unique voice for having such a message heard, speaking as the voice of the larger Michigan business community, rather than a narrow group of businesses, a corporate PAC, or an individual. No substitute existed for the Chamber's unique position and voice. Thus, a law intended to restrict certain voices perceived to "dominate" the debate merely kept a highly relevant voice from being heard. No alternative voice was "enhanced" by this silencing of one relevant voice. Another recently popular proposal in campaign finance, restricting donations from outside the district, would also have blocked the Chamber ad. Yet the Chamber ad was clearly relevant to the voters within the district—indeed, it was arguably the fact that it came from a voice outside the district that made it both unique in its perspective and relevant to the race. It is this type of government error, as much as any nefarious government intention, that suggests the wisdom of the framers in passing the First Amendment. Assurances to the contrary, government is uniquely ill suited, and far too much an interested party, to act as a benign "parliamentarian" in the debate.

Similarly, the 1996 presidential election campaign showed how campaign spending promotes public airing of diverse views in the political process. In the campaign, Republican candidate Steve Forbes sought to bring public attention to a proposed "flat tax" on income, that is, a federal income tax with no deductions and only one tax rate. When Forbes first declared his candidacy, it drew little media attention. His flat tax idea was derided by one network television commentator as "wacky." Forbes responded with an advertising campaign that exceeded, by some accounts, $23 million in the Republican primaries.[33] As a result, he was able to rise in the polls, and his flat tax was widely discussed. Yet Forbes's spending did not "drown out" other candidates—indeed it may have heightened interest in the campaign, helping other candidates to be heard. Before Forbes's spending, Senator Bob Dole was considered a virtual shoo-in to take the Republican nomination. And though Senator Dole did eventually win that nomination, Forbes's spending drew attention not only to Forbes but to other candidates. Once Forbes shattered Dole's appearance of inevitability, a spirited contest arose not only between Dole and Forbes but also with Pat Buchanan and Lamar Alexander. Similarly, Forbes's own low initial standing in the polls was not the result of his voice being drowned out. Rather, it was the result of his being unknown. In other words, if Forbes had not been allowed to spend his own money, but all other candidates had had their spending limited, there is no reason to believe that Forbes would have drawn media or public attention. His money did not drown out others, but it allowed his candidacy to float. In doing so, it probably helped other second-tier candidates to be heard, as well.

At the same time that money allows added voices to be heard, there is ample evidence that the type of regulation and bureaucracy required to limit campaign contributions and spending tends to intimidate and silence voices, especially political amateurs (disproportionately, one suspects, the poor and middle class) who might otherwise participate in politics. Regulation of political speech tends to benefit those already familiar with the process and with the money or expertise to hire the lawyers, lobbyists, consultants, and accountants to comply with the ensuing regulatory burden.[34]

151

In summary, the idea that the voices of some may be restricted to "enhance" the voices of others is not only, as the *Buckley* court put it, "wholly foreign to the First Amendment."[35] It is also based on erroneous assumptions about the effects of both money and regulation in practice. It is extremely unlikely that campaign finance regulation has enhanced, or will enhance, public debate in the United States. And the fact is that the published statements of proponents of the "enhancement" theory provide ample grounds to believe that the purpose of the enterprise is less to "enhance" public debate than to guarantee a favored set of winners in the political process. Indeed, it is hard to see how (or why) such "enhancement" could (or would) otherwise be conducted.

The bias that regulatory advocates such as Owen Fiss seek to introduce into the process; the failure of regulators to recognize that the very idea of "enhancement" rests on the denial of "content neutrality"; and the manner in which campaign finance regulation tends to limit the breadth of political discussion and disproportionately burden "grassroots" voices—all are testimony to the wisdom of the founders in passing the First Amendment to prohibit, not authorize, government involvement in policing political speech.

The First Amendment is not merely a representation of values, as regulatory supporters such as Neuborne, Fiss, and Sunstein seem to imply. It is a structural part of the Constitution that governs our nation. The plain purpose of the amendment was to limit the authority of government to regulate speech. For all the complaints these limits generate today, they have served our country well for over two hundred years.

The Fourteenth Amendment Formulation

A second approach to the constitutional problems of campaign finance regulation aims to sidestep these First Amendment difficulties altogether by relying on the Fourteenth Amendment, which prohibits governments from denying to persons "equal protection of the laws." Under this theory, the concept of equal protection permits, or even requires, the government to silence some to assure equality for others. Unlike the First Amendment theories of Sunstein, Fiss, Neuborne, and others, which aim to "enhance" "underrepresented" voices, this approach relies on supressing voices to assure equal political "influence" at some point prior to voting.[36] Several of the prominent supporters of this theory have put forth detailed proposals for the overhaul of the American system of financing political campaigns, replacing private funding with a system of total government funding. Those proposals center on the proposition that no individual should have more money to spend on political speech than any other individual. Richard Hasen calls his proposal one for "an egalitarian pluralist political market"; Edward Foley titles his proposal, "Equal Dollars per Voter." Jamin Raskin and John Bonifaz term their proposal one for "Democratically financed elections."[37] Each proposal takes, as a starting point, the view that voter equality demands full public funding of campaigns, and the elimination of private campaign contributions. Before proceeding, it is worth reviewing these proposals to illuminate the scope of ambition burning in these scholars.

Richard Hasen proposes a tax-financed system, under which each voter would receive a government voucher for some politically determined sum. Voters could then give their dollars to candidates, "licensed interest groups," or political parties. "All campaign contributions and independent expenditures in support of or in opposition to a candidate must be made with voucher dollars." Furthermore, "only licensed interest groups could collect voucher dollars from others to run independent expenditure campaigns." An individual could volunteer his or her own time to work on a campagn. Other in-kind contributions would be prohibited.[38]

Hasen constructs a system that is hardly comforting to those whose primary concern is free speech; in order to make the voucher system work, Hasen would restrict all direct and indirect political donations, organizational money, in-kind contributions, honoraria, and expenses from whatever source, other than government-provided vouchers. Interest groups of whatever kind would, in order to participate in politics, need to be licensed by a special federal agency, which agency would also maintain an investigatory antifraud unit. Recently, Hasen has expanded his proposal to argue that media endorsements should also be prohibited unless the publication pays for its own space with government-issued vouchers.[39]

Edward Foley, arguing for a similar voucher-type proposal, goes even further, including in his proposal a ban not only on media endorsements but even on the "publication of . . . statements of support or opposition

153

[of a candidate or ballot proposal]."[40] It is unclear exactly how a newspaper could manage to report on politics under such a standard.

There should be no obfuscation of what Hasen and Foley are proposing: they propose to ban most partisan political activity in the United States, beyond a minimal expenditure allowance that each citizen obtains from the federal government, with modest allowances for people to donate time, if that is their pleasure, they can afford to do so, have the health to do so, and their talents have some value in the political arena. These proposals, appearing in some of the nation's most prestigious law reviews, are so audacious it is hard for most casual observers to take them seriously. Yet they are taken seriously by those coordinating the movement to regulate political speech. Both men have signed statements touted by the Brennan Center for Justice, a leading "reform" group, that have sought to convince Congress that it has the authority to limit political speech.[41] Foley formerly sat on the advisory board of the National Voting Rights Institute, and is now Ohio's state solicitor. Both men routinely speak at conferences on the issue, and Foley has addressed the national conference of the Council on Government Ethics Laws, a leading gathering for state and local officials, to promote his theories. These theories are taken seriously.

Raskin and Bonifaz outlined their proposal in an article in the *Columbia Law Review*. Their plan, which basically mimics one made by an ad-hoc group of campaign finance reform activists calling itself the Working Group on Electoral Democracy, calls for public funding of elections. The proposal also calls for forced participation in broadcast debates, free media time, and cash subsidies aimed at covering living expenses for "poor" people running for office. Although Raskin and Bonifaz call the system "voluntary," in fact it so severely penalizes a candidate for opting out of the plan that the right to opt out is meaningless. For example, the proposal provides for up to triple expenditures for the opponent of a candidate who chooses private financing, extra reporting requirements for those who reject public funds and their accompanying spending limits, and a limit on total expenditures during the last two weeks of the campaign for those who reject public funds. With such provisions, no candidate would realistically refuse public financing. As Raskin and Bonifaz admit, the goal is to make certain that no candidate will refuse the "volun-

154

tary" spending limits. They write that under their proposal, "the attractions of [private financing] would fade."[42]

As can be seen, these are radical proposals indeed, calling for a complete shake-up of American politics and the elimination of nongovernmental approved speech that requires any contribution of money. Is this truly what the Fourteenth Amendment contemplates?

From a constitutional perspective, Raskin and Bonifaz are the most ambitious, arguing that the Constitution's equal protection clauses already *require* that private funding of campaigns be abolished. There are several reasons why this proposition is wrong.

At the outset, before the Constitution's equal protection clause comes into play, there must be some form of government action. The Constitution prohibits government—not private citizens—from denying equal protection under the law. It is difficult to find government action in campaign finance, given that these advocates' admitted goal is to use the Equal Protection Clause to make the government act affirmatively—by financing campaigns—where it now refrains from doing so. However, in an effort to find government action in the current system of campaign finance, Raskin points to what he calls "state subsidies" to incumbent congressmen. These include a salary well in excess of $100,000, which may be drawn while campaigning; over a half million dollars per year in personal staff expenses; over $150,000 per year in district office expenses; and a mail allowance of approximately $200,000. Raskin's "extremely conservative" estimate of the total value of such perks toward reelection is $200,000 every two years.[43] Thus, he argues, government has acted, and in doing so has treated some citizens (incumbents) differently from others (nonincumbents).

Although there is no denying the advantages of incumbency, such advantages cannot coherently amount to the type of state action that would invoke equal protection guarantees for all nonincumbents. In essence, Raskin is arguing that the mere creation of a Congress—which necessarily requires at least minimal staff and office or desk space, and includes an express constitutional mandate for a salary—mandates government-funded campaigns. But while the Constitution provides for a Congress and congressional salaries, it does not provide for government funding of campaigns. Finding state action in the mere fact that some people are officeholders seems a dubious proposition, for it would place state action at the center of all aspects of public discourse.

Raskin, however, sees a broader form of state action at work, not only in "the public self-subsidy granted to incumbents in Congress" but also in "the enactment of legislation which may benefit donors," the need of candidates to raise money to be "effective," and the involvement of public officials in each of the above.[44] In other words, he argues that because politicians are, if elected, part of the government, any government policy that may affect electoral outcomes must constitute state action in the realm of electoral laws. This theory raises more questions than it answers. It would suggest, for example, that if an incumbent votes for popular measures and is effective in office, a challenger who lacked the public office to take such vote-winning actions must be compensated for this "unequal" treatment.

In arriving at this far-reaching definition of state action, Raskin draws heavily on the Supreme Court's "white primary" cases from the middle of the twentieth century, in particular *Terry v. Adams*.[45] The "white primary" cases were a series of Supreme Court decisions that, pursuant to the Fourteenth Amendment, barred party primaries limited to white voters. In Southern states, where the Republican Party was at the time all but nonexistent, victory in the Democratic Party primary was tantamount to election. State Democratic parties in the South argued that as private entities they could exclude black voters from their primaries. In *Nixon v. Herndon*, the Supreme Court struck down a state law that prohibited blacks from voting in party primaries. In *Smith v. Allwright*, the court went on to invalidate a Democratic Party rule that limited the primary to white voters, arguing that the primary was part of the electoral process of the state. *Terry v. Adams* posed yet another challenge for the Court, however, for *Terry* involved a scheme to exclude black voters from the Democratic Party's nominating process without directly involving the state electoral machinery.[46]

In *Terry*, white citizens in Fort Bend County, Texas, had organized the Jaybird Democratic Association which for more than sixty years had dominated county politics. During that period, every single Democratic Party primary winner had been the endorsed candidate of the Jaybird Association and, indeed, "other candidates almost never file[d] in the

Democratic primary." The association's membership consisted, according to its rules, of all members of the county's white voting-age population, according to county government poll lists. Each spring, before the official Democratic party primary, the association would hold its own primary, using the same process provided for by Texas state law governing primary elections. Despite the association's status as a private organization, the Supreme Court held that its activities, combined with the Democratic Party primary structure and the general election structure, functioned to deprive negro citizens of their right to vote.[47] Using *Terry* as his foundation, Raskin argues that state action exists in the system of private campaign financing, first, because the government has allowed a system to develop in which "wealthy private social groupings are permitted to exclude . . . the poor . . . from 'an integral part' of 'the elective process' "; second, because the campaign finance system has become "part of the machinery for choosing officials"; and third, because public officials receive and spend private campaign donations.[48]

There are a number of problems with Raskin's analogy of the campaign finance system to the activities of the Jaybird Democratic Association. First and foremost is the question of context. According to the census of 1950, the entire white voting age population of Fort Bend County was just 18,242.[49] Although these voters may have differed in their views on many issues, they were united in their hostility to the Republican Party and to the county's African-American population. Because the Republican Party lacked any base of support in the white community, victory in the Democratic primary was tantamount to election. But in order to assure that the county's majority white vote would not be split among several candidates in the primary, thus allowing a minority candidate to capture the Democratic Party nomination with a bare plurality of the total (white and black) vote, it was necessary to hold what might be termed a "preprimary" to assure that whites would unite behind a single candidate. This was the function of the Jaybird Association. The list of those eligible to vote in the Jaybird primary was supplied by county election officials; the primary was private but run in accordance with Texas state laws governing official elections, except for the exclusion of minority voters. In virtually every case, losers in the Jaybird primary did not enter the official Democratic party primary, thus assuring only one white candidate on the ballot. In other words, within the small community of Fort Bend, white citizens had conspired to create a public election system that disenfranchised minority voters for over sixty years. They created an ostensibly private organization, which in fact included every white citizen registered to vote, whether or not that citizen sought out membership, for the purpose of holding whites-only elections. Other than disenfranchising negro voters, they operated the system exactly as a state election, and relied on county officials to determine who would be "members" by informing the association of those white citizens eligible to vote in the official, government election. At this point, it should be apparent that the finding of state action in *Terry* (and the other white primary cases) was significantly dependent on the type of activity occurring: all of the white power structure, with the cooperation of the government, was engaged in a systematic effort to deprive negro citizens of the right to vote. Yet even under these circumstances, the court had to strain mightily to find state action, and its finding has remained controversial. Many have argued that the white primary cases were wrong in stretching to find state action in the affairs of the private Jaybird Association. Indeed Justice Minton, dissenting in *Terry*, wrote, "the majority have found that this pressure group's work does constitute state action. The basis for this conclusion is rather difficult to ascertain. Apparently it derives mainly from a dislike of the goals of the Jaybird Association. I share that dislike. I fail to see how it makes state action." Other commentators have shared that view. Nevertheless, the Court has shown no inclination to disavow the white primary cases, which are generally viewed "as one of the bright spots in the history of the Supreme Court." Thus, in responding to Raskin's argument, I think we must accept that the white primary cases, however problematical, are correctly decided.[50]

Raskin relies most heavily on Justice Frankfurter's concurrence in *Terry*, in which Frankfurter found state action because "somewhere, somehow, to some extent, there [is] an infusion of conduct by officials, panoplied with state power . . . in an effort to . . . subvert what is formally the law of the State." However, unlike *Terry*, where the "subversion" is relatively apparent, Raskin does not explain how lawful private campaign contributions "subvert what is formally the law of the state," other than to claim that they discourage some candidates from running, and that not all persons have equal financial resources.[51] Thus the comparison of campaign finance to *Terry* merely begs the question that Raskin hopes to answer—are all citizens entitled to equal financial resources when seeking public office? On this key issue, Frankfurter's concurrence offers him no support.

Indeed, Frankfurter's opinion explicitly distinguished the type of situation in *Terry* from that which exists in campaign finance. Wrote Frankfurter: "This is not a case of occasional efforts to mass voting strength. Nor is this a case of boss-control. . . . Nor is this a case of spontaneous efforts by citizens to influence votes or even continued efforts by a fraction of the electorate in support of good government. This is a case in which county election officials have participated in and condoned a continued effort to effectively exclude Negroes from *voting*."[52] In contrast, campaign contributions are efforts to, as Frankfurter would say, "mass voting strength" and "support [differing views of] good government." They entail no effort to shut another group out of similar participation in the political process. Nor do they entail any effort to "subvert what is formally the law of the state." Indeed, if anything, campaign fund-raisers seek to bring people into the political process, by seeking out new donors and then using those funds to encourage citizens to vote, rather than by preventing people from voting. Certainly no group is denied the vote.

Although the Court continues to cite approvingly *Terry* and the other white primary cases, in fact recent cases make it clear that the finding of state action in those cases is not being expanded. In *DeShaney v. Winnebago Dept. of Social Services*, the court found no state action where government officials failed to remove a child from family custody when the child was beaten and severely, permanently, injured. In other recent cases the Court has held that a private school that receives much of its budget in government funds is not a state actor, and that Congress's grant of a trademark monopoly did not make an organization a state actor.[53] Professor Raskin recognizes these precedents, but argues that the court has not "abandoned its sweeping 'state action' holdings in the specific field of elections and political process."[54]

159

But, in fact, the Court has effectively moved away from such a broad definition of state action in a series of cases that uphold the associational rights of political parties against state regulation. In *Democratic Party of the United States v. Wisconsin*, the Court prohibited judicial enforcement of a state law that violated a political party's internal rules for delegate selection to the national convention. In *Tashjian v. Republican Party of Connecticut*, the Court held that a party could, contrary to state law, include independents in its primary. In *Eu v. San Francisco Democratic Central Committee*, the Court struck down a state statute that prohibited party endorsements in primary elections. Each of these cases suggests strongly that the Court views political entities not as state actors but as private actors with a right to association free from government interference. That being the case, it seems unlikely that the Court would about-face and find state action in a system of private donations to campaign organizations that are not part of the governmental apparatus. Thus the state action needed to assert an equal protection claim is lacking.

Supporters of the equal protection thesis seem to assume that their most difficult hurdle is the question of state action and that, once crossed, their position is clearly correct. Although the state action problem is a very high hurdle, even if the issue is conceded no equal protection violation exists. For in order to find an equal protection violation, there must also be an unjustified infringement on a constitutional right. Even if state action could be found in a system of private campaign finance, the action will be scrutinized solely to determine if it has a rational basis, unless those claiming discrimination constitute a "suspect class," or the matter involves a fundamental right.[55] By "suspect class," the Court means a discrete, insular minority subject to majority discrimination. Generally, such classes are limited to those defined by race, sex, or in some cases, religion and national origin. The Court has refused to recognize such an indiscrete group as "poor" people as a suspect class, and it is hard to know how such a class could be recognized or defined if it did.[56] Therefore, unless a "fundamental" right is involved, government "action" of the type described by Raskin will be subject only to the lenient "rational basis" test. There is surely a rational basis for government to pay salaries, provide office space, staff, and mail allowances, and pass at least some legislation. Thus, even if correct, the strained effort to find government action may be for naught, unless it can also be shown that a fundamental right is being burdened by the government "subsidy" to incumbents.

Raskin purports to find a fundamental right in the right to vote, and the concept of one person/one vote.[57] But this position seems prima facie wrong. No one is denied the right to vote by a system of private campaign finance, and all votes are counted equally.

Despite the prima facie improbability of the argument, Raskin argues that the right to vote is burdened by what he terms the "wealth primary." He argues that the need to raise campaign funds excludes certain citizens from the political process, because many citizens are unable to raise substantial sums to run for office. But here he is vague. At times he seems to be saying that individuals are deprived of a fundamental right because they are unable to raise enough money to run effective campaigns. At other times, he seems to argue that voters as a whole are denied a fundamental right to choose candidates because certain candidates cannot raise the money to compete effectively.[58] Both approaches fail.

In *Clements v. Fashing*, the Supreme Court specifically rejected the notion that running for office is a fundamental right. Nor, in any case, is a claim that individuals cannot compete in fund-raising ability the same as saying the candidates are unfairly discriminated against. Candidates begin campaigns with a variety of advantages and disadvantages. The ability to raise money (or to spend one's own money) is a potential advantage. Other advantages may include, but certainly are not limited to, good looks, speaking ability, powerful friends, a fractured opposition, a friendly media corps, appeal to large numbers of students (who often have time to volunteer to campaigns), and simplistic but popular and easy-to-understand positions on issues. The mere lack of a valuable political asset does not create an equal protection violation. Such a theory, if adopted as a constitutional proviso, would seem to suggest that officeholders must be selected by lottery, given that any system for elections will favor some candidates and parties over others.

Raskin's second formulation is that voters are denied choices because some candidates are unable to raise money. Again, this reaches too far. Voters are also denied choices when individuals choose not to run for office because they lack some other quality, such as popular political views.

Further, Raskin fails both to identify which policy choices are not available to voters and to explain why the lack of such options are linked to contributions, rather than, say, the unpopularity of the options he has in mind. Raskin seems to suggest that it is "poorer" people, or "people of ordinary means" who find their views underrepresented.[59] He is never clear however, on just who constitutes the "poor" nor on exactly what views they hold that are radically different from the rest of the population. One can glean from his writing that he thinks "the poor" would favor a sort of socialist redistributive policy, along with what is generally thought of as a strong liberal perspective on the environment and other issues. Tipping his hand, he goes so far as to argue that "the goal of campaign finance reform ought not be "good government" but "how to dismantle the regime of plutocracy which overlays our democratic ideals."[60] In any case, such liberal views seemed to be well represented in the political world in the late 1990s by, among others, such high-profile politicians as Jesse Jackson and House minority whip David Bonior. So it is hardly clear that such views are not represented.

On the whole, money in elections tends to flow to candidates who are popular or who are seen as having a good chance to win. Raskin seems to be of the opinion that there are popular candidates who cannot win because they cannot raise money. He cites no examples, nor does he explain why they cannot raise money (even in very small contributions) if they are popular, nor why voters are so easily duped by opponents' campaign advertising that they choose to vote, and have voted for many generations, against their own views and interests. In short, other than the fact that Raskin seems unhappy with the political direction of the country, he supplies no evidence to support his contention that candidates are excluded from the process or that large numbers of voters are regularly being denied access to the candidates for whom they would otherwise prefer to vote. In the words of one skeptic, "these critics are like annoying children who whine at their parents, 'you're not listening to me,' when what they really mean is 'however much I go on, you don't think I'm right.'"[61]

Still, theorists such as Raskin and Bonifaz are undeterred. They argue that wealth, or access to it, is not a constitutionally permissable barrier to electoral success. In other words, all candidates must have at least "adequate" funds, provided by the government if necessary. For this proposition, they rely primarily on *Bullock v. Carter*, which, they state, "forms the basic theoretical structure for our argument."[62] In *Bullock*, the Supreme Court struck down a Texas law that required candidates to pay primary election filing fees ranging from $150 to $6,300. Candidates could not appear on the ballot without paying the fees. Chief Justice Burger, writing for the Court, found that the fees constituted an "exclusionary mechanism" that kept some candidates from running and, further, that the candidates so prevented from running would, by definition, be poor. He further found that the burden fell disproportionately on the "less affluent," on the theory that the candidates they would like to support would be less likely to be able to pay the filing fees.[63]

However, just two years later the Court clarified *Bullock* in *Lubin v. Panish*. In *Lubin*, an indigent candidate contested a state statute that required a filing fee of just over $700. The Court did not hold that *Bullock* disposed of the case; in fact, it specifically denied that it did. Unlike *Bullock*, in which the court struck down the entire filing fee system, in *Lubin* it held only that an indigent candidate must be given some alternative way to appear on the ballot other than by paying the fee, or the fee must be waived for such a candidate.[64] The Court rejected the proposition that an equal protection violation could be found in the mere fact that the filing fee fell more heavily on some candidates than on others. Absent a complete inability to appear on the ballot, a candidate could be assessed a filing fee, despite the fact that it might fall harder on candidates with fewer resources than on those with greater resources. In other words, the fact that a $3,000 filing fee is more burdensome for a candidate with just $10,000 than for a candidate with $50,000 does not create an equal protection violation. Thus, *Bullock* and *Lubin* do not stand for the proposition that candidates have some constitutional right to financial equality. Quite the opposite, they specifically recognize that candidates will have differing financial strengths, and that a system that allows those differences to exist does pass the constitutional test under equal protection

163

analysis.[65] Only if a candidate has no legal means of getting his name on the ballot is an equal protection issue raised. Once the candidate can have his name placed on the ballot, discrepancies in campaign resources are no concern of the Constitution. The Constitution requires no more than the minimal ability to appear on the ballot. It suggests nothing about the ability to campaign on equal terms.

Bullock and *Lubin* actually shut the door on the equal protection clause as a hook to justify campaign regulation. What the Court struck down as violating equal protection was a direct, state-imposed barrier (filing fees) that denied the opportunity to appear on the ballot at all. In this respect, the cases are similar to *Harper v. Virginia State Board of Elections*, in which the Court struck down a poll tax that prevented some from voting at all. But what Raskin and others want to claim violates equal protection is precisely what the Court did not find to be an equal protection violation; namely, the fact that private campaign contributions allow some candidates to raise more money to pay campaign expenses, whereas other candidates find it more difficult to pay expenses due to lack of financial resources. This is true even where the campaign expenses are, like ballot access fees, the direct result of the state electoral laws—unlike most campaign expenses, which are discretionary. Indeed, the ballot cases cut even further against Raskin's position, because they clearly establish that the government may pass laws that raise the cost of campaigning, without violating the rights of poorer candidates. In both *Bullock* and *Lubin*, the Court endorsed, as an alternative to filing fees, a requirement that a candidate collect signatures to appear on the ballot, a requirement that requires considerable time and money, typically in excess of $1 per required signature.[66]

Unlike the white primary cases, the "wealth primary" of which Raskin and Bonifaz complain is not the result of any one group acting specifically to exclude another group of voters from the electoral process. No fundamental right is violated. Voters are not denied the right to vote, nor to participate in politics. To find a "fundamental" right, then, reformers perform a linguistic sleight of hand. They describe an unquestioned political skill—fund-raising—in electoral terms. But the fact that some candidates are better than others at raising money does not burden the right to vote.

One can call it a "primary" if one likes, but in fact, no such "primary" is held. Candidates raise money, make their case to the voters, and all voters then go to the polls, where each voter has an equal vote. The candidates do not stuff dollar bills into ballot boxes, and no voter is excluded at the point at which ballots are cast. Neither candidates nor parties are excluded from the ballot. There is no more a "wealth" primary than a "good looks" primary or a "media" primary.

Even if this hurdle, like the hurdle of state action, could be crossed, Raskin and his fellow theorists are not out of the woods. For even if we assume that this is state action burdening a fundamental right, the traditional remedy is to remove the offending state action—not to require additional state regulation of private activity. Any offending state behavior could be limited, for example, by eliminating the franking privilege or restricting the contents of franked mail, or by cutting congressional staff and more closely restricting staff time spent on campaign-related activities.

Ultimately, the idea that the Fifth and Fourteenth amendments to the Constitutution already prohibit what some have dubbed the "wealth primary" is simply not supported by existing case law or the language of the Constitution. The *Buckley* Court got it right: "the concept that government may restrict the speech of some elements of our society in order to enhance the relative voices of others is wholly foreign to the First Amendment."

Conclusion

Limits on political contributions and spending infringe on the right to free speech. The Supreme Court's *Buckley* decision was correct in rejecting the specious equality arguments advanced as a justification for restraining rights otherwise guaranteed by the First Amendment. What is suspect in the Supreme Court's jurisprudence is the notion that an unproven interest in preventing corruption is sufficient to justify infringements on First Amendment rights.

The First Amendment was written so as to keep government out of the business of deciding who may speak when, how, and how much, on public issues. If that barrier is broken down, there is little between voters and outright censorship. And, indeed, "reform" measures are moving fast in the latter direction. Bill Bradley, a serious contender for the 2000 Democratic Party presidential nomination, proposed a 100 percent tax on issue speech. John McCain, a serious contender for the Republican nomination in 2000, expressed his desire to ban all negative ads, if he could figure out how to do it constitutionally.[67] What can we expect, what might happen, if *Buckley* is overruled in the direction favored by those urging greater regulation of political speech and campaigns?

PART III
REAL AND IMAGINED REFORM OF CAMPAIGN FINANCE

Chapter 9

Unfree Speech: The Future of Regulatory "Reform"

Despite numerous court defeats, the constitutionally suspect premises behind campaign regulation, and the abject failure of past regulatory regimes to accomplish their goals, there has been little or no reassessment by the campaign finance "reform" movement of its operating assumptions, its stated objectives, or its legislative approach. Rather, the emphasis has been on more and heavier regulation, aimed at closing "loopholes" in the law. On both the political and academic fronts, the leading advocates of increased regulation have used a two-prong strategy to attempt to drum up political support. First, they have emphasized over and over the "corrupt" nature of "the system," without specifying which, if any, legislators have actually been corrupted. Next, they have promised to "fix" the problem, while sometimes appearing to deflect attention from the actual measures proposed and the probable consequences of those measures.

The purpose of this chapter is to ask some questions about the future of reform, and to point out some potential problems. For we are rapidly heading down a path from which it will be very difficult to make the return journey. We had best be certain that we want to reach the destination that lies ahead.

Why Spending Really Rises

In earlier chapters we have seen some of the problems with past efforts at campaign finance regulation. In chapter 2 we examined the long, steady rise in spending on political campaigns, without asking why spending had increased. If we are to understand the enormous task facing would-be regulators, it is important to understand why spending increases.

There is little doubt that campaign spending has gone up dramatically over the past two hundred years. The exact amount of this increase is hard to pin down, however, because until the last half century, much political spending was hidden and very difficult to track. Thus, early estimates of political spending are unreliable and probably understated. As an example of this unreliability, George Thayer points out that most scholars believe that the total cost of James Buchanan's 1856 presidential campaign was approximately $25,000; yet one prominent Democrat of the time stated that Buchanan's victory was helped by spending $50,000 *more* than his Republican opponent, John Fremont. If true, that would suggest that Buchanan spent much more than twice the amount that scholars have previously estimated. Similarly, Abraham Lincoln paid most of the travel costs in his congressional campaign of 1846 from his own pocket, and did not record them or even seem to view them as a "campaign" expense.[1] If early spending was higher than most published estimates, and there is reason to believe that it was, then spending has, quite obviously, not increased as much as the published figures show.

Whatever the actual increase, much of that increase is due to ordinary, mundane factors. The most obvious, of course, is general inflation. One dollar in 1900, adjusted for inflation, would be about twenty dollars a century later. Furthermore, since the 1980s at least, prices for such indispensable campaign items as paper, postage, and media advertising have risen faster than general inflation, so one would expect political spending to rise at a rate faster than the general inflation rate.

A second reason for the general growth of campaign expenditures is the growth of the electorate. The few dozen pounds that George Washington spent on his 1757 campaign for the Virginia House of Burgesses, a race with just 391 eligible voters, would amount to over two dollars per eligible voter in 1999 dollars. Today, many, if not most races that involve such small electorates are conducted for less money, which suggests that much of the spending growth in congressional and legislative races is due to larger electorates.

Part of the growth of the electorate, of course, is pure population growth. The electorate has grown at a faster rate than the populace, however, for reasons that most people quite rightly approve. Early elections were limited, in most states, to white male property owners. This began to change during the early nineteenth century and accelerated through the Jacksonian era. States gradually dropped religious and property qualifications for voting.[2] The Fifteenth Amendment to the Constitution, ratified in 1870, did away with formal bans on voting based explicitly on race. The Nineteenth Amendment, ratified in 1920, enfranchised women, and the Twenty-Sixth Amendment gave eighteen-year-olds the vote in 1971. Statutory changes have also tended to expand the franchise. Especially notable was the Voting Rights Act of 1964, which was a stunning success in eliminating legal barriers to black voter registration in the South.[3] The Supreme Court also expanded the electorate through a series of decisions that struck down literacy tests, whites-only primary elections, bans on voting by citizens in the military, poll taxes, and unduly long residency requirements.[4] Thus candidates are required to reach a far greater number of voters than their predecessors.

These larger electorates also make it less likely that a candidate will personally know any substantial percentage of the electorate. This makes increased advertising necessary if voters are to gain information on the candidates. Thus, the larger electorate should be expected not only to increase total advertising expenditures but to increase expenditures on a per-voter basis, as well. In fact, the amount spent per voter is considerably

171

higher than in our nation's early days. Yet over the past twenty years, a period marked by great concern over political spending, the amount spent per eligible voter has remained quite stable. Since the Voting Rights Act and the Twenty-Sixth Amendment greatly expanded the electorate in the 1960s and early 1970s, the amount spent per eligible voter in congressional races, in constant dollars, has hovered in a range from approximately $2.50 to $3.50 per eligible voter, inching up slightly in the highly competitive elections of 1994 and 1996, but stabilizing—indeed declining—in another highly competitive election in 1998.[5] On a per-voter basis, political spending in the United States remains lower than in many other democracies, including some that are considerably poorer, such as Venezuela, Italy, and Israel. Many countries spend substantially more, on a per-eligible-voter basis, than the United States.[6]

Not only has the electorate grown but the number of political offices that are filled by popular election is also significantly higher today than in the early days of the republic. In colonial America, most offices were appointed, and this changed only gradually after the Constitution was ratified. Not for many years did a majority of states provide for popular election of presidential electors. Not only are more offices elected but there are also more primary elections than before, especially at the presidential level. Not until the 1960s did primaries become particularly important in presidential races. A primary, of course, requires added spending, and spending on political activity naturally rises with the number of offices up for election.

Another factor in the long increase in spending is the gradual democratization of campaign methods. Early campaigns, as noted, were fought out primarily through highly partisan newspapers and circulars. The campaign of 1840 is notable for the first large-scale use of buttons, banners, parades, and memorabilia. In 1860, Stephan Douglas became the first presidential candidate to campaign extensively in person, but personal campaigning was again eschewed as a major tool until the candidacy of William Jennings Bryan in 1896, and remained rare until well into the twentieth century.[7] The new style of campaigning has given voters more direct exposure to the candidates, and has created an atmosphere in which candidates are expected to communicate directly to voters. This style of campaigning had raised costs long before the advent of radio and televi-

172

sion, but these forms of mass communication would come to drive costs considerably higher. By 1928, nearly 20 percent of the Democratic National Committee's budget went to bring presidential candidate Al Smith's voice "into every home in the United States."[8] By the election of 1952, television had become as important to candidates as radio, and by the mid-1960s, most Americans relied on television as their primary news source.[9] Today, a candidate in a closely contested congressional campaign will spend one-half to three-quarters of his or her budget on television advertising. Similarly, more and more local candidates rely on television than in the past. This increase, though substantial, is not uniform, as many candidates for local office still do not use television, especially in less urbanized areas.[10]

Yet another new expense that has driven up campaign costs is the cost of compliance with campaign finance regulations. Since the 1970s, candidates for federal offices, and in many states for state and local office, have faced substantial legal obligations to track and report on contributions and expenditures, which has created accounting, reporting, and legal expenses that were unheard of in earlier days. In the presidential election of 1992, the two major party candidates spent $11 million dollars on compliance costs, or roughly 10 percent of their total campaign budgets.[11]

In addition to factors that have directly raised the cost of campaigning, campaign spending has probably grown simply because the supply of funds available has increased. The ability, and desire, to spend money on political activity will naturally be lower when the material standard of living is lower. As the standard of living increases, more money should be available for such discretionary, nonessential activities as politics. As a percentage of gross domestic product, the amount spent on politics remains trivial. We now spend approximately .05 to .06 percent of gross domestic product on political activity, an increase from .03 percent in 1968.[12] As a society becomes richer, it is likely to have more discretionary income, and to spend more of that discretionary income on political activity. This is not a bad thing and, as has often been pointed out, the amounts spent on political campaigns are far less than the amounts spent on other types of advertising, or on most popular consumer products, including Barbie Doll products, potato chips, and similar nonessentials.[13]

173

But for all this, there is one other factor that has contributed mightily to the growth of political spending: the growth of government.[14] Indeed, this factor seems to outweigh all of the others. The more that government has the power to bestow benefits on the populace, or to regulate human endeavors, the greater the incentive for citizens to attempt to influence the government and the election of persons to fill government offices.[15] According to studies by John Lott, an economist working out of Yale Law School, 87 percent of the increase in federal campaign spending between 1976 and 1994 could be attributed to rising federal government expenditures. Similarly, most of the spending growth in state legislative and gubernatorial races can be explained by increases in state spending.[16] This causal effect is only common sense. When the federal government has, or at least claims, the power to nationalize whole industries such as health care; when it threatens to use its powers in an effort to destroy a long-standing legal industry, such as tobacco; when it spends over $1.8 trillion per year, redistributes income freely to politically favored groups, and regulates or claims the right to regulate virtually all aspects of human endeavor, including what methods of birth control may be used, who may carry a weapon, whether or not individuals may smoke, drink, or take particular drugs, the grounds on which one may refuse to hire employees or lease an apartment, local educational standards, farmland use, and more—then it is only natural that groups and individuals will find it worthwhile to spend increasing amounts in an effort to influence who holds office.[17]

Of all the reasons for the growth of spending, this is the most important when it comes time to consider campaign finance regulation, because the level of government spending can only be controlled by dramatically changing other substantive government policies. All of this suggests that efforts to limit legal expenditures and contributions, if not accompanied by a reduction in the size of government, will only result in opening up new avenues of political spending and contributions. And that is exactly what has happened.

Since the reforms of the 1970s attempted to limit contributions to candidates, there has been a substantial growth in alternative forms of political expenditures, or what one Supreme Court justice has dubbed "covert" speech.[18] These noncandidate expenditures, in the form of "issue ads" and independent expenditures, are the direct result of efforts by citizens to engage in political participation in the face of contribution and spending limits. Bundling is another technique designed since the reforms of the 1970s in an effort to keep money available to candidates. Banning such tactics in a manner consonant with the First Amendment is all but inconceivable, not only on constitutional grounds but for practical reasons. For example, in the early 1980s, one proposal to combat "independent expenditures" was to give added government funds, or to allow large contributions to be made to the opponent of a candidate benefiting from the independent expenditures. One political consultant pointed out that if Congress were to pass such a law, he would simply run ads that on their face supported the candidate he opposed but that were poorly done, and that trumpeted unpopular actions and positions taken by the candidate. The result would be that the ads would be more likely to hurt than to help the ostensible beneficiary, while at the same time triggering more federal money or looser fund-raising rules for the truly favored candidate.

This type of creativity was not a surprise to the Supreme Court when it extended full constitutional protection to issue ads and independent expenditures. The Court well understood that talking about politics might affect federal elections. But it was precisely for this reason that strong First Amendment protection must be extended to campaign speech. For the determination to close "loopholes" could otherwise lead to the wholesale regulation of core First Amendment political speech.

If efforts to shut off the flow of legal contributions are futile so long as government continues to grow, this argues for disclosure, and disclosure alone, as the appropriate solution to concerns about corruption. The most credible argument for regulating campaign finance, and the only one recognized by the Supreme Court, is the prevention of corruption and its appearance. Disclosure solves this problem by exposing potential or actual conflicts of interest. Disclosure allows individuals and groups to fulfill their desire to participate freely in the system. Some, of course, may still want to hide their activity, but doing so becomes the difference between legal action and illegal activity, a potentially high cost for the slightly added benefit of nondisclosure. Assuming that the contributor's primary goals are to affect who is elected to office and what policies are pursued by the government, the added burden of disclosure is relatively little. Because the basic desire to participate can be fulfilled legally, so long as contributions are disclosed, most contributors and candidates will comply with disclosure requirements.[19] For those overly concerned about the "corrupting" influence of contributions, this disclosure provides voters with information that should deter improper legislative behavior.

This link between the growth of government and campaign spending poses an even greater dilemma for reformers concerned about political equality. Many of those who urge campaign finance on equality grounds also favor redistribution of wealth and activist government to assure economic equality.[20] To the extent that that is true, their efforts on the economic front will encourage more spending in the political arena. This, in turn, suggests that ever harsher regulatory measures will be required to achieve the desired political equality.

Given this, it is no surprise that the pressure for campaign finance reform really began, and has grown, with the growth of government, which took off in the latter part of the nineteenth century. Since then, and especially since the explosion in the size of the federal government concurrent with Lyndon Johnson's Great Society programs of the 1960s, the campaign finance "reform" movement has urged increasingly stringent controls on campaign finance and limits on citizen speech. Unfortunately, as we have seen, these controls have caused more problems than they have solved. But we also ought to be asking ourselves: if campaign spending is an inevitable result of government spending and lawmaking, where do controls on political speech come to an end? Indeed, is there any point at which we will have enough controls in place? How much regulation will be enough?

The Beat Goes On: More Restrictions on Giving

On the national political level, the primary vehicle for added regulation in the 104th, 105th, and 106th Congresses was a series of bills commonly referred to by the names of their primary sponsors, Senators John McCain and Russell Feingold in the Senate, and Representatives Christopher Shays and Marty Meehan in the House of Representatives. Both the House and Senate versions underwent numerous changes over time, so that at any given moment it could be quite difficult for the casual observer to know what exactly was in the McCain-Feingold or Shays-Meehan bills. However, the various permutations of these two bills nevertheless represent a good view of late-twentieth-century regulatory thinking.

Much of what these bills offered up as "reform" is the same approach that reformers had previously tried for years. For example, as first introduced in the 105th Congress in 1997, the Shays-Meehan and McCain-Feingold bills would have set overall spending limits on congressional campaigns. In order to comport with *Buckley v. Valeo*, these spending limits are ostensibly "voluntary." In fact, however, they include a number of punitive provisions intended to assure that no candidate could refuse to comply with them. For example, if a candidate were to spend more than the "voluntary" limit, the bills provided that his or her opponent could increase spending to match the noncomplying candidate. Additionally, the noncomplying candidate's opponent would have been allowed to accept contributions two to eight times larger than the noncomplying candidate would be allowed to receive.[21] Thus a candidate would rarely refuse to accept the limit unless he or she could be confident of raising money competitively while being limited to much smaller contributions. This approach was included even though most observers agree that such limits work to entrench incumbents in office.[22] Indeed, the early 1997 versions of the Shays-Meehan and McCain-Feingold bills would have established spending thresholds at the very point where challengers become competitive. Shays-Meehan used a $600,000 figure for House races: roughly 40 percent of challengers who had spent more in the previous election cycle had won, while only 3 percent of challengers who had spent less won. Similarly, all 1994, 1996, and 1998 Senate challengers who spent less than the limits in the McCain-Feingold bill as introduced in the 104th and 105th Congresses lost, but all incumbents spending less than those limits won.

The abolition of political action committees, or PACs, remains another goal, despite, or perhaps because, PACs allow small donors to band together to increase their political clout. At one point, the McCain-Feingold bill would have abolished all PACs.[23] Even the bill's named sponsors admitted that such a ban was probably unconstitutional, a sign of the cavalier attitude that some regulatory zealots have taken to the First Amendment issues involved. But the attempt illustrates fundamental issues that would exist with or without the restraints of the Constitution. PACs are one of the primary means by which ordinary citizens of modest means can pool their resources to add to their political clout. Does it make sense to abolish the most practical method for organized citizen cooperation and action in candidate races? In addition to providing a means for participation in politics, PACs have provided citizens with information on politics. In essence, ordinary citizens, who generally lack both the time and inclination to study candidates and issues carefully, have "hired" PACs to do that for them. Is it advisable to ban such methods of voter organization?

Furthermore, banning PACs, in and of itself, would seem to accomplish little, for one would expect groups quickly to find ways around the ban. Indeed, one such evasion is already well known: the practice of bundling. Bundling, recall, occurs when a group solicits individual contributions to a candidate, then delivers those contributions together to the candidate. A tactic pioneered by the liberal women's group, Emily's List, bundling has proven to be a very effective means of organizing certain groups of individuals with common interests, in a coordinated strategy to elect like-minded people to Congress. A ban on PACs would almost certainly lead to an increase in bundling. Bundled contributions, in turn, are generally harder to trace than straightforward PAC contributions, since they come in the form of many separate checks that may not have a readily apparent common interest once "unbundled." Not surprisingly, then, some early versions of the McCain-Feingold bill attempted to ban bundling. This proposed ban was quickly dropped, however, due to the objections of key Democratic cosponsors. Bundling, it turns out, is a fund-raising technique that has been used most effectively by Democratic Party constituencies, such as Emily's List and the trial lawyers. This decision to drop the bundling ban from the bill, like the proincumbent spending limits, illustrates the difficult problem of trusting government to regulate political speech in a neutral manner. In any event, a ban on bundling would be almost impossible to enforce. Nor is it at all apparent that the legislature could, in accordance with the Constitution, make it illegal for two or more individuals to put their separate personal checks to candidates into a single envelope, or to enter a congressman's office together.

178

Another twist on contribution limits is to limit out-of-district contributions to candidates, either by banning them entirely or limiting them to a fixed percentage of total candidate receipts. Such a proposal was also included in some early versions of the Shays-Meehan and McCain-Feingold bills, which attempted to limit out-of-district contributions to 40 percent of a candidate's total.[24] Such a rule could be a reporting nightmare, especially for first-time candidates with less compliance experience. But the rule raises other problems, as well. In many districts, such a rule would only entrench existing elites against challenges. After all, it is easier to exercise dominance when fewer potential donors are available. With the source of dollars depleted, candidates might feel even more inclined to accommodate special interests in return for contributions. Such a limit would, once again, reward certain elites at the expense of the ordinary voter: for example, such a rule would not prohibit celebrities, athletes, or other politicians from campaigning in the district, nor would it prohibit national or regional news media from making endorsements or skewing reports on the campaign.

The idea that candidates should not accept donations from outside of their electoral district, like many other regulatory proposals, confuses voting with campaigning. Only the electorate in a given district may participate in the final decision—the vote to elect a candidate—but it seems absurd, and patently unconstitutional, to limit the ability of others to speak in the district. Certainly we know that citizens all across the country are affected by the votes of members of Congress from Massachusetts or Connecticut. Why should these citizens not be permitted to express their concerns to the voters of the district? Indeed, in many cases it is precisely the fact that these voices come from outside the district that makes their participation important: absent their participation, there may be no substantial voice for many concerns that elected officials are called on to deal with.

Another favorite idea is to lower still further the $1,000 individual contribution limit, to amounts as low as $100, or in the most extreme cases even $5 or $10.[25] This approach has been especially popular in the states. This also favors incumbents, strengthens narrow organized interests at the expense of broader interests, and encourages interests to seek legislative influence rather than electoral results, thus working directly contrary to the goals of anticorruption reformers. It also requires candidates to increase the time spent fund-raising, which, paradoxically (or perhaps not) then becomes a justification for still more regulation.[26]

There is little reason to believe that these added limits, if passed, would resolve the types of problems of which the regulatory advocates complain. Indeed, as with the 1974 reforms, they would quite likely exacerbate the problems they are intended to solve. They would, however, seriously cut into the rights of ordinary citizens to engage in political debate. Nevertheless, their potential impact pales when compared to an even more ambitious "reform" agenda—the regulation of "issue ads" and "soft money."

Issue Ads and Soft Money

A favorite target of reformers since the mid-1990s has been issue ads. Issue advocacy is political discourse that does not expressly support or oppose a candidate but that has the potential to influence voters' thinking about a candidate.[27] The widespread use of issue ads is itself an outgrowth of the current regulatory climate. Such ads have always been lawful, but they were rarely used prior to the mid-1990s. As campaign costs continued to rise, however, the 1974 FECA contribution limits remained static, not even adjusted for inflation. This created a growing search for new ways to participate in and to finance political activity. Issue ads were one answer. By discussing a candidate's record or views on some issue in favorable or unfavorable terms, groups realized that they could influence the results of upcoming elections. In 1996, issue ads were used extensively by groups as diverse as the AFL-CIO, the Sierra Club, Handgun Control, the National Education Association, the National Abortion Rights Action League, Citizen Action, the National Rifle Association, and the Christian Coalition.[28] What distinguishes unregulated issue ads from regulated campaign ads is that the former do not ask the audience to vote in any particular manner. Typical issue ads would include ads run by the tobacco industry in the summer of 1998, which urged viewers to oppose a tobacco bill pending in Congress, or the famous 1993–1994 "Harry and Louise" ads run by the Health Insurance Association of America, in which a young couple nervously voiced their concerns over President Clinton's proposal for nationalized health care. These ads probably affected election results—almost certainly the "Harry and Louise" series soured some voters on Bill Clinton and the Democrats, which probably added to Republican gains in Congress in the 1994 elections. But issue ads can also be more overtly aimed at defeating particular candidates. Typical ads may excoriate a candidate's record on some issue of importance, such as social security, and conclude with a tag line such as, "Call Congressman X, and tell him to keep his hands off your benefits." To campaign finance regulatory enthusiasts, these ads are not issue ads at all but rather "so-called issue ads," "sham issue ads," "phony issue ads," or "campaign ads masquerading as issue ads."[29] They argue that the ads are intended to influence federal elections, and so both the ads themselves and the contributions used to fund them may be regulated under the framework of *Buckley v. Valeo*. In fact, we have been down this road before, and the advocates of regulation are wrong.

An often overlooked feature of *Buckley v. Valeo* is that the decision dealt directly with the question of regulating what we now call "issue advocacy." It seems to have been forgotten that in the 1974 FECA amendments Congress sought to limit issue ads, just as many do now. Section 608(e)(1) of FECA, as amended provided that "no person may make any expenditure . . . relative to a clearly identified candidate during a calendar year which, when added to all other expenditures made by such person during the year advocating the election or defeat of such candidate, exceeds $1,000." In other words, any expenditures about a candidate would be defined as contributions to a candidate's campaign. The Court noted that "the plain effect of Section 608(e)(1) is to prohibit all individuals, who are neither candidates nor owners of institutional press facilities, from voicing their views." Because such expenditures are made independently of a candidate's campaign, the Court held that such expenditures do not pose the same danger of quid-pro-quo corruption as campaign contributions.[30] Therefore, such a broad restriction on independent expenditures was held to be constitutionally impermissible.

In addition to upholding the people's rights to make unlimited expenditures independently of a candidate's campaign, the Court also held that "the use of so indefinite a phrase as 'relative to' a candidate fails to clearly

181

mark the boundary between permissible and impermissible speech,"[31] that is, between campaign contributions, whose size can be regulated, and independent expenditures, which cannot be regulated because they do not pose the same threat of corruption. The Court then rejected the argument that this vagueness problem could be saved by looking at other manifestations of the speaker's intent in an effort to determine if the ads were intended to affect federal elections, or had some other purpose. The use of subjective manifestations of intent would do nothing to take away the chilling effect of such regulation:

> Whether words intended and designed to fall short of invitation would miss that mark is both a question of intent and of effect. No speaker, in such circumstances, safely could assume that anything he might say upon the general subject would not be misunderstood by some. . . . In short, the supposedly clear-cut distinction between discussion, laudation, general advocacy, and solicitation puts the speaker in these circumstances wholly at the mercy of the varied understanding of his hearers and consequently of whatever inference may be drawn as to his intent and meaning.
>
> Such a distinction offers no security for free discussion. In these conditions it blankets with uncertainty whatever may be said. It compels the speaker to hedge and trim.[32]

Thus, the Court correctly concluded that, "Constitutional difficulties can be avoided only by reading Section 608(e)(1) as limited to communications that include explicit words of advocacy of election or defeat of a clearly identified candidate for federal office." Therefore, the Court limited the application of Section 608 (e)(1) to "communications containing express words of advocacy of election or defeat, such as 'vote for,' 'elect,' 'support,' 'cast your ballot for,' 'Smith for Congress,' 'vote against,' 'defeat,' [and] 'reject.' " Ads that did not use such explicit language were exempt from regulation as campaign contributions. Nor was *Buckley* a close decision on this point—at least seven, and possibly all eight, of the justices who heard the case agreed on this issue.[33]

The Court's narrow reading of Section 608(e)(1) is eminently sensible. Political speech, after all, is at the core of the First Amendment, a simple fact long accepted by the Court.[34] All discussion of public issues has the potential to influence federal elections, simply by affecting how listeners think about the issues that are supported or opposed by particular candidates. The discussion of issues, in turn, is routinely tied up in the discussion of candidates for office. Indeed, the purpose of discussing issues is often, if not usually, to influence who will be elected to office. Although aggressive issue ads targeted at specific campaigns are often portrayed as a new threat to the integrity of the campaign finance system, which was not addressed in *Buckley*, in fact the *Buckley* Court was well aware that discussions of issues could be intentionally used to influence election outcomes. Wrote the court: "the distinction between discussion of issues and candidates and advocacy of election or defeat of candidates may often dissolve in practical application. Candidates, especially incumbents, are intimately tied to public issues involving legislative proposals and governmental action. Not only do candidates campaign on the basis of their positions on various public issues, but campaigns themselves generate issues of public interest."[35] Nor was the Court oblivious to the fact that its ruling would open a major "loophole" in the law. One reason that the Court, in *Buckley*, struck down an expenditure limit on independent "express advocacy" was because it recognized that "issue advocacy" could and would be used effectively to influence elections. Having placed issue advocacy within the protections of the First Amendment, the Court realized that a ban on expenditures for independent express advocacy would serve little purpose: "It would naively underestimate the ingenuity and resourcefulness of persons and groups desiring to buy influence to believe that they would have much difficulty devising expenditures that skirted the restriction on express advocacy of election or defeat but nevertheless benefited the candidate's campaign."[36] Therefore, the court also struck down expenditure limits on express advocacy.

In short, the Court held that although issue ads might affect elections—intentionally or unintentionally—this alone is not a sufficient basis to justify the chilling effect that the regulation of issue ads would have on political speech. In the years since *Buckley* was decided, both the Supreme Court and lower courts have, time and again, reaffirmed both the reasoning and holding of that decision as it pertains to issue advocacy, including the necessity of requiring express words of advocacy before any regulation of a communication is constitutionally permissible.[37]

Proposals to limit issue advocacy speech are perhaps the greatest threat to liberty of all campaign finance regulation proposals, because virtually all political discourse is carried on in the hopes of eventually electing or defeating candidates. For example, one version of the Shays-Meehan bill would have allowed the FEC to limit speech "made for the purpose of advocating the election or defeat of the candidate, as shown by one or more factors, such as a statement or action by the person making the communication, the targeting or placement of the communication, or the use by the person making the communication of polling, demographic, or other similar data relating to the candidate's campaign or election."[38] But one of the main reasons that people discuss political issues at all is to advocate the election or defeat of a candidate, and almost any statement about political issues has the potential to affect an upcoming election. This standard would raise precisely the type of uncertainty that *Buckley v. Valeo* insists must be avoided.

Another formulation being promoted by regulators and used in some versions of Shays-Meehan and McCain-Feingold is to regulate any speech that mentions the name of a clearly identified candidate within sixty days (or ninety days, or thirty days, in various versions) of an election. This would have the bizarre effect of granting political speech less protection at the time of political campaigns—the exact moment that people are most focused on, and most interested in discussing, political issues.

Regulation of issue advocacy has been consistently struck down by the courts in part because it all but cries out for political abuse. For example, in 1996, a variety of liberal and conservative groups ran issue ads in certain Wisconsin races. Under a state statute purporting to regulate issue ads, the state prosecuted the Wisconsin Manufacturers' and Business Association, but not the Sierra Club, which ran nearly identical ads—for the other candidate—in the same race. Eventually, the Wisconsin Supreme Court held the law unconstitutional, but the case illustrates the potential for partisan enforcement.[39]

What should also be recognized about these proposed restrictions is that they have been proposed not only for television ads but also for other forms of communication, including "scorecards" that record a candidate's voting record. For example, some versions of the McCain-Feingold bill attempted to limit any scorecards that only recorded the votes of one candidate. Yet it is a common method of ranking incumbents to record their votes in scorecard form. Challengers will often lack any such record of votes to record even if the group putting out the scorecard desired to do so. Some proposals for regulation would ban the use of any language in the scorecards that described candidate votes or positions, so that a scorecard touting some votes as, for example, "pro-taxpayer" (or "pro-choice," or "pro-education") would count as campaign contributions, or independent expenditures subjecting them to the regulation and limits of FECA. This type of regulation would allow incumbent politicians to protect themselves from criticism, and its express purpose is to limit the sources of information available to voters and to give candidates "control" over their campaigns. But the First Amendment does not leave it to the politicians to decide who will say what about them. Such decisions are intended to be left to the public.

The twin evil accompanying issue ads is so-called "soft money." Soft money is itself a product of the late 1970s, originally aimed at increasing grassroots activity. Despite the catchy name, at bottom soft money is simply money. What makes it the target of so much indignation is that it is money that is unregulated by FECA. Any money that is not contributed directly to a candidate's campaign or used expressly to advocate the election or defeat of a candidate constitutes a form of soft money, although the term is used most often when discussing such donations made to political parties. Parties may use soft money to fund party activities such as voter registration drives, get-out-the-vote drives, generic advertising, and slate cards. Regulatory advocates view this as a loophole that allows candidates and parties to circumvent spending and contribution limits. They argue that it reintroduces quid-pro-quo corruption as candidates seek donations, and works against equality by allowing wealthy individuals, corporations, and unions to contribute large amounts.[40]

At first blush, it can be difficult to see what the soft money fuss is about. In the 1996 election cycle, for example, soft money constituted less than 10 percent of spending on congressional races, and about 13 percent of total spending on all federal races. In many ways, soft money might be seen as preferable to direct candidate contributions, as it works against many of the evils that allegedly exist in the system. Because the money is given to the parties, it cuts against any "war-chest" effect that the regulatory advocates believe discourages competitive elections. It is given not directly to candidates but to the parties, so that any threat of quid-pro-quo corruption is ameliorated by the presence of the party intermediary. It reduces the time that candidates must spend raising campaign funds. And to the extent that it is used for voter registration drives, get-out-the-vote drives, and grassroots support such as buttons and bumper stickers, it seems to be the kind of spending the proregulatory interests favor over television ads.

Much of the near hysteria over soft money, it seems, is based on the fact that soft money can also be used for issue advocacy. Indeed, in the elections of 1996, 1998, and 2000 both the Republican and Democratic parties made major use of issue ads to support their party messages. What is important to note is that the Supreme Court has held that parties have the same rights to engage in political advocacy as other groups. As the Court put it, in *Colorado Republican Federal Campaign Committee v. Federal Election Commission*, "The independent expression of a political party's views is 'core' First Amendment activity no less than is the independent expression of individuals, candidates, or other political committees."[41] Indeed, it would be a bizarre result if were not, for it would mean that groups such as the Sierra Club and the Health Insurance Association of America would have greater rights and ability to campaign during an election season than the political parties themselves.

Advocates of this type of speech regulation also attempt to argue, however, that limits on soft money may be allowed to combat what they dub "conduit corruption." The argument is that large donations to parties "corrupt" the parties, which then put pressure on officeholders to make decisions favorable to donors.[42] In short, the party is both the bagman and the enforcer in a quid-pro-quo arrangement.

But what does it mean to say that a "party" is corrupted? Political parties do not make governmental decisions; rather, those decisions are made by officeholders who usually (though not always) are members of a political party. These officeholders may simultaneously be members of the American Civil Liberties Union, the American Association of Retired Persons, the Sierra Club, Common Cause, and any number of other groups. To suggest that contributions to a political party for issue advo-

186

cacy may be limited because officeholders may feel an obligation to the party would be to undercut the entire rationale behind *Buckley* and its many progeny. For just as surely, office holders may feel obliged to any individual or group that conducts an issue advocacy campaign that has the effect of turning the public in favor of those issues supported by the office holder/candidate, or against the issues supported by the office holder/candidate's opponent. So "conduit corruption" turns out not to be a new theory at all but merely the same theory of corruption behind the original, 1974 ban on issue advocacy struck down in *Buckley*. Can the discussion of issues be considered campaign contributions, subject to limitation and regulation, if it mentions a candidate or otherwise has the potential to affect the outcome of a federal election? The Court has considered this, and responded with a resounding "no!"

Nevertheless, a number of scholars organized by the Brennan Center for Justice, a group that argues in favor of campaign finance regulation and has litigated—with little success—several cases in the field, have argued that soft money contributions can be banned to prevent the "corruption" caused by large corporate contributions.[43] These scholars state that "the most relevant Supreme Court decision is ... *Austin v. Michigan Chamber of Commerce*, in which the Supreme Court held that corporations can be walled off from the electoral process by forbidding both contributions and independent expenditures from general corporate treasuries."[44] Indeed, *Austin* is the only case cited in support of their position that soft money may be banned. This assertion reads far too much into *Austin*. *Austin*'s holding comes in the context of express advocacy, that is to say, a corporate advertisement that very clearly urged voters, in large bold type, to "Elect Richard Bandstra."[45] A ban on this type of corporate expenditure is consistent with *Buckley v. Valeo*, which allowed greater restrictions on direct candidate advocacy than on other political speech. But although *Austin* upheld the state ban on express advocacy made from corporate treasuries, in other cases the Supreme Court has flatly rejected a ban on issue advocacy paid for from general corporate treasuries. In *First National Bank of Boston v. Bellotti*, the Court struck down a ban on corporate issue advocacy pertaining to a voter referendum. The Court wrote that when public issues are being discussed, "the inherent worth of

187

the speech in terms of its capacity for informing the public does not depend on the identity of its source, whether corporation, association, union, or individual." In *Austin*, the Court perceived a danger of corruption in large corporate sums in candidate races. But in *Bellotti*, it rejected the notion that corporations can corrupt the discussion of public issues, stating that "the risk of corruption perceived in cases involving candidate elections simply is not present." It should be noted that the issue advocacy of the corporations in *Bellotti* pertained to a referendum appearing on the November 1976 ballot, along with numerous races for federal office. Thus, commentary on the ballot issue certainly had the potential to affect these simultaneous federal races. But the Court emphasized "the fact that advocacy may persuade the electorate is hardly a reason to suppress it."[46]

Driving the point home, just three years later the Court struck down a limit on the size of contributions, including corporate contributions, to a group engaged in issue advocacy related to a ballot measure. In *Citizens against Rent Control v. City of Berkeley*, the Court held that "whatever may be the state interest or degree of that interest in regulating and limiting contributions to or expenditures of a candidate or a candidate's committees there is no significant state or public interest in curtailing debate and discussion of a ballot measure."[47] Discussion of a ballot measure is, of course, issue advocacy, and by affecting the electorate's view of candidates who support or oppose the issue, and by altering voter turnout, such discussion can certainly influence federal races. Indeed, campaigns on ballot issues often feature, in their advertising, endorsements from popular candidates for federal office.

In response to all this, regulatory advocates led by House Democratic leader Richard Gephardt actually proposed an amendment to the Constitution that would have, in essence, repealed First Amendment protection for political speech. Former Senator Bill Bradley, a 2000 presidential candidate, argued in the fall of 1999 for a 100 percent tax on issue ads.[48] Such efforts to ban soft money and issue advocacy strike at core First Amendment values. If successful, they would regulate a huge swath of hitherto inviolate political speech. Not since the Alien and Sedition Acts more than two hundred years ago have the rights of citizens to speak out on political issues and to criticize the actions of elected officials been so threatened by official action.

Government Funding and "Free" TV

One long-term goal within the campaign finance "reform" movement has been to provide for tax funding of all campaigns. With political support for such a measure lacking,[49] in recent years some have begun to advocate the allocation of television time to candidates, free of charge, as a substitute.

The attraction of free television seems to be that it is politically more palatable than other forms of government subsidies. Conceptually, however, it adds little to the debate. "Free" TV is nothing more than a government subsidy to campaigns. This can be quickly illustrated by considering the following example: suppose that rather than order broadcast stations to grant thirty minutes "free" time to candidates, Congress instead purchased television time from the stations, and then provided each candidate with vouchers good for up to thirty minutes of television time. The net effect is the same: the candidates receive a subsidy equal to thirty minutes of television air time from the government. The difference is that in the first case, the tax to pay for the subsidy is levied only on broadcasters, which effectively cede to the government advertising revenue for those thirty minutes, whereas in the second example it is levied on taxpayers more generally. Thus "free" TV is just a peculiar variation of government campaign subsidy—peculiar, because it requires the subsidy to be used for television advertising at a time when many think that campaigns are already too oriented toward television, and because the tax falls on a single industry.

So the question is whether public subsidies, either through "free" TV or direct cash grants, can solve the problems of money in politics. In chapter 5, we saw that there is serious reason to doubt that the political system will yield up a workable system of government-financed campaigns that improves on a deregulated system in any of the key criteria of administrability, flexibility, opportunity, competitiveness, and communication.

Moreover, taxpayer funding has drawbacks from which there is no escape. It forces large numbers of Americans to finance the dissemination of political views that those Americans find to be wrong or even abhorrent. Thomas Jefferson once wrote, "To compel a man to furnish contributions of money for the propagation of opinions which he disbelieves, is sinful and tyrannical," and many Americans still feel that way today. Whether or not they should feel that way is not terribly important to this debate—they do, and that imposes a very real cost to public funding. Indeed, that may be one of the major reasons why there has traditionally been so little public support for taxpayer funding of campaigns.

A second problem is that public funding places demands on the public purse. This concern is probably exaggerated in public debate—as we have seen, total political spending in the United States amounts to no more than a few billion dollars per year, a mere drop in the bucket where the federal budget is concerned. Still, this too is a real cost. For example, in early 2000 a proposal to reduce the federal tax on gasoline by 4.3 cents per gallon met stiff resistance in Congress because it would have cost the government less than $10 billion per year. Members argued that despite federal budget surpluses substantially in excess of $10 billion, the loss would have a "devastating" impact on road repair.[50]

Yet another cost is the role of regulation in fostering litigation. Any system that requires a number of rules and some enforcement body to interpret those rules is open to abuse. As we have seen, litigation has become an important campaign tactic under the current rules, and there is no reason to think that that would change with taxpayer financing—indeed it would probably increase if government financing was accompanied by more complex regulations.

Beyond these specific problems, there is little reason to believe that government-funded campaigns, unless accompanied by sweeping (and almost certainly unconstitutional) reform will actually promote the equality or anticorruption interests that justify its imposition.

For example, government financing does not necessarily promote equality in political races, and in many cases it can further inequality between candidates. Some of these problems are specific to particular government-financing systems, whereas others are inherent in the concept of government financing. The system of matching funds used in American presidential primaries, for example, tends to reward those who have already raised the most money—the candidate who has raised more money can normally expect to receive more in matching funds, adding to his spending advantage. The system also rewards candidates who raise money in larger contributions: a contribution of $250 is matched with

190

$250 of federal money, whereas a contribution of just $25 is matched with just $25 federal dollars. As it is often suggested that one purpose of taxpayer funding is to reduce reliance on large contributions, this is a rather quirky system to adopt.[51]

But a system that provided for grants of equal size would not necessarily promote equality, either. For example, if a candidate is endorsed by the largest newspaper in the district, and candidate spending is otherwise equalized, is the campaign equal? Of course not. Private spending at least opens the possibility that the nonendorsed candidate can compete on equal footing. Differences in money can make a campaign more equal or less equal, depending on how other resources and candidate advantages are distributed. Equalizing expenditures, as most taxpayer funding proposals would do (at least for the major party candidates), is simply no guarantee of equality. At best, if funding levels are sufficiently high, it can help to assure competitiveness by giving all candidates the resources to take their message to the public. But it does not solve the problem of unequal resources and advantages between candidates.

Finally, as discussed in chapter 5, government subsidies have not, in the past, generally solved the problems of corruption or unequal political influence that are alleged to exist due to private funding of campaigns. Moreover, so long as issue advocacy remains constitutionally protected, government financing is unlikely to solve those problems.

It is perhaps for these reasons that extreme proposals now favor curbing the ability of the press to make political endorsements.[52] Yet even these proposals, if enacted under an amended Constitution (almost certainly a necessity), wouldn't solve the "problem" because the main complaint with the influence of the press is not over its overt editorializing but rather over its coverage and selection of news.[53] There are numerous other ways to sidestep even these draconian types of regulation. Given the size and scope of modern government, there is no reason to think that those who seek to influence who holds power in this monumental government will not be creative enough to circumvent the regulations.[54]

A system that makes participation harder, and perhaps less effective, may of course, eventually reduce or eliminate such participation. After all, if issue ads had to be run at least sixty days before an election, they may not be as effective, resulting in a decline in their use. One who is convinced that federal representatives are easily bought and purchased may find this a worthwhile endeavor.

I think, rather, that our experience with campaign finance laws indicates that any number of things could go wrong with this manner of reform. Making such political activity less effective may just increase the amount of it, in order to achieve the same results. It may lead to the creation of other advertising means that can affect federal elections—indeed, wherever the line on express advocacy is drawn, it will not be hard for political operators to stand at the edge of the new line. Restrictions on private financing may increase the influence of groups with a strong, permanent presence in Washington, rather than increasing the influence of more decentralized groups that rely on a large membership base and a PAC funded by small contributions. Such restrictions might also inhibit the arrival of a well-financed hero to channel their energies, much as large contributions to the Gene McCarthy campaign in 1968 brought together disparate, scattered antiwar sentiments into a meaningful, anti-Vietnam War political campaign. This is particularly true if, as with the McCarthy campaign, key issues come to the fore too late for a would-be candidate to comply with the government-financing scheme. Restrictions may simply drive expenditures further underground.

To the extent that government financing aims to prevent potential corruption or equalize voices, it presupposes that other expenditures will be stopped, either by law or "voluntarily," through incentives to limit spending. But simply mandating an end to private expenditures is unconstitutional, and with good reason. And the only real voluntary spending limit comes when those who care about politics decide not to spend any more. Everything else is a coercive limit on political speech, or else it would not need to be included in the law. Because the limit is not voluntary, and because we have a First Amendment allowing free discussion of political issues, a way will be found around that limit. So long as this is the case, the goal of reducing the political influence of "special interests," whether we define that influence as creating an equality problem or a corruption problem, is not going to be met merely through government financing.

Tax funding can be enacted, of course, with or without the types of restrictions now in place or those being proposed by regulatory advocates.

But to the extent that it is enacted without such restrictions, one should not expect the clamor for more restrictive "reform" measures suddenly to cease. Government subsidies are not, in and of themselves, sufficient to assure a reduction in the alleged corrupting effects of campaign contributions, nor do they necessarily equalize campaigns. To the extent that government financing may be enacted with such restrictions, the same problems of equity and First Amendment rights will exist whenever existing regulations are enforced or new regulations proposed. Thus the question of government subsidies, whether in cash or "free" TV time, merely distracts from the main issue this book seeks to address: can political speech be regulated in a manner consonant with the First Amendment?

The Next Wave of "Reform": The Law Reviews

Efforts to regulate campaign finance further—to close "loopholes" in the law—are alarming not only because of the burden that the they place on First Amendment rights, but because they seem to have no stopping point, and tend to flow so naturally from the assumptions and goals underlying campaign finance regulatory efforts. Since the passage of the 1974 FECA amendments, campaign finance has been much more heavily regulated than ever before. Yet we are constantly barraged with calls for still more regulation to close alleged loopholes. If the most extreme versions of the various proposals suggested earlier in this chapter were enacted, individuals would not be able to contribute more than $100 to any candidate; any such contribution would be subject to rigorous disclosure requirements, despite the possibility for retaliation; contributions could not be made to candidates—even personal friends and family—running in other districts; citizens would be limited in their ability to speak about pending legislation if, in doing so, they mentioned the name of a candidate; voter scorecards would be regulated if they contained any words of praise or criticism; citizens could no longer pool their resources to run advertisements supporting or opposing candidates or to make a single contribution to the candidate that would indicate their common interest and the political concerns motivating their support; and interest groups would be limited in their ability to communicate with voters, including even their own members.

193

And yet, even if all of these regulations were in place, would the solution be adequate to meet the demands of regulatory advocates? I think not. It is simply absurd to think that private actors will ignore rents made available to them by government action,[55] and even more absurd to think that individuals or interests will allow the government to tax or regulate them, sometimes to the point of economic extinction, without attempting to influence who holds the reigns of power. Thus, if the most egregiously partisan issue ads were banned, we would expect to see money flow into other means of affecting elections. This might mean only slightly less obvious issue ads. Would these then be banned, too, further restricting the ability of citizens to discuss issues? If ads mentioning candidates were limited in the sixty days leading up to an election, wouldn't we simply see a barrage of such ads from sixty one to ninety days before the election? Would the ban then need to be extended to ninety days? And what would be the probable result then in the timing of issue ads?

Large membership organizations such as unions or the National Rifle Association or American Association of Retired Persons might step up highly partisan membership communications, making sure that excess copies happen to be available and are left at strategic locations. Or would we prohibit such groups from communicating with members? Outright old-fashioned bribery might return, as it did during prohibition, as businesses and unions seek to protect their interests. We might see an increase in the publication of anonymous campaign literature, which some feel is more scurrilous and less accountable than other publications, because it avoids disclosure problems altogether. Another possibility is a return to the purchase or subsidy of partisan newspapers, radio, and television stations, for example. Would it then become necessary to censor these media outlets? The ingenuity of those who seek to influence political outcomes knows few bounds, and given the power wielded by government, the incentive will exist to find the inevitable loopholes.[56]

Proposals such as the Shays-Meehan and McCain-Feingold bills seem comprehensive, but it quickly becomes apparent that they will fall short of achieving their goals. When they do, we can be sure that a new wave of legislation to close loopholes will follow. Indeed, law reviews, which often form the vanguard for future trends in legislation, are already brimming with ideas to further regulate political speech.

One "hot" idea in academia is to limit all campaign spending except for a small amount made available to each voter through a government-issued voucher.[57] For example, under Richard Hasen's proposal, discussed in chapter 8, each voter would receive a $100 voucher from the government, and no other monetary or in-kind contributions could be expended to influence federal elections. Nor could vouchers be supplemented from private funds. Interest groups could collect vouchers in order to make independent expenditures in support of candidates. However, in order to monitor the system and prevent fraud, these interest groups would be licensed by the federal government.[58] Hasen does specify that licensing decisions could not be made on political grounds, but it is hard to believe that this could be enforced. History is replete with government power being used to attack political opponents, including Franklin Roosevelt's use of the FBI to pressure newspaper editors; the Kennedy administration's use of the IRS to harass opponents and of the Federal Communications Commission to silence conservative radio stations; and President Nixon's use of the IRS, FBI, and CIA against political opponents. Though it has not been proven, some claim that President Clinton may have done the same.[59] Given the history of abuse of the IRS and other government agencies to harass political opponents, Hasen's sanguinity may be misplaced.

However, even if it is possible to have what election law attorney Jan Baran has dubbed a "benign political police,"[60] Hasen's proposal, as comprehensive as it seems to be, would not necessarily satisfy the reformers. For example, he does not deal with the question of "issue advocacy" that so perturbs the current wave of reformers.[61] That such a thoroughgoing proposal as Hasen's would probably fail to satisfy reformers indicates just how dangerous it is to tread down the regulatory path where political speech is involved. Further, even if Hasen's proposal were modified to include a broad, intrusive, Shays-Meehan-type definition of expenditures "in support of or in opposition to a candidate," it would probably fall short of its stated goals, because he excludes from his proposal political advocacy related to ballot issues—at least he does for now, although he expresses a willingness to ban that, too, if state-level issues can be brought in under the regulation.

Ballot issues, however, are already a common means by which individuals seek to build support for a current or future candidacy. For example, in the 1970s, a Michigan insurance executive, Richard Headlee, achieved political prominence in the state through his authorship and promotion of a state tax limitation measure. In 1982, Headlee was the Republican nominee for governor. Established politicians can also use the tactic; California governor Pete Wilson used his support for initiatives limiting affirmative action and public benefits to immigrants to boost his political fortunes. With other forms of financial participation shut off, it is easy to see ballot initiatives being used more explicitly to promote candidacies—by featuring or mentioning candidates in ads, for example—unless this, too, were precluded by a broad definition of issue advocacy. This could mean that if a popular governor running for U.S. senator were to oppose a state constitutional amendment, ads by groups opposing the amendment would probably be barred from featuring, or even mentioning, the governor's opposition. For example, in 1996, Ohio governor George Voinovich took a high-profile role in opposition to a state constitutional amendment to allow gambling in the state. Had he also been a candidate for federal office—or even reelection, if the same principles are applied to state elections—ads by gambling opponents that featured the governor would probably be deemed a contribution to his campaign. In fact, Voinovich, though not yet an officially declared candidate, had made clear even before the 1996 elections that he would run for the U.S. Senate in 1998.[62]

Furthermore, if the aim of reform is equality, why shouldn't restrictions also be levied on ballot issues? If inequality of wealth "distorts" the election of candidates, thereby indirectly "distorting" the laws that are passed, shouldn't the application of wealth to politics also be banned where it directly "distorts" laws and governance? Indeed, for this very reason, another voucher proponent, Edward Foley, argues that ballot issues should be included in any voucher scheme. Like Hasen, Foley is not entirely clear on what he would do with issue ads that have the potential to affect elections, though one might glean from his general thesis and his inclusion of ballot issues that these ads, too, would have to be limited.[63]

Even if a voucher program were applied to limit political communication that involves candidates and ballot issues, including issue advocacy, this would also not seem to satisfy the regulators. For example, the issue of internal communications would remain. Groups with large memberships such as the NAACP, NRA, American Association of Retired Persons (AARP), Christian Coalition, and labor unions could still have "undue influence" through their ability to spend large sums on member education and endorsements—some of which would almost surely leak into the general populace.[64] Membership magazines and literature are easily put into general circulation. Suppose, for example, that a group such as the League of Women Voters or AARP urged its members to provide free copies of group literature to libraries, hotels, and physician waiting rooms, or to abandon copies on buses, subways, and airplanes? Even if the casual placement of literature might not be viewed as a problem, would an organized campaign to leave literature lying about in this fashion create a violation of the law? Or suppose the organization made it easy to download its publications, and encouraged members to download and then post its literature to Internet sites and discussion groups? Would that violate the law? If not, wouldn't candidates still seek out such endorsements as having special value? Wouldn't that be "undue influence?"

Thus membership communications have also become a target of reformers. For example, in the 1994 elections, the Federal Election Commission applied an extremely narrow definition of "membership" to argue that the U.S. Chamber of Commerce and the American Medical Association should be prosecuted if they published endorsements to thousands of their dues-paying members—many of whom undoubtedly joined precisely to get such information. Both organizations decided not to make the communications rather than risk possible fines and penalties. Fortunately, a federal court later struck down the FEC's membership definition as overly restrictive.[65]

Newspapers and other media present another thorny problem. If all other avenues of financial participation are sealed, might not groups and individuals purchase media outlets for the sole purpose of promoting a partisan view, candidate, or group of candidates? Richard Hasen admits that this is a "large loophole," but originally suggested that he would allow it because "newspapers and other news media are a valuable source of information for the public," and "help people overcome collective action problems in acquiring information, a classic public good."[66] Of course, the same is true of party, candidate, and issue group advertising,[67] so the exception doesn't really add up. Hasen has since recognized this, but rather than retreat from his proposals to limit speech instead he modified his thinking to argue that newspapers should also be regulated, after all. It is interesting that Hasen apparently noticed the need to regulate newspapers only when it came to his attention in the form of Rupert Murdoch, a conservative media magnate.[68] So long as media had remained safely in control of fellow political liberals, it appears that Hasen had not seen the contradiction. Edward Foley, however, had seen the problem, and so included newspaper editorials within the limits of his system from the start.[69] Newspapers would have to "pay," with vouchers collected from the electorate, to run their own editorials. This misses the central purpose of newspapers editorials, which is to persuade, not merely to reflect those views already held by the citizenry. But would even this draconian provision satisfy the reformist goals of equality or preventing corruption? I think not. For example, the primary complaints one hears about media influence do not regard editorials but the slant of news coverage.[70] Foley suggests that "it will be difficult at times to tell whether what a newspaper has written is merely reporting the facts relating to an electoral race or, instead, is a thinly disguised attempt to persuade voters to support or oppose a particular candidate."[71] I suggest that it is not only difficult but in most cases impossible. Foley calls the potential chilling effects of such regulation "the necessary price we must pay in order to have an electoral system that guarantees equal opportunity for all."[72] Perhaps Foley's greatest contribution to the debate is to show how high that price might be.

In considering further regulation—loopholes that will need to be closed—I do not mean to suggest that all reformers are hopelessly trapped on a slippery slope. For example, many reformers may wish to ban soft money contributions to parties, but remain squeamish about attempts to redefine issue advocacy, for precisely the types of reasons I have suggested. But I do wish to suggest the quixotic nature of efforts to purify politics or equalize influence through the campaign finance system. There will always be loopholes. If rent seeking is unavoidable under a powerful, activist state; if equal political influence is both a flawed and unattainable goal; and if reform measures have both failed in the past and seem unlikely to accomplish their goals in the future, we must ask if the freedoms already sacrificed are worth the gain, and how far down the slope we will go in pursuit of an unattainable goal.

The potential for "corruption," in that odd sense of the word in which it is used in this debate, will exist so long as the state retains tremendous power not only over wealth but also over such personal decisions as whether or not to consume alcohol, tobacco, or drugs, or to own guns, or to read pornography. The potential will exist because the incentive to "corrupt" will exist. This does not mean that we must live in a libertarian state. There may be other goals besides reducing rent seeking or maximizing economic efficiency, and it may be that we would sacrifice economic growth and property rights to achieve those goals. But the founders were not blind to the problem of rent seeking, even in the minimalist state that existed at the time. Madison's famous *Federalist No. 10* is largely about how the Constitution seeks to prevent rent seeking through federalism, separation of powers, and the size of the union.[73] Like the founders, we need to recognize the trade-off. One price of an activist state is that people will attempt to turn that power toward their private ends.[74] In a futile effort to prevent rent seeking, reformers suggest that we should sacrifice our liberty of speech and political action, as well.

Similarly, egalitarian reformers also seek to promote a type of political equality at the expense of liberty. They hold forth the dream of a world in which all people have "equal" influence, or at least the opportunity for equal participation. Yet reaching that utopia is always, it seems, one more campaign finance "loophole" away. Some, such as Fiss and Dworkin, respond that they are not taking away freedom but granting it. Dworkin argues that political practices must "treat all members of the community as individuals, with equal concern and respect," and that this requires restrictions on political participation through campaign giving.[75] But this merely begs the question: are all individuals treated with equal concern and respect when they are not allowed to employ equally the fruits of their labors and talents to political action?

Fiss's argument doesn't beg such questions, but as a result is even more disturbing. He argues, "we may sometimes find it necessary to restrict the speech of some elements of our society in order to enhance the relative voice of others, and that unless the Court allows, and sometimes even requires, the state to do so, we as a people will never truly be free."[76] As Fiss makes clear, what he has in mind by "freedom" is not freedom as it has historically been accepted in the United States, and it is not the historic interpretation of the First Amendment. Indeed, as the Supreme Court noted in *Buckley*, "the concept that government may restrict the speech of some elements of our society in order to enhance the relative voice of others is wholly foreign to the First Amendment." And it is good that this is so. For as George Mason University Law School's Daniel Polsby has written, "Almost every country in the world, including those behind the iron curtain, can display a constitution that guarantees freedom of expression to the people—to the extent, of course, that the people's representatives may deem proper. . . . [W]e can boast that our Constitution protects something far scarcer in history than that sort of freedom. And with the knowledge of the caliber of people who sometimes get their hands on our government, it is well that this is so."[77]

Before heading off down a road, it is fair to ask about the destination. Before rushing off on another round of increased regulation passing as reform, Americans should consider the ugliness of the vision held by self-styled "reform advocates." Where is it intended to end? And if we do not like the end destination—a state in which no political speech is allowed except with prior approval of the government—we must ask again, where have the "reformers" gone wrong?

Chapter 10

REAL EQUALITY, REAL CORRUPTION,
REAL REFORM

Political Equality in the United States

There can be no doubt that many of those active in
the campaign finance reform movement despise the
inequalities of wealth that a system of democratic
capitalism produces. Many of the reform articles
demonstrate a strong bias against money and
wealth.[1] The question, however, becomes why this
single source of unequal political influence should
be removed from the process. Personal hostility to
wealth hardly seems a sufficient basis to ban it from
the political arena. Besides, there are many other
sources of political influence, including but not limited to fame, time, holding political office, the ability
to write law review articles, and skill at obtaining
foundation grants that permit one to spend one's

days lobbying Congress for campaign finance reform. Many persons are hostile to these forms of influence, yet there is little talk of banning them. Why should access to money be singled out? What are the characteristics that allegedly make money a particular vice in the political system?

Money, they say, is "the root of all evil." The rationale for this hostility to money is difficult to fathom. Money, in the sense of physical currency and coin, is merely an object, in modern society made of the same stuff as the pages of this book and components of the lamp by which you read these words. Economists point out that almost any relatively scarce object can serve as money, and note that some societies have used dried cod, tobacco, or livestock as money.[2]

Money is a tool of exchange. It is what has allowed the human race to move beyond a barter economy and to develop the specialization of labor.[3] It enables this author to survive by writing law review articles and torturing students with Socratic dialogue on obscure nineteenth-century Supreme Court decisions, all without the slightest clue as to how to make candles (let alone produce electricity), grow food, or turn plants and animals into clothing. Money allows individuals, quickly and easily, to convert the things that they produce efficiently, and which other people value, into those things that they value but are not able to produce, at least not with any degree of efficiency or quality. Money is the medium through which the labor one puts forth and the talents one possesses are stored and transformed into those goods and services one desires but lacks the talent to produce.

Money, then, is the single most important means by which people who lack talents with direct value in the political arena, such as production of advertising, writing, campaign organization, speaking, and the like, can participate in politics beyond voting. This would, on its face, seem to be a positive thing.

One of the earliest efforts to rationalize the prejudice against money as a political asset was that of David Adamany and George Agree. Writing in 1975, Adamany and Agree argued that money is different from other forms of political influence because "money can buy most non-economic political resources. It can pay canvassers, or skilled campaign managers, or publicists, or researchers. It cannot endow a candidate with intelligence, but it can buy him a brain trust. It cannot change his voice or face, but it can hire a make-up man, a voice coach, and a clever film editor. Those with money can buy virtually any of the resources that other citizens give directly."[4] In addition, Adamany and Agree argued, money is more liquid than other sources of political influence, being easily moved across states or across the country. This is an alluring argument, but one that ultimately fails.

First, it is not at all clear that the characteristics which they attribute to money are, in the political context, unique to money. True, money may be exchanged for noneconomic political resources, but noneconomic resources may equally be traded for money. Volunteer canvassers can raise money or recruit still more canvassers; skilled campaign managers and publicists can devise ads and themes that raise money. A brain trust can think up popular or innovative ideas that raise money or bring favorable, and free, press coverage. A winning personality, good looks, or a good voice can all be used to gain access to the media, volunteer or paid labor, or other elements of political success. Success in electoral politics generally comes from capitalizing on the assets with which a candidate begins to create the necessary assets the candidate initially lacks. History is replete with fund-raising champions such as John Connally, Oliver North, and Phil Gramm, who had the ability to raise money but lacked the ability to convert that money into other assets needed for victory.[5]

Nor is money uniquely liquid, as Adamany and Agree suggest. Other political attributes are moved across borders or distances with the same ease, or nearly so, as cash. Hollywood celebrities campaign around the country; producers and publicists can perform their jobs anywhere, sending only the final product to the targeted area; phone banks staffed by volunteers can be run from a variety of locations inside or outside the district or state; a brain trust can operate in almost any location; national media in far off places can influence races through their coverage. In any case, money's liquidity is an asset that increases political participation. For example, money contributions are the only way for most citizens to participate in the crucial New Hampshire presidential primary, or in important races affecting national politics, such as the 2000 New York Senate race that included Hillary Clinton.

In addition, Adamany and Agree argue that money is more difficult to trace than other forms of political influence.[6] This last problem is easily solved by disclosure, and to the extent that campaigns and donors might violate the law by failing to disclose, it is hard to see that the situation would be any different regardless of what laws might exist against the use of private money in campaigns. Adamany and Agree are simply wrong in thinking that the characteristics they describe are unique to monetary contributions.

Even if these characteristics were, to at least some degree, unique to monetary contributions, all that Adamany and Agree have done is to state why money may be particularly valuable to a campaign. This does not, however, explain the prejudice against allowing monetary contributions, nor explain why we should deny this form of political influence to individuals. There are various ways to contribute to campaigns, and different types of contributions have differing values to those campaigns, depending both on the supply of the items or talents in question in the market, and the campaign's demand for such items or talents. Many individuals, such as small-business owners, have time constraints that prevent them from working on a campaign. Most individuals lack skills directly transferable to political campaigning. For such individuals, money contributions are the primary source of political participation. A ban on this form of participation can hardly be justified on the grounds that such participation is, in many campaigns, particularly valuable.

What Adamany and Agree consider a vice of money contributions is, then, precisely the virtue of money contributions. Money, by design, allows people to use talents in one field to fulfill desires in another. Banning private monetary contributions would, in effect, turn politics into a barter system, with everyone excluded who does not possess attributes that can be directly bartered into political access and influence. That is to say, a ban on private monetary contributions may favor students and retirees, who have volunteer time, over working people, who may have less time but more discretionary income. It favors persons who are skilled in producing political advertising over persons skilled in producing plastic injection-mold products. It favors skilled writers over skilled plumbers. But plumbers and owners of small injection-mold companies can participate effectively through money contributions. That money can pay canvassers, or campaign managers, or publicists, is a virtue that broadens opportunities for political participation. It is not a vice.

Unable to recognize this virtue of monetary contributions, regulatory advocates respond to this problem of nonmonetary influence in two ways. The first is simply to ignore it. This is the approach not only of reform advocacy groups but also of many in the academy. For example, in their respective plans to ban all private giving (discussed in chapters 8 and 9), save for that authorized through government vouchers, both Hasen and Foley take a very pragmatic view: administratively, it is just too hard to ban most nonmonetary contributions. Indeed, the professors each recognize that inequalities will still exist. But neither offers any compelling rationale why these inequalities are acceptable but monetary inequalities—which, we now recognize, are also difficult to ban—are not. Implicit in their argument, however, is the belief that eliminating one form of inequality—money—will make everyone more equal, even though other forms of inequality remain.[7]

At work here is a fundamental failure to analyze correctly the workings of politics. It is simply wrong to assume that eliminating money as a form of influence will, in some way, increase the influence of citizens whose economic means limit them to, at most, a relatively modest contribution. To illustrate the point, a favorite story of regulatory advocates quotes a legislator's reaction on returning to his office: "You get back from lunch. You've got fourteen phone messages on your desk. Thirteen of them are from constituents you've never heard of, and one of them is from a guy who just came to your fundraiser two weeks earlier and gave you $1,000. Which phone call are you going to return first?"[8]

It's a catchy story, but really tells us very little. Suppose, for example, that all private monetary contributions were banned. Now the legislator returns to his or her desk, and finds fourteen phone calls, of which one is from the editorial board of the *Washington Post*. Which will be returned first? What if one is from a lobbyist for the national union whose local represents workers at the largest manufacturing facility in the district; which is returned first? What if it's from a well-known citizen activist with a talent for organizing rallies and gaining media attention? From a top outside media aide? A prominent business person? The leader of the Sierra Club? The pastor of a large church? A personal friend? In each case, we know which call will be returned first, and we know who will have the most influence on the legislator's thinking and behavior, all other things remaining equal. We could also arrange to have twelve calls from unknown individuals, one from a donor and one from another person of "influence" in the community. I think it is very hard to say that the candidate will return the donor's call before that of the local Sierra Club president, or pastor, or union leader, and so on.

We could go still further and imagine the enactment of a voucher system such as that envisioned by Hasen, in which all contributions must be paid for with government-issued vouchers. Thirteen calls are from constituents; the fourteenth is from a consultant who brokers campaign vouchers, much as Emily's List now bundles political contributions. Is there much doubt whose call is returned first? So although reformers suggest that the elimination of monetary contributions will help make all citizens politically equal, it remains an Orwellian sort of equality, in which "all . . . are equal but some . . . are more equal than others."[9] Academicians such as this author are, fortunately, in the more equal group. We have, for example, the time and skills to write law review articles and newspaper editorials, to prepare and give congressional testimony, or to file amicus briefs in lawsuits with important ramifications for public policy. We also have a captive audience for six to eight hours a week to which we can espouse political views, and we are sometimes invited to speak at public gatherings. I do not mean to suggest that there is any conscious effort by academics who write in favor of regulation to increase their personal influence. Nor do I think that journalists who editorialize for regulation are consciously trying to increase their political power. But such people have a natural tendency to view their sources of influence as legitimate, and others' sources of influence, of which money is the most obvious, as illegitimate. That this prejudice against money exists does not mean that it has been justified.

Restricting private monetary campaign contributions does not empower the "average constituent," however defined. Rather, it increases the relative influence of an even smaller elite: media people and others whose skills are directly valuable to a candidate or legislator.[10] The best way to assure that a representative does not shirk the public interest for that of narrow interests is to provide as many points of influence as possible. Efforts to ensure equality of inputs to the campaign process are less

206

likely to guarantee popular control than is the presence of multiple sources of political power.[11]

Regulatory advocates offer a second response to the question of other sources of influence. They argue that the unequal distribution of other political resources does not create the same problems as the unequal distribution of wealth because "inequalities of money are probably greater," and because money is less evenly distributed across society than are "inequalities in time, energy, education, and personal traits."[12] Both assertions are, I think, quite obviously wrong, at least at the point where it matters for politics. Indeed, I would posit quite the opposite: from the standpoint of political participation, citizens are more equal in their financial capabilities than in their campaign capabilities.

First, it should be obvious that citizens are not equal in their ability even to engage in such routine, "unskilled" campaign activity as walking a precinct or stuffing envelopes. A great many people have disabilities or serious time constraints that preclude their doing so. I doubt seriously that the number of people capable of devoting an afternoon to walking a precinct is any greater than the number of people capable of making a $40 campaign contribution. Both are minor contributions that have value to the campaign and that give the contributor some small level of "influence." But very few citizens have the talent, physical and personal attributes, luck of time and place, or wealth to influence political affairs substantially. Thus, a relatively small number of individuals will always have political influence far exceeding that of their neighbors. Activist/celebrities such as Barbra Streisand or Warren Beatty, writers such as Elaine Goodman or George Will, campaign managers such as James Carville and Mary Matalin, consultants such as Dick Morris, or talented lawyers specializing in campaign law will have far more influence. These individuals, we might suggest, are the equivalent of the $5,000, $50,000, or even the $200,000 financial donor. A high-powered campaign strategist such James Carville or Mary Matalin has enormous political influence relative to most other citizens, including millions who may be equally fervent in their beliefs and support for a candidate but who would not be good campaign managers. People in this latter group can, in most cases, seek influence only through a monetary gift to the campaign. There are far more people who can give a candidate money to help hire a James Carville than there are James Carvilles.

When we are warned, then, that "just" 235,000 people contributed one-third of all private money for federal campaigns in 1996 in contributions of $1,000 or more,[13] we must ask why this is a matter of concern, rather than a good thing. For even leaving aside the fact that millions of Americans contributed the remaining two-thirds, it would appear that 235,000 is a considerably larger number than those given op-ed space in daily newspapers, or the number of people who served as managers for political campaigns, or who filed amicus briefs in the United States Supreme Court, or who sat on the boards of foundations that awarded six-figure grants to groups that lobby for campaign finance reform. Indeed, 235,000 large financial donors would seem to be a considerably larger number than all of the other groups listed combined. Yet these 235,000 probably still have less influence than the other groups listed.

To the extent that wealth is a source of political power, there are more citizens of wealth (however that might be defined—$1,000 donors seems like a low threshold to me) than there are citizens capable of running a political campaign, producing quality political advertising, writing newspaper editorials, coaching voice, and so on. One recent study suggests that 30 million Americans could make a $1,000 contribution without affecting their lifestyle. The number of top-quality political consultants, attention-grabbing celebrities, and television news anchors is far smaller than the number of "rich people." The number of people capable of meaningful nonmonetary contributions to a campaign—that is, the type of contribution that will give the individual some extra say in policymaking—is much smaller than the group of monied people. In fact, because achievers in any field that has substantial value in politics (whether they be producers, celebrities, writers, lawyers, campaign consultants, or whatever), tend to be rewarded monetarily for their success, persons with other forms of political influence tend to be a subset of those capable of making $1,000 donations.

Not only is wealth the most widely dispersed form of influence, but the views of the "rich" are, it appears, much less homogenous than the views of many other groups with a large amount of political influence. Richard Briffault echoes a popular theme when he notes that donors to political

campaigns are more likely to be "affluent, men, whites . . . more conservative . . . more Republican" than the public at large.[14] But in other ways,
these donors are more like the American public than those with disproportionate influence stemming from other sources. They are less likely to
work for government, less likely to be college professors, more likely to
have business management experience, more likely to live outside political
capitals, and less likely to be Democrats than those with considerable
nonmonetary sources of influence, notably members of the press and
those with access to it. For example, one survey of Washington press corps
reporters and bureau chiefs found that 89 percent voted for Bill Clinton
in 1992, as against just 43 percent of the general population, and that
only 2 percent considered themselves to be conservative, as against 34
percent of voters nationally. Academics lean overwhelmingly to the political left, with as many as 80 percent identifying themselves as Democrats.
Hollywood celebrities seem to tilt sharply to the political left, despite the
occasional Schwarzenegger or Heston. On the other hand, corporate
PACs, which presumably might be considered a voice of the rich, routinely
give 40 to 60 percent of their contributions to Democratic Party candidates, despite the general belief that the Republican Party favors corporations and those with high incomes.[15] That the wealthy should be less homogenous than other political elites is no shock. Because wealth stems
from many sources, the wealthy probably represent a greater cross section
than do, say, network news anchors, political consultants, or professional
activists, which are smaller, more select groups. Furthermore, because of
the fluidity of wealth in American society, many of the rich will have been
born poor or middle class; be just one or two generations away from such
state; or have family and friends still in that economic condition.[16]

Even the availability of time can be very unevenly distributed in favor
of certain points of view. For example, a sole proprietor may have less
time to devote to political activities than his hourly employees. However,
he may also have more money to contribute. Thus, restrictions on campaign contributions may benefit organized labor relative to small business. Or, as executives of large corporations may have more time than
entrepreneurs, it may benefit both organized labor and big business over
small business. Similarly, a Hollywood celebrity's time spent campaigning
is far more valuable than any time a typical butcher can donate to a cam-

paign. Thus a limit on donations will not resolve the inequalities between them. Indeed, if looked at closely, we see that all that Adamany and Agree are saying is that money does what money is intended to do—it allows citizens to convert their talents in one field into something else. By allowing monetary contributions, all persons may put their personal talents to use in the political arena. Thus, although individual inequalities abound, overall equal protection is enhanced through political giving.

Equality is not likely to be enhanced by driving one form of political influence—the one which, next to voting itself, is probably most widely distributed—from the field. Indeed, money contributions are the single most common way, short of voting itself, in which Americans formally attach themselves to political candidates. We will not reach political equality by treating political talents as inherently more worthwhile than other talents.

This difficulty that regulatory advocates have with monetary gifts to campaigns is the result not only of a failure to appreciate that money itself is a source for expanding political influence beyond a narrow political caste, but also a failure to understand, and indeed an active mischaracterization of, traditional American notions of political equality. Historically, American political equality has hinged on the idea that each voter is entitled to a single, equal vote.[17] That is to say, each person is an equal at the ballot box. The framers certainly never intended that each person should have equal political influence. Indeed, it is not even clear what "equal influence" might mean. As one skeptic has written, "if being a 'political equal' means that one cannot legitimately attempt to acquire or exercise political influence, what reason would there be to engage in political deliberation?. . . At what point would effective participation in political debate become transformed into 'undue influence'? On the other hand, if everyone had the same amount of political influence, would not the very concept of 'political influence' itself be oxymoronic?"[18]

What this points out is that the very notion of politics presumes that some will have more influence than others. The traditional notion of political equality is not that that each person has equal influence at all stages of the process, but that each has a right to vote, and to have that vote weighted equally with those of others. But citizens are free to use their differing abilities, financial wherewithal, and personal disposition to become more or less active in political life, and to attempt to persuade their fellow citizens to vote in a particular manner. The question for campaign finance reform is whether or not those with substantial influence beyond the act of voting will be drawn from a narrow caste of those with political skills or from a wider group that includes those with money earned through nonpolitical talents.

Over the course of time, this country has gradually abolished restrictions on the right to vote. By constitutional amendment and statutory changes, the franchise has been extended to blacks, women, young adults, and persons without property. The courts have also played a role, striking down white primaries, state poll taxes, restrictions on voting by military personnel, unnecessarily long residency requirements, excessive filing fees, and malapportioned legislative districts that made one vote worth more than another. Reformist commentators often write and speak as if the elimination of private financing is the logical next step in the campaign for voter equality.[19]

But there is a fundamental difference between campaign finance reform and the rightly treasured judicial decisions banning poll taxes, white primaries, residency requirements, and the like. In the latter category of cases, the court acted to remove impediments that prevented individuals from casting a vote *at the ballot box*. Similarly, in the Supreme Court's redistricting cases of the 1960s, which gave us the now famous judicial rule of "one person/one vote," the Court acted to remove legislative impediments that literally made one person's ballot, cast *at the ballot box*, count for more than another's.[20] In the ballot access cases, the Court only went so far as to declare that there must be a means for a candidate to appear on the ballot *at the ballot box*; but the remedy applied by the Court in *Lubin v. Panish* did not require that every aspect of the electoral system be equal in its impact on candidates or voters. Indeed, the Court has made clear that so long as a party can gain access to the ballot, the disparate impact on the party of election laws is not grounds for striking down those laws.[21]

Equality-driven reformers tend to blur with rhetoric this important distinction between campaign and ballot box. Raskin and Bonifaz, for example, speak of a "wealth primary." But in fact, there is no such primary, if by "primary" we mean what one normally means and what the one person/one vote cases meant: an election in which people vote. There are no property qualifications for voting, let alone an election in which voters stuff dollars into a ballot box according to their financial means and political desire. Jezer, Kehler, and Santuria argue that the rich must be denied the ability to "vote with their money," and "ballots, rather than dollars," should determine who gets elected.[22] But metaphors aside, the rich do not vote with their money; they go to the polls and mark a ballot, like everyone else; and the election *is* won by counting ballots, rather than campaign donations or the aggregated wealth of the voters on each side.

What the campaign finance reformers seek, then, is not equality at the ballot box, or one person/one vote, but equality at stages of the process that precede actual voting. And although Foley, for example, states repeatedly that such equality is "the bedrock principle" upon which American democracy rests,[23] such a principle is nowhere to be found in the Constitution, was not how campaigns were conducted at the time the Constitution was passed, or when the First or Fourteenth amendments were adopted, and bears no resemblance to how campaigns have ever been conducted in this country. Further, as we have seen, efforts to put such a principle into place by restricting monetary contributions in politics threatens to have precisely the opposite effect of that intended. Such efforts further limit the number of people with political influence, thus increasing the influence of a smaller elite and restricting the number of competing voices and viewpoints active in politics. This deprives voters of information and, therefore, goes much further to making their *votes* "meaningless" in determining public policy than the speech of others in the campaign.

The 1938 United States Supreme Court decision in *United States v. Carolene Products Company* is generally considered to be the birthing ground of modern equal protection jurisprudence under the Fourteenth Amendment. In the most famous line of that opinion, the Court stated: "legislation which restricts those political processes which can ordinarily be expected to bring about the repeal of undesirable legislation [may] be subjected to more exacting judicial scrutiny under the general prohibitions of the Fourteenth Amendment than are most other types of legislation."[24] Campaign finance regulations are exactly that: state action intended to prevent individuals from spending money to, among other things, repeal "undesirable legislation" through the election of different

212

representatives. The Supreme Court has been quite correct in applying strict scrutiny to such restraints. The Court's pronouncement in *Buckley*, that "the concept that government may restrict the speech of some elements of our society in order to enhance the relative influence of others is wholly foreign to the First amendment,"[25] is equally appropriate when applied to the equal protection clauses of the Fifth and Fourteenth amendments.

Few concepts are more elusive than that of political equality. Government, by definition, presupposes unequal influence, for the influence of those holding high office must far exceed that of most other citizens. Historically, political equality in America has meant equality at the ballot box, and equality before the law, including the right of each citizen to speak freely on public issues. Regulators, erroneously equating campaigning and persuading with voting, will not enhance equality at the ballot box but would instead sacrifice the equal right of citizens to speak out on public issues.

Corruption in the United States

Advocates of campaign finance regulation routinely refer to "corruption" within the system. But the term is kept remarkably vague. Ask just who is corrupt, and one will rarely find a straight answer. Rather, one is told that the "system" is corrupt. But one ought not call a system corrupt if it does not lead to acts of corruption, and if acts of corruption exist to the degree commonly claimed, one would think it would be possible to name names and acts.

This is not to say that no corrupt officials are ever elected to office, or that acts of corruption do not take place. But what is interesting is that such acts are still rare enough to be the cause of outrage and a great deal of press attention. Furthermore, most such incidents involve true corruption outside of any question of campaign finance, such as the 1977 Abscam scandal, which involved good old-fashioned bribery of public officials.

Although they can't name names, regulatory zealots claim to see corruption everywhere. How can this be so? Consider again the telling quote from Ann McBride, former president of Common Cause, discussed in

213

chapter 1. Appearing on the *Newshour with Jim Lehrer* in the fall of 1996, McBride stated, "at the same time there are efforts to regulate them . . . you have all the major interests that have an outcome in the election and an outcome in policy being able to pour this money in . . . , money affecting federal elections. . . . It's corrupting, the American people understand it, and it has really got to be changed."[26] Consider for a moment the ramifications of the concept of corruption advocated by McBride. What she is saying is that if a party has an interest in government policy, that party should forfeit its right to speak during a campaign or to lobby after the election. Such an understanding of "corruption" turns American democracy on its head. The First Amendment guarantees not only the right to speak out but also the right to petition government. The essence of American democracy has always been that the people have a right to a say in the policies that may affect their well-being. McBride seems to suggest that individuals and interests affected by government action should sit idly by and take whatever comes their way. They should make no effort to persuade their fellow citizens of the rightness of their cause, because to do so is corrupting. This is the direct opposite of participatory democracy. In McBride's world, we seem to have gone from "no taxation without representation" to "no representation if possible taxation."

In short, for at least some campaign regulation advocates, it appears that democracy itself is the problem. If individuals and groups are allowed to spend money campaigning, they might succeed in convincing voters to vote in certain ways; if they are allowed to lobby their representatives, they might persuade those representatives to support or oppose legislation. This "has really got to be changed." Democracy itself is corrupt.

Not only is such a conception of democracy totally unworkable, of course, but it needlessly impugns the motives and integrity of millions of Americans who donate to campaigns and thousands of political candidates who seek public office. When reformers say that the system is corrupt, perhaps they reveal more than they intend. They reveal a profound lack of faith in the American people, and in the wisdom of voters to elect good men and women to office and to oust scoundrels who slip through the cracks. What the reformers are now calling "corruption" is what separates the United States from dozens of petty dictatorships around the world—the right of the people to participate in political life free from

214

government interference. We should consider that the greatest corruption is likely to result from a system that gives lawmakers the power to determine who will spend how much in a campaign against them; or who will criticize their stands on public matters in the form of issue advocacy.

The final irony of the great quest for campaign finance "reform" is that it may be leading to an increase in traditional, old-fashioned corruption, such as bribery and vote fraud. There is no corruption when a citizen, a group of citizens, or even a corporation or union contributes $10,000 to the political party that shares the same general ideology as the donors. Yet such donations—otherwise known as "soft money"—have been the subject of countless editorials and investigative reports. This media and advocacy group focus on the noncorruption of campaign finance reform has obscured, and perhaps even contributed to, an alarming increase in many types of real corruption thought to be long banished from the American political scene, recently documented by political scientist Larry J. Sabato. Such corruption includes vote fraud, buying and selling of votes and endorsements, and gross abuses of government power.[27] Left unchecked, such abuses will do far greater damage to American democracy than a few large, publicly disclosed campaign donations. The law is far better equipped to deal with these problems than it is with trying to perfect political speech. And indeed, the founders seem to have recognized as much, for they added the First Amendment to the Constitution.

Real Reform

Successful reform of campaign finance requires an honest assessment of the problems we seek to address. Regulatory advocates have misinterpreted the effects of money on political equality and corruption. Having done that, it is no surprise that the solutions imposed have made the problems worse. Campaign finance regulation has helped to insulate incumbents, hindered grassroots political activity, infringed on free speech, and made campaigns longer and devoid of content. What should be done now?

First, we must recognize that campaign contributions are not the same as votes. Money is not stuffed into ballot boxes; winners are not determined simply by counting donations or net worth. Voter equality comes at the ballot box, where each vote is weighted the same. It makes no more sense to try to create equal influence before the vote by limiting money than it would to try to create equal influence by limiting newspaper columnists to one column, requiring television stations to randomly select citizens to choose the night's news stories and write the copy, or to require consultants such as James Carville or Mary Matalan to divide their time evenly between Democrats and Republicans. True, money might be used to bribe county officials around the country who are responsible for administering elections and tabulating votes, but such vote fraud is addressed by other laws, and that is not what regulatory advocates mean when they claim that "money buys election." What these advocates mean is that money creates inequality in political participation. But there are many sources of political inequality: celebrity; media access and attention; writing ability; time; friendship; lawyering skills; institutional presence at the seat of government; organizational ability. Money is simply one more.

Second, we must realize that monetary contributions are one of the most popular, and egalitarian, ways in which Americans participate in political campaigns. When other sources of political power, such as media access or friendship with office holders, are unequally distributed, as they usually are, money is as likely to be an equalizer as it is to be a source of inequality. When fewer people are able to exert any sort of political influence, the chance that some small group will divert government power to serve its parochial interests increases.

Money, on the other hand, is more broadly distributed, and monetary participation is one of the few avenues of political participation that is realistically open to most Americans. If, as I have suggested, the 235,000 donors of $1,000 or more in 1996 is a greater number than those writing opinion columns in newspapers, running advocacy groups, hosting their own talk radio programs, or working as campaign consultants, then banning or limiting contributions will reduce, rather than increase, the number of persons capable of exercising substantial political influence. And these 235,000 are only the tip of an iceberg. Behind them are millions more who contributed less than $1,000 each, but two-thirds of the total, to campaigns, and other millions with the financial resources to contribute, but who choose not to contribute. If these millions more exceed the number who volunteered labor to campaigns, as I am quite sure that they do, then we need to stop the nonsense that an unregulated private financing system reduces the role of average citizens in political campaigns and the discussion of political issues. Reducing the amount of money in politics will not increase the number of people who can exercise influence in others ways. It will not increase the number of television news anchors, press reporters, celebrities, professors, or others who are positioned to exert more political influence than their fellow citizens. One goal of campaign finance reform should be to increase the number of people who can participate in politics. Money is the single easiest method for most people to participate directly in political campaigns. Indeed, for a great many Americans, it is the only realistic form of direct political participation. For an American who wants to help a presidential candidate in the New Hampshire primary, for example, a monetary contribution is usually the only option available.

Third, we must make an honest assessment of the level of corruption that exists in government. Editorialists and campaign finance reform advocacy groups suggest that corruption is rampant among public officials in the United States. But we must remember that what they mean by "corruption" is not that officials are taking bribes or lining their own pockets. That type of behavior, once again, is illegal under other laws having nothing to do with campaign finance.

Rather, by corruption they mean that legislators are voting or acting in ways that the legislators themselves believe are bad for the country, and are opposed by their constituencies, in exchange for contributions to their campaigns. When stated this way, the proposition that a large number of lawmakers is corrupt seems highly improbable. Do we really believe that large numbers of elected officials vote against both their own consciences and the wishes of voters in their districts? If so, why aren't they voted out of office? Serious discussion of campaign finance reform requires us to admit that the vast majority of local, state, and national officials in the United States are honorable men and women who sincerely believe in what they are doing. This is not to say that men are angels—certainly the founders were not so naive. The various agendas that men and women take to public office can be public spirited or venal. These agendas can be aimed at looting the wealth of their fellow citizens, or simply obtaining power over others. But there is relatively little reason

217

to think that these agendas are radically altered by campaign contributions. As discussed in chapter 3, systematic studies of legislative behavior indicate that contributions have little effect on legislative behavior, at least when compared to such influences as party loyalty, personal ideology, and constituent desires.

In fact, if campaign contributions really affected much legislative behavior, we should expect to see far more spent on politics. After all, in every two-year election cycle the federal government alone spends approximately one thousand times as much money as is spent on all political activity—local, state, and federal—in the country. If campaign contributions were really an effective technique for buying government favors, we almost certainly would see far more money spent.

Incidents of "corruption" that involve campaign finance are rare enough that they are, in fact, scandals that bring an outpouring of public shock. It has been over a decade since the so-called Keating Five scandal broke, and in the ensuing years there has been no congressional scandal approaching it. And yet that "scandal" involved just five senators, and at least one of the five, John McCain, had only the most peripheral involvement. The extent of McCain's "improper" behavior involved little more than attending a meeting with federal regulators to discuss the investigation of Keating's Lincoln Savings and Loan. Nor is there evidence that any of the senators had much impact on government policy; after meeting with the senators, Federal Home Loan Bank Board Chairman Edwin Gray terminated an audit of Lincoln Savings and Loan, but also referred Keating and Lincoln Savings and Loan to the Justice Department for possible prosecution.[28]

Similarly, in the 1996 elections much was made of the fact that large donors to President Clinton's reelection campaign were invited to spend night's in the Lincoln Bedroom at the White House. I am not sure which is more remarkable: that this simple act, which apparently involved no official actions by the president, was considered scandalous; or that this treatment of major campaign supporters had apparently not been used by prior presidents. In any case, if this is a scandal, it suggests, if anything, that campaign contributions have little to do with dictating government policy. Americans do not seem concerned enough to make fund raising a priority when it comes time to vote.

There simply is very little evidence, or reason to believe, that even the type of corruption envisioned by the campaign finance regulatory lobby exists to any great extent. This is why specific examples of corruption are virtually never referred to by the regulatory lobby. Campaign contributions are just one of many considerations for a legislator, and by all evidence and common sense a relatively minor one. Nor is it clear that it is always inappropriate for a legislator to consider campaign contributions. After all, contributions can reveal both the extent and intensity of public support or opposition on any given issue.

Fourth, we must appreciate the fact that campaign finance regulation falls most heavily on political novices and grassroots political organizations. It is no surprise that a majority of the examples cited in chapter 1— stories of people such as Margaret McIntyre, Leo Smith, Edward Cozzette, the National Committee for Impeachment—involve spontaneous political activity by ordinary Americans. In most states today—that is to say, in states that have imposed FECA-like regulation on campaign finance—an idealistic individual who decides to run for state representative or county commissioner, or who organizes a campaign to lobby on an issue associated closely associated with an incumbent seeking reelection, must begin his or her campaign by hiring a lawyer. Rather than add more regulation, we ought to be seeking ways to lower the burdens on these truly grassroots activists. Similarly, we need to recognize that limiting contributions has rewarded incumbents and other candidates who start out with high name recognition and has increased the influence of other elites, especially the media.

Having faced these realities, is there, then, nothing that can be done about campaign finance? The purpose of this book has not been to deny that campaign contributions might affect the functioning of the legislature, though I have attempted to show that the problem is not nearly so serious as has been claimed, and not sufficiently serious to justify the intrusions on First Amendment rights included in both existing campaign finance law and in most proposals for further regulation. The purpose of this book has not been to suggest that political equality is not a potentially valid objective of public policy. Quite to the contrary, I have attempted to show that regulatory advocates have simply given too cramped a definition to equality, and further, to show that even on their own terms,

219

equality will be fostered by including more people and types of participation in the process, rather than trying to exclude people or disfavor one type of participation. If these goals have some merit, is there not some role for regulation?

In *Buckley v. Valeo*, Chief Justice Burger argued that a system of full disclosure would meet the legitimate concerns about possible corruption while still offering substantial protection to First Amendment rights. In constitutional parlance, Justice Burger saw disclosure as the "narrowly tailored" solution to the compelling state interest in preventing "corruption" or the "appearance of corruption."[29] Disclosure, when not accompanied by limits on spending and contributions, leaves citizens free to speak, and so appears to be less of an infringement on constitutional rights than such limits. Disclosure may be justified by thinking along agency principles. Just as agents are required to disclose potential conflicts of interest to their principles, it may be appropriate that elected officials, as "agents" for voters, disclose campaign contributions as potential conflicts of interest. As the *Buckley* majority put it:

> Disclosure requirements deter actual corruption and avoid the appearance of corruption by exposing large contributions and expenditures to the light of publicity. This disclosure may discourage those who would use money for improper purposes either before or after the election. A public armed with information about a candidate's most generous supporters is better able to detect any post-election special favors that may be given in return. . . . In enacting these requirements [Congress] may have been mindful of Mr. Justice Brandeis' advice: "Publicity is justly commended as a remedy for social and industrial diseases. Sunlight is said to be the best of disinfectants; electric light the most efficient policeman."[30]

Disclosure has proven to be a popular remedy even with those generally skeptical of campaign finance regulation.[31]

Ironically, a limited, disclosure-only regime of campaign finance regulation has never been seriously tried at the federal level—prior to 1971, there were no effective disclosure laws, and by 1974, contribution and spending limits were in place. However, during the brief experiment with a system based primarily on disclosure, it seemed to work. The disclosure of large—but legal—contributions to the Nixon campaign, including over $2 million from insurance executive Clement Stone and $250,000 from oilman Leon Hess, was a major source of controversy and contributed to erosion of the president's support during the Watergate scandals.[32]

But disclosure, too, has serious limits. As the *Buckley* Court realized, it does infringe on First Amendment liberties, even if the Court found those infringements justified.[33] Indeed, many of what seem to be the more outrageous incidents of campaign finance enforcement involve disclosure laws. It was under Ohio's disclosure law, for example, that Margaret McIntyre, the Westerville housewife passing out homemade leaflets against a local tax increase, was prosecuted. If the burden of regulation falls most heavily on newcomers to the political process, and on local grassroots activists such as McIntyre, it is in large part because of the requirements of disclosure laws, including filing, tracking, and compiling data, registering with the state, and knowing when one must register and when and how to report information. For this reason, some advocates of disclosure have suggested that any reporting threshold be set as high as $25,000 or $50,000 in total election-related expenditures per cycle.[34] This would alleviate the burden on grassroots and incidental activity. However, it would do so at a cost in enforcement. Even though the law could presumably be structured to include the expenditures of all affiliated groups, it would be relatively easy for large donors to avoid detection by contributing to many small groups.

Nor would a disclosure-only regime totally eliminate the contentious question of issue advocacy, or what constitute the "election-related" expenses that must be disclosed. Lines would still need to be drawn as to exactly which activity was included in the reporting requirements. Of course, it might well be that disclosure of the financing of issue ads would be less of an issue than efforts to ban them outright. But it is not obvious that this is so. In *McIntyre v. Ohio Elections Commission* and the 1999 case of *Buckley v. American Constitutional Law Foundation*, the Supreme Court reaffirmed a constitutional right to engage in anonymous speech on political issues, following its earlier decision in *Talley v. California*. The Court was quite correct when it stated in *McIntyre*, "anonymity is a shield from the tyranny of the majority. It thus exemplifies the purpose behind the Bill of Rights, and of the First Amendment in particular: to protect unpopular individuals from retaliation—and their ideas from suppression—at the hand of an intolerant society. The right to remain anonymous may be abused when it shields fraudulent conduct. But political speech by its nature will sometimes have unpalatable consequences, and, in general, our society accords greater weight to the value of free speech than to the dangers of its misuse."[35] Indeed, prior to *Buckley*, the Court had only once upheld a law compelling the disclosure of the names of people engaged in political association, against a First Amendment challenge. In that case, *Communist Party v. Subversive Activities Control Board*, the Court made an exception where the organization "operate[ed] primarily to advance the objectives of that movement, that is, the overthrow of existing government by any means necessary and the establishment in its place of a Communist totalitarian dictatorship."[36] It is probably fair to say that most campaign regulatory enthusiasts would not view *Communist Party* as one of the Court's proudest moments, and in any case no one has suggested that campaign contributors are dedicated to the violent overthrow of the government. In *NAACP v. Alabama*, *Bates v. Little Rock*, *Louisiana ex rel. Gremillion v. NAACP*, and *Gibson v. Florida Legislative Commission*, the Court had rejected efforts to compel disclosure.

Forced disclosure holds the danger of government retaliation for unpopular speech—and certainly *McIntyre* itself is indicative of that. In that case, Margaret McIntyre had been opposing a local school millage: school board officials filed the complaint against her after the election, which suggests that their primary aim was retaliation.

Nor is the harassment problem limited to official retaliation. As Chief Justice Burger noted in *Buckley*, "rank-and-file union members or rising junior executives may now think twice before making even modest contributions to a candidate who is disfavored by the union or management hierarchy." Even reform advocates such as Burt Neuborne recognize this danger, noting that managers can feel pressured to make donations to company PACs, and corporations to legislators. Neuborne's odd solution, however, is not to question disclosure but to question the right to contribute.[37]

Indeed, even in the context of express advocacy of the election or defeat of candidates for office, the Supreme Court has carved out an ad hoc exception to the disclosure rules. In *Brown v. Socialist Workers '74 Cam-*

paign Committee, the Court, following hints it had given in *Buckley*, held that the Socialist Workers Party could avoid disclosure as a "minor party" with a history of "harassment."[38]

Given these problems, it may be worth reconsidering the rationale even behind disclosure laws. The Supreme Court tells us that the purpose of the law is to "deter actual corruption" and "detect any postelection special favors." But as we have seen, corruption in the sense of personal enrichment is already covered by bribery laws. As to postelection special favors, we might ask why they should especially matter. After all, opening meeting laws, roll-call votes, and actual results should tell us about postelection special favors. How does one tell a "postelection special favor" from a "sound policy decision" without making some value judgment about what one wants the legislator to do? To one voter, a decision to support ethanol subsidies or sugar quotas is a special favor. To another, it is a sound policy decision to support family farms or promote clean energy sources. And it is to determine questions such as these that we have elections. Is it not the policies, rather than the names of contributors, that should be most important? As one wag recently put it; "A candidate who favors freedom and fair play is a hero even if his campaign money came from Satan, Chiquita or the National Education Association. A candidate who favors corporate welfare or sweetheart union deals is a bum, even if his campaign was financed by $10 donations from a million nuns."[39]

The reason that we care about knowing who has contributed what to whom cannot really be that it helps us to weed out corruption in the old-fashioned meaning of the world, for the truly corrupt will simply not disclose their bribes. And whether we are happy or disappointed with an office holder's performance in office should ultimately depend on what he does in office rather than on the identity of his contributors. If we favor more road building, it shouldn't really matter to us if the legislator favors bigger highway budgets in order to assure contributions from construction unions and truckers or out of concern for urban sprawl. If we oppose those budgets, it shouldn't terribly matter whether the legislator opposes them out of a desire to please the mass transit lobby or because of an ideology opposed to government spending generally. The primary reason for caring about who has contributed what to whom, then, is not really that it will prevent old-fashioned bribery, or even give us particularly valuable information on our legislators' activities that is not available elsewhere. It would seem that the interest identified by the *Buckley* Court doesn't really exist at all. In fact, focusing on the sources of money may simply distract voters from analyzing the underlying issues. Every news report or story on money in politics is a story that could have been devoted to candidates' speeches or analysis of issues. Viewed in this light, a focus on disclosure of contributions may actually impoverish debate. One reason that the *Federalist Papers* were published anonymously was to force readers to focus on the arguments therein, rather than on attacking the writers.

But there is a simple and legitimate, though hardly flattering, reason for favoring disclosure. It is that we, as voters, are lazy. Keeping up on the activities of particular legislators—particularly in the modern era when government has its hands into so many activities—is hard, time-consuming work. Knowing the sources of a candidate's campaign funds provides us with a shorthand method for estimating a candidate's probable stand on a variety of issues. A candidate who receives large donations from the National Rifle Association is likely to oppose gun control efforts. A candidate who receives donations from the Sierra Club is likely to have a strong environmental record. Contributions, in short, are a bit like endorsements. We rely on our knowledge about the endorser to make quick, relatively effortless judgments on the candidate. Thus, there may be modest benefits to be had from a system that provides voters with information on the sources of campaign funds, through mandatory disclosure. Curiously, if we limit private political donations, we may lose this source of voter information, because we lose this simple method of determining what groups or individuals are supporting or opposing a given candidate and how intense their support or opposition is.

Whether or not this is a strong enough government interest to justify a regime of disclosure, given the burdens that disclosure places on grassroots political activity and its infringement on First Amendment liberties, is hardly an easy question. It may be time to question whether even disclosure is worth the cost, or at least to consider other options. Ian Ayres and Jeremy Bulow, for example, have suggested taking the route opposite from disclosure. They argue that retaliation could be avoided and alleged corruption deterred by mandating that all contributions be made in blind trusts.[40] Although skeptical that this is the solution, either, it represents the type of creative thinking, that may deserve more attention, rather than efforts to ratchet up the level of regulation.

Whether or not we ultimately decide that mandatory disclosure is justified, it is time to move away from the failed approach of the past. More regulation is not the answer. Command and control regulation cannot hope to close the "loophole" of issue advocacy or solve the problems of unequal, nonmonetary influence, at least not in a manner compatible with the First Amendment rights of Americans to engage in political speech.

There is a system, however, that can meet the criteria of a successful regulatory system—that is, one that is flexible and easy to administer; that provides adequate information to voters; that lowers barriers to political activity and fosters competitiveness; that combats alleged influence peddling and increases official accountability; and that promotes true equality. It is one with which Americans are familiar, even if it has, at times, been forgotten in the enthusiasm to regulate campaign finance in recent years: the First Amendment.

The First Amendment begins "Congress shall make no law. . . ." We must take that strict prohibition seriously. It is true that "no law" cannot be interpreted in the most absolute sense. There seems to be little disagreement but that persons can be held accountable for making statements that can be proven to be false, such as shouting "fire" in a crowded theater, or publishing libelous material. But these exceptions are narrow in scope. A person generally cannot be punished for falsely yelling "fire" in a crowded theater if the person honestly and reasonably believed that there was a fire. Proving libel of a public figure, such as a political candidate, requires not only that the statement be false but that the speaker act with malice, indicated by the knowledge that the statement is false or with reckless disregard for its truth or falsity.[41] And prior restraint of speech is allowed only under the most exceptional circumstances.

Proponents of campaign finance regulation tend to frame their First Amendment argument in terms of "values." They argue that the purpose of the First Amendment is to promote the discovery of truth, or to ensure that all voices are heard, or to promote democracy. And surely all such concerns are important, and probably did influence the writing of the Constitution and the First Amendment. But they are not themselves the

First Amendment. The First Amendment is still that tricky little phrase that begins, "Congress shall make no law." Over time, many have come to view the actual language of the First Amendment as little more than an outdated barrier to the "values" present in the First Amendment. This is wrong.

Of course, the First Amendment is concerned with values, in particular with individual rights and liberties. But it is important to remember that the Constitution is, first and foremost, a governing document. As a governing document, it specifies certain things that the government may and may not do. The First Amendment, then, is not merely a libertarian barrier to government action reflecting some odd paranoia of the framers, but a considered response to the problems inherent in any democratic system of governance, including the conduct of fair elections.

By assuring freedom of speech and of the press, the First Amendment provides voters with information needed to address the alleged corruption seen by campaign finance regulators at the polls, if the voters so desire. There is no shortage of newspaper articles reporting on candidate spending and campaign contributions, and the candidates themselves frequently make such information an issue in campaigns. By keeping government out of the electoral arena, the First Amendment allows for a full interplay of political ideas and prohibits the type of incumbent self-dealing that has so vexed the reform movement. It allows challengers to raise the funds necessary for successful campaigns and keeps channels of political change open.

By prohibiting excessive regulation of political speech and the political process, the First Amendment prevents true grassroots political activity from being squashed by the heavy hand of regulation. And because the First Amendment, properly interpreted to protect both political contributions and spending, makes no distinction between different types of political influence, it allows a maximum number of voters to participate and helps to prevent any one faction or interest from gaining the upper hand in political debate.

What the First Amendment does not do is promise a neat and tidy system of elections. Campaign finance regulators, focusing on the untidiness of the process, which they have erroneously labeled "corruption," have responded with an ever-growing web of regulation. This has served

226

only to distance Americans from politics and politicians and has thus led to a decline in the public's trust in government.

Issues pertaining to political campaigns in the twenty-first century are unlikely to be resolved by piling still more regulations on top of a failed system of campaign finance regulation. The problems with this approach are, I hope, convincingly documented in the preceding pages. But beyond all the failures of this approach to accomplish its goals, and beyond the distorting, deleterious effects it has had on elections, the greatest danger with this regulatory approach is that there is always one more loophole to close. Since 1907, Federal election law has been amended twelve times, with at least four major overhauls in 1907, 1925, 1971, and 1974. When laws become complicated and difficult to follow, as the Federal Elections Act most certainly is; when they fail repeatedly to achieve their purported goals; and when they are in constant need of revision to plug and ever-changing series of loopholes, one must consider that it is the laws, and not the people, that are flawed.[42]

The attempt to regulate political speech in the guise of campaign finance reform has been a folly. Fortunately, the solution to this folly is readily at hand. Most Americans, indeed, know its opening line by heart: "Congress shall make no law. . . ."

Notes

Chapter 1
Introduction

1. *Federal Election Commission v. Central Long Island Tax Reform Immediately Committee.*
2. *McIntyre v. Ohio Elections Commission.*
3. Federal Electoral Commission, *Advisory Opinion 1998–22,* November 12, 1998.
4. See *Reno v. American Civil Liberties Union.*
5. *Congressional Record,* March 18, 1997.
6. Nancy Gibbs, "The Wake-Up Call," *Time,* February 3, 1997, 22.
7. Paula Kane Allen, "Fellow Freshmen Focus on Campaign Reform."
8. *Newshour with Jim Lehrer,* October 18, 1996.
9. Martin Shapiro, "Corruption, Freedom and Equality in Campaign Financing," 393.

Chapter 2
Money Talks

1. *See* Robert J. Dinkin, *Campaigning in America,* 1–30.
2. George Thayer, *Who Shakes the Money Tree?* 25; See for example, Dinkin, *Campaigning in America,* 3;

Robert Mutch, *Campaigns, Congresses and Courts: The Making of Federal Campaign Finance Law,* xv; Charles S. Sydnor, *Gentlemen Freeholders,* 55.

3. See, Dinkin, *Campaigning in America,* 14–30; Herbert E. Alexander, *Financing Politics: Money, Elections, and Political Reform,* 77; Thayer, *Who Shakes the Money Tree?,* 26; Timothy D. Johnson, *Winfield Scott: The Quest for Military Glory,* 84.

4. Chilton Williamson, *American Suffrage: From Property to Democracy 1760–1860.*

5. Donald B. Cole, *The Presidency of Andrew Jackson* 17–21; Thayer, *Who Shakes the Money Tree?,* 28–29; Dinkin, *Campaigning in America,* 40.

6. Alexander, *Financing Politics,* 77, 80, Table 5–1.

7. Ibid., 9–10, 24; Mutch, *Campaigns, Congresses and Courts,* xvi; Dinkin, *Campaigning in America,* 40, 73; Congressional Quarterly, *Congressional Campaign Finances: History, Facts and Controversy.*

8. Jasper P. Shannon, *Money and Politics,* 21. See also Thayer, *Who Shakes the Money Tree?,* 35, 39, 40.

9. Nathan Miller, *Stealing from America: A History of Corruption from Jamestown to Reagan* 255. See also Mutch, *Campaigns, Congresses and Courts,* xvii; David J. Rothman, *Politics and Power: The United States Senate 1869–1901,* 185.

10. Thayer, *Who Shakes the Money Tree?,* 40, 42.

11. Ibid., 48; See also, Dinkin, *Campaigning in America,* 106; Alexander, *Financing Politics,* 12–13, 80, Table 5–1.

12. Mutch, *Campaigns, Congresses and Courts,* 3; Alexander, *Financing Politics* 13; Thayer, *Who Shakes the Money Tree?,* 51.

13. Mutch, *Campaigns, Congresses and Courts,* 3; Dinkin, *Campaigning in America,* 106; Frank J. Sorauf, *Inside Campaign Finance: Myths and Realities,* 3.

14. Mutch, *Campaigns, Congresses and Courts,* 2–3, 6, xvii; *Perkins v. Moss.*

15. Mutch, *Campaigns, Congresses and Courts,* 166, citing to a quote in *Fortune* by Duncan Norton Taylor, May 1956.

16. Congressional Quarterly, *Congressional Campaign Finances,* 31; Mutch, *Campaigns, Congresses and Courts,* 14.

17. Louise Overacker, *Money in Elections,* 271; *United States v. Newberry.*

18. Thayer, *Who Shakes the Money Tree?,* 52, 58–59; Robert K. Murray, *The Harding Era: Warren G. Harding and His Administration,* 28–29, 472.

19. Interestingly, Sinclair had not contributed to Harding's presidential campaign; Murray, *Harding Era.* See also Larry J. Sabato and Glenn R. Simpson, *Dirty Little Secrets: The Persistence of Corruption in American Politics,* 12–13.

20. Alexander, *Financing Politics,* 25–26.

21. Sorauf, *Inside Campaign Finance,* 6.

22. Alexander, *Financing Politics,* 14.

23. Thayer, *Who Shakes the Money Tree?,* 71; Mutch, *Campaigns, Congresses and Courts,* 33–35.

24. Alexander, *Financing Politics*, 14; Thayer, *Who Shakes the Money Tree?*, 73; Mutch, *Campaigns, Congresses and Courts*, 155.
25. *See United States v. Congress of Industrial Organizations*, Mutch, *Campaigns, Congresses and Courts*, 156–58.
26. *United States v. United Auto Workers*.
27. Alexander, *Financing Politics*, 82, Table 5–2.
28. Sorauf, *Inside Campaign Finance*, 4.
29. John Gardner, *In Common Cause*, 33, 55.
30. Alexander Heard, *The Costs of Democracy*, 388.
31. Congressional Quarterly, *Congressional Campaign Finance*, 39–40.
32. Alexander, *Financing Politics*, 37–38.
33. Ibid., 30–32; Congressional Quarterly, *Congressional Campaign Finance*, 41–42.
34. *See Buckley v. Valeo*. The 1974 amendments also repealed the 1971 limits on media spending. See, Congressional Quarterly, *Congressional Campaign Finance*, 44–45.
35. Alexander, *Financing Politics*, 38.
36. Ibid., 54–55. The spending level of the challenger is generally far more important in determining the outcome than is the spending of the incumbent or the ratio between the two. Alan I. Abramowitz, "Explaining Senate Election Outcomes"; Gary Jacobson, "Money and Votes Reconsidered: Congressional Elections 1972–1982"; Jacobson, "The Effects of Electoral Campaign Spending in Congressional Elections."
37. *Buckley v. Valeo*, 39–51.
38. Ibid., 42–44 n. 52.
39. See, for example; Alexander, *Financing Politics*, 51–54; 2 U.S.C. Sec. 432 (8)(B)(x)–(xi); 431 (9)(B)(viii); Federal Election Commission, *Advisory Opinion 1978–10*; Donald Simon, "Beyond Post-Watergate Reform: Putting an End to the Soft Money System," 175.
40. John H. Fund, *Term Limitation: An Idea Whose Time has Come*, 5; Fred Wertheimer and Susan Manes, "Campaign Finance Reform: A Key to Restoring the Health of Our Democracy," 1,133; "FEC Reports on Congressional Fundraising," available at www.fec.gov; Vincent Blasi, "Free Speech and the Widening Gyre of Fund-Raising: Why Campaign Spending Limits May Not Violate the First Amendment After All."
41. "FEC Reports"; *McIntyre v. Ohio Elections Commission*, Sara Fritz and Dwight Morris, "Federal Election Panel Not Enforcing Limit on Campaign Donations"; *United States Chamber of Commerce v. Federal Elections Commission*; *Pestrak v. Ohio Elections Commission*; Stephanie D. Moussalli, *Campaign Finance Reform: The Case for Deregulation*, 9.

Chapter 3
Faulty Assumptions

1. *See* Vincent Blasi, "Free Speech and the Widening Gyre of Fund-Raising: Why Campaign Spending Limits May Not Violate the First Amendment After All";

Jamin Raskin and Jon Bonifaz, "The Constitutional Imperative and Practical Superiority of Democratically Financed Elections, 1,187. For the proposition that this has not historically been a major argument for reform, See Robert E. Mutch, *Campaigns, Congresses and Courts: The Making of Federal Campaign Finance Law*, 1–53, and John W. Gardner, *In Common Cause*.

2. *St. Louis Post-Dispatch*, October 23, 1994, 1B. Also see Lydia Saad, "No Public Outcry for Campaign Finance Reform" (79 percent favor spending caps in campaigns); "Seventy Percent Want Spending Limits," (70 percent favor spending caps).

3. Marlene A. Nicholson, "Continuing the Dialogue on Campaign Finance Reform: A Response to Roy Schotland," 474–75; see, for example, Debra Burke, "Twenty Years after the Federal Election Campaign Act Amendments of 1974: Look Who's Running Now," 375–76; Fred Wertheimer and Susan W. Manes, "Campaign Finance Reform: A Key to Restoring the Health of Our Democracy," 1,132–33; Kenneth J. Levit, "Campaign Finance Reform and the Return of Buckley v. Valeo," 473 ("excessive campaign spending . . . compromi[ses] the electorate's confidence in the democratic process"). See also Frank J. Sorauf, "Politics, Experience, and the First Amendment: The Case of American Campaign Finance," 1,357 ("a consensus agenda for mainstream reform . . . includes . . . a reduction in the total sums being raised and spent").

4. Don Van Natta, Jr., "Spending By Candidates May Pass $3 Billion," quoting several experts, including Herbert Alexander, Larry Mackinson, and Fred Wertheimer.

5. Clare Ansberry, "The Best Beef Jerky Has Characteristics Few Can Appreciate," citing annual spending on chips in excess of $4.5 billion; Roy A. Schotland, "Proposals for Campaign Finance Reform: An Article Dedicated to Being Less Dull Than Its Title"; *Wall Street Journal*, "Sony's Statesmanship," Roxanne Roberts, "The Remote Controllers."

6. Ilya Somin, "Voter Ignorance and the Democratic Ideal," (on voter ignorance); Annelise Anderson, *Political Money: The New Prohibition*, 7–8 (on cost of campaign).

7. See, for example, Victor Kamber, *Poison Politics: Are Negative Campaigns Destroying Democracy?*; Stephen Ansolabehere and Shanto Iyengar, *Going Negative: How Political Advertisements Shrink and Polarize the Electorate*.

8. Bruce L. Felknor, *Political Mischief: Smear, Sabotage and Reform in U.S. Elections*, 29–44.

9. Gary Jacobson, *Money in Congressional Elections*, 31–32; Stephen E. Gottlieb, "The Dilemma of Election Campaign Finance Reform," 266; Fred Wertheimer and Randy Huwa, "Campaign Finance Reform: Past Accomplishments, Future Challenges," 58, saying that greater use of television advertising increases the electorate's knowledge about candidates and issues, and stimulates interest in the campaign; citing Atkin and Heald, "Effects of Political Advertising," 40 *Public Opinion Quarterly* 40 (1976); Jean Crete, "Television, Advertising, and Canadian Elections in Media and Voters";

John J. Coleman and Paul F. Manna, "Congressional Campaign Spending and the Quality of Democracy."

10. Frank Sorauf, "Politics, Experience and the First Amendment: The Case of American Campaign Finance," 1356; see also Raskin and Bonifaz, "The Constitutional Imperative," 1, 180–82 (arguing that a system funded by large contributions depresses voter turnout because it fails to provide voting alternatives to "poor" people); Edward Foley, "Equal-Dollars-per-Voter: A Constitutional Principle of Campaign Finance," 1,204 ("the electoral system must be wealth neutral in order to be fair"). Compare E. Joshua Rosenkranz, "Faulty Assumptions in 'Faulty Assumptions': A Response to Professor Smith's Critiques of Campaign Finance Reform," 887, where he writes, "I know of no respected reformer who subscribes to this view," but in the next sentence adds, "there are, of course, numerous reform proposals directed at encouraging a broader participation in the political process through small contributions," and later, "these reform proposals are intended to expand the pool of contributors." Rosenkranz concludes by noting that this interest exists separately from concerns about corruption: "There are *also* those who believe that low contributions limits will reduce corruption in government"; emphasis added.

11. Frank Sorauf, *Inside Campaign Finance*, 29–30. This figure has been quite stable for three decades. Ruth S. Jones, "Contributing as Participation," 27.

12. Sorauf, *Inside Campaign Finance*, 4; Michael J. Malbin, "Most GOP Winners Spent Enough Money to Reach Voters," 8, 9. It is interesting to note that despite his reliance on small donations from a large donor base, North was roundly castigated by many campaign finance reformers for the high cost of his campaign.

13. George Thayer, *Who Shakes the Money Tree?*, 54–57.

14. Herbert Alexander, *Financing Politics: Money, Elections, and Political Reform*, 20; Stephanie D. Moussalli, *Campaign Finance Reform: The Case for Deregulation*, 4; Gary C. Jacobson, "The Effects of Campaign Spending in House Elections: New Evidence for Old Arguments," 342–43.

15. Malbin, "Most GOP Winners," 8, 9. See also Political Finance and Lobby Reporter, "Late Money Key to House Races," 3, 5–6; and "Money in House Seat Turnovers," 3, 4; information complied from FEC reports.

16. Philip L. Hersch and Gerald S. McDougall, "Campaign War Chests as a Barrier to Entry in Congressional Races," 630–37, 640, examining U.S. House races in the 1988 election cycle. Hersch and McDougall define (635) a "war chest" as the amount of cash on hand eleven months before the election, a time when challengers must normally decide whether or not to pursue a campaign.

17. See Gary C. Jacobson, "Enough Is Too Much: Money and Competition in House Elections," 179, concluding that $500,000 was needed for a challenger to have a realistic chance of success in a U.S. House campaign in 1986; Larry Sabato, "Real and Imagined Corruption in Campaign Financing," 169,

suggesting that $150,000 was the bare "minimum financial base needed to conduct a modern campaign."

18. Sorauf, *Inside Campaign Finance*, 175–76, 178.
19. Quoted in Wertheimer and Manes, "Campaign Finance Reform," 1,128–29. For more quotes, see Rosenkranz, "Faulty Assumptions," 876–80.
20. Holly Bailey, "Top Gun"; Dan Balz, "Why Consumers Should Care about Campaign Finance Reform."
21. See Thomas F. Burke, "The Concept of Corruption in Campaign Finance Law," 139 n. 45 and cites therein (indicating that "contributions do influence representatives, but less than many suppose"); see also Stephan G. Bronars and John R. Lott, Jr., "Do Campaign Donations Alter How a Politician Votes? Or, Do Donors Support Candidates Who Value the Same Things That They Do?" 346 (concluding that empirical data fail to support the notion that campaign contributions buy politicians' votes).
22. See, for example, Rosenkranz, "Faulty Assumptions," 877.
23. Quoted ibid., 876–77; see ibid., 875–77 for other, similar quotes.
24. U.S. Congress, Senate, Committee on Rules and Administration, *Hearings on Campaign Contribution Limits*, 106th Cong. (March 24, 1999), 6.
25. Bruce Cain, "Moralism and Realism in Campaign Finance Reform," 116.
26. See for example, Sabato, "Real and Imagined Corruption," 160; Moussalli, *Campaign Finance Reform*, 6; Frank Sorauf, *Money in American Elections*, 316.
27. Sanford Levinson, "Electoral Regulation: Some Comments," 412; See, for example, George Zodrow, "Economic Analysis of Capital Gains Taxation: Realizations, Revenues, Efficiency and Equity," 429–30.
28. See, for example, Sorauf, *Inside Campaign Finance*, 166; Sorauf, *Money in American* 307–17; Commin Cause, "National Rifle Association Gives Large Amounts of Soft PAC Money."
29. Daniel H. Lowenstein, *Election Law: Cases and Materials, Teachers Manual*, 116; Max Gates, "FTC Targets Buyer's Guide Violations"; David Hendee, "Defending the Sugar Program."
30. *See* John Stuart Mill, "Considerations on Representative Government," 323, noting that some representatives "feel bound in conscience to let their conduct, on questions on which their constituents have a decided opinion, be the expression of that opinion rather than of their own"; Edmund Burke, "The English Constitutional System," 175, stating that although the opinion of constituents is "weighty and respectable," the notion that a representative is "bound blindly" to obey is "unknown to the law."
31. See *Hearings on Campaign Contribution Limits*, testimony of former senator Dan Coates: 6 "A contribution is by no means necessary to obtain a meeting, and a meeting by no means guarantees results."
32. Common Cause, "Channeling Influence: The Broadcast Lobby and the $70-Billion Free Ride"; Center for Responsive Politics, "Banking Deregulation"; Charles Lewis, *The Buying of the President 2000*; Lewis, *The Buying of the President*.

Chapter 4
The Folly of Reform

1. Michael Malbin, "Most GOP Winners Spent Enough Money to Reach Voters," 9; See "Constitutional Implications of Campaign Finance Reform," 169 (comments of Robert Peck).
2. See George Thayer, *Who Shakes the Money Tree?*, 55; Deposition of Eugene McCarthy, Ex. C at *Buckley v. Valeo*; affirmed in Deposition of Stewart R. Mott, Ex. D at ¶ 11, *Buckley v. Valeo*. See generally Stewart R. Mott, "Independent Fundraising for an Independent Candidate," 138–41.
3. Daniel H. Lowenstein, "A Patternless Mosaic: Campaign Finance and the First Amendment after Austin," 399–401; Stephan E. Gottlieb, "The Dilemma of Election Campaign Finance Reform," 224; Bradley A. Smith, "Money Talks: Speech, Corruption, Equality, and Campaign Finance," 79 n. 233.
4. See, for example, Jeffrey Milyo, *The Electoral Effects of Campaign Spending in House Elections: A Natural Experiment Approach*; Steven Levitt, "Congressional Campaign Finance Reform"; Levitt, "Using Repeat Challengers to Estimate the Effects of Campaign Spending on Election Outcomes in the U.S. House"; Gary C. Jacobson, *The Politics of Congressional Elections* 54, 132; Jacobson, "The Effects of Campaign Spending in House Elections: New Evidence for Old Arguments," 342–43; Jacobson, "Money in the 1980 and 1982 Congressional Elections," 57; Jacobson, "The Effects of Electoral Campaign Spending in Congressional Elections"; Filip Palda, *How Much Is Your Vote Worth?*, 48–50; Alan I. Abramowitz, "Explaining Senate Election Outcomes." But see Donald Green and Jonathan Krasno, "Salvation for the Spendthrift Incumbent: Reestimating the Effects of Campaign Spending in House Elections." The declining marginal utility of money is especially rapid for incumbents—Jacobson finds that incumbent spending matters very little. Jacobson, "Enough Is Too Much: Money and Competition in House Elections," 176: "With the challenger's level of spending (the best measure of the strength of a challenge) controlled, the effect of the incumbent's spending is, in virtually every model or election year, very small and statistically indistinguishable from zero."
5. Jacobson, *Politics of Congressional Elections*, 50, 53; Jacobson, "Money in the 1980 and 1982 Congressional Elections," 62–63, finding that challengers gained approximately 3.5 percentage points for each $100,000 spent, whereas incumbent vote totals actually went down with higher spending.
6. See James C. Miller III, *Monopoly Politics*, 90–91; John R. Lott, Jr., "Explaining Challengers' Campaign Expenditures: The Importance of Sunk Nontransferable Brand Name"; Jacobson, *Politics of Congressional Elections*, 53.
7. See *Political Finance and Lobby Reporter*, "Money in House Seat Turnovers."
8. See *Gable v. Patton*.
9. Mandatory spending ceilings are not allowed under *Buckley*, but voluntary ceilings created by offering public subsidies to candidates who agree to abide by the ceiling are a common feature of many reform proposals. See

Marlene A. Nicholson, "Continuing the Dialogue on Campaign Finance Reform: A Response to Roy Schotland," 473–75; Fred Wertheimer and Susan W. Manes, "Campaign Finance Reform: A Key to Restoring the Health of Our Democracy," 1,149–54. Many of these "voluntary" proposals would be prime candidates to be struck down by the Supreme Court as violating the "unconstitutional conditions" doctrine. Typically, they are so punitive toward candidates who do not opt into the system that voluntary limits are, in effect, mandatory. See, for example, David Mason and Stephan Schwalm, "Advantage Incumbents: Clinton's Campaign Finance Proposal," 9–11; Daniel H. Lowenstein, "On Campaign Finance Reform: The Root of All Evil Is Deeply Rooted," 335.

10. Larry Sabato, "Real and Imagined Corruption in Campaign Financing," 169.

11. Debra Burke, "Twenty Years after the Federal Election Campaign Act Amendments of 1974: Look Who's Running Now," 357, noting that over half of U.S. senators are millionaires. In 1994, Huffington spent approximately $24 million of his own fortune to run for the U.S. Senate. By September 30, 1994, Kohl had contributed almost $4 million to his 1994 reelection effort. Edward Kennedy and Mitt Romney each loaned or contributed $2 million to their campaigns for the U.S. Senate in Massachusetts. *Political Finance and Lobby Reporter*, "Senate Candidates Add $31.5 Million to Their Own Election Campaigns." Physician Bill Frist of Tennessee ($3.75 million) was another big spender. See Edward Roeder, "Big Money Won the Day Last November." On the House side, Republican Gene Fontenot ($2 million) and Democrat Robert Schuster ($1.1 million) provided much of their own campaign financing. Edward Zuckerman, "Money Didn't Matter for Most Challengers Who Won."

12. Martha T. Moore, "Main Goal: Carry Banner of Supply Side Economics"; Alan Elsner, "Running for the White House Will Take Megabucks This Time."

13. The current, heavily regulated system, however, works against many of these potential challengers, especially those who begin with low name recognition. See Bradley A. Smith, "Faulty Assumptions and Undemocratic Consequences of Campaign Finance Reform," 1,072.

14. At the height of the campaign season, a majority of persons of voting age cannot name either major party congressional candidate in their district. See Ilya Somin, "Voter Ignorance and the Democratic Ideal."

15. This has been shown in numerous studies that emphasize the need for political challengers to spend enough to cross a viability threshold. Once across that threshold, they have a legitimate chance of winning; below that threshold, defeat is all but certain. See Bradley A. Smith, "A Most Uncommon Cause: Some Thoughts on Campaign Finance Reform and a Response to Professor Paul," 853 n. 94 and sources cited therein.

16. See Miller, *Monopoly Politics*, 37–38, regarding the similarity of commercial and political markets.

17. See, for example, Gottlieb, "Dilemma of Election Campaign Finance Reform," 221. It is worth noting that this dynamic would exist, albeit to a lesser extent, even at a lower contribution limit, such as $100 or even $50.

18. Clifford W. Brown, Lynda W. Powell, and Clyde Wilcox, *Serious Money: Fundraising and Contributing in Presidential Nomination Campaigns*, 30–31; Herbert Alexander, *Financing Politics: Money, Elections, and Political Reformat*, 74.

19. It may be worthwhile to consider the proposition that PACs have a less corrupting influence on incumbent legislators than those legislators have on PACs. See David A. Strauss, "Corruption, Equality, and Campaign Finance Reform," 1,380–82.

20. Vinceny Blasi, "Free Speech and the Widening Gyre of Fund-Raising: Why Campaign Spending Limits May Not Violate the First Amendment after All."

21. See, "E.T.: Prototypical '80s Celeb"; see also, "Celebrity Hearings: Much Show, Little Go," noting that Meryl Streep and Steven Spielberg both admitted their lack of relevant knowledge during their testimony before congressional committees.

22. David W. Adamany and George E. Agree, *Political Money*, 3.

23. *Austin v. Michigan State Chamber of Commerce.*

24. See Stanley Moister, "Public Found to be More Cynical Than Press," noting that only 5 percent of journalists, versus 39 percent of the public, describe themselves as politically "conservative." For an ex-journalist's view of this power, see Jonathan Rowe, "The View of You from the Hill," 47.

25. Several proposals to limit in-kind contributions have been made. See, for example, Carville B. Collins, "Maryland Campaign Finance Law: A Proposal for Reform," 544–46; Wertheimer and Manes, "Campaign Finance Reform," 1,557–58. For a more theoretical discussion of the administrative problems involved with limiting in-kind contributions, see Edward B. Foley, "Equal-Dollars-Per-Voter: A Constitutional Principle of Campaign Finance," 1,246–49.

26. Looked at from the campaign's point of view, one might argue that the law student's real contribution is only what it would cost the campaign to have someone else to do the same job. The hypothetical remains the same, of course, if the body shop owner's contribution is merely reduced to this amount.

27. See generally, Gottlieb, "The Dilema of Election Campaign Finance Reform," 271–72; see also *The Federalist No. 10* (James Madison).

28. See Mott, "Independent Fundraising," 135.

29. See, for example, "Amicus Brief of American Civil Liberties Union of Ohio Foundation, Inc." at 12–14, *Pestrak v. Ohio Elections Commission*, Nos. 88–3131 and 88–3132.

30. *See* Sara Fritz and Dwight Morris, "Federal Election Panel Not Enforcing Limit on Campaign Donations."

31. Edward Zuckerman, "Speechless in D.C.," The regulation in question was struck down by the D.C. Circuit approximately one year after the 1994 elections. See *United States Chamber of Commerce v. FEC*.

32. Quoted in Nancy Gibbs, "The Wake-up Call," *Time*.

Chapter 5
Government Financing

1. One can argue that we already have a system of government financing that substantially favors incumbents, in the form of franking privileges, free web sites, paid time off to campaign, and so on, so perhaps this suggestion is not so far fetched. See Jamin Raskin and John Bonifaz, "Equal Protection and the Wealth Primary," 289–91, which estimates the political self-subsidy of congressional incumbents to be $200,000 during a two-year period.
2. See Richard Briffault, "Public Funding and Democratic Elections."
3. Bradley A. Smith, "Faulty Assumptions and Undemocratic Consequences of Campaign Finance Reform," 1,082–83.
4. Arguments have been made against even disclosure; see *McIntyre v. Ohio Elections Commission*, upholding the right to engage in anonymous speech on non-candidate-specific political issues; and Amicus Curiae Brief of Gun Owners of America et al. at 25–29, *Nixon v. Shrink Missouri Government PAC*, arguing that forced disclosure of campaign contributions violates the First Amendment.
5. See Federal Election Commission, *Budget Request, for Fiscal Year 2000*, which allocates 2 percent of the budget to campaign fund administration, while over 75 percent goes to enforcement, disclosure, and audits.
6. *Buckley v. Valeo*, 58.
7. *See* FEC Reports, "Top 50 House Receipts," http://www.fec.gov/press/hserec98.htm.
8. Annelise Anderson, *Political Money: The New Prohibition*, 7–8.
9. See, for example, *Gable v. Patton*, 947–49, discussing the extent of the financial pressure Kentucky's campaign finance scheme puts on all candidates to participate.
10. For example, ossified campaign finance laws, along with many other practices, helped to lock in a Democratic majority in the U.S. House in the 1970s and 1980s. See Larry J. Sabato and Glenn R. Simpson, *Dirty Little Secrets: The Persistence of Corruption in American Politics*, 49–57.
11. See Federal Election Commission, *Advisory Opinion 1999-9* at 4–5; and *Advisory Opinion 1999-06*.
12. See Sabato and Simpson, *Dirty Little Secrets*, 50–53.
13. See, for example, Daniel Hays Lowenstein, "On Campaign Finance Reform: The Root of All Evil Is Deeply Rooted," 335–36.
14. See Samuel Issacharoff and Pamela S. Karlan, "The Hydraulics of Campaign Finance Reform," 1705 ("Electoral reform is a graveyard of well-intentioned plans gone awry"); Lowenstein, "On Campaign Finance Reform," 302–3; Cass R. Sunstein, "Political Equality and Unintended Consequences," 1,400–11.
15. Raskin and Bonifaz, "Equal Protection," arguing that financial resources are a decisive factor in elections.
16. See 26 U.S.C. §§ 9004, 9033(b), 9037(1994).
17. See Jacqueline Salit, "Breaking Bread with the Devils of Politics."

18. See 26 U.S.C. § 9004(a) (1994); Elizabeth Rada et al., "Access to the Ballot," 808.
19. See *Clean Money, Clean Elections Act*, S. 982, 106th Cong. § 502 (1999).
20. See Public Campaign, "Clean Money Campaign Reform Annotated Model Legislation: comment to §103 (A)(2)."
21. See ibid.: "It's common knowledge that many people will sign anything but that very few people will contribute even a couple of dollars to a person or project they aren't in favor of."; see also Daniel H. Lowenstein and Robert M. Stern, "The First Amendment and Paid Initiative Petition Circulators: A Dissenting View and a Proposal," 199–200, arguing that factors other than public support determine the success of a petition; and Philip L. Dubois and Floyd F. Feeney, *Improving the California Initiative Process: Options for Change*, 84: "signatures . . . are simply not meaningful gauges of public discontent or even interest."
22. Briffault, "Public Funding."
23. See Daniel Hays Lowenstein, *Election Law: Cases and Materials*, 654–58; Daniel Hays Lowenstein and Richard Hasen, *Election Law Supplement*, 1999–2000, 84; Gary C. Jacobson, *The Electoral Origins of Divided Government: Competition in U.S. House Elections, 1946–1988*, 26–29, reporting that the percentage of marginal incumbents—those winning with less than 60 percent of the two-party vote—declined dramatically from 1974 to 1988.
24. See, for example, Jacobson, *Electoral Origins*, 133.
25. See Norman J. Ornstein et al., *Vital Statistics on Congress, 1997–1998*, 87.
26. Patrick D. Donnay and Graham P. Ramsden, "Public Financing of Legislative Elections: Lessons from Minnesota," 362.
27. Kenneth R. Mayer and John M. Wood, "The Impact of Public Financing on Electoral Competitiveness: Evidence from Wisconsin, 1964–1990," 70, 86.
28. Kenneth R. Mayer, *Public Financing and Electoral Competition in Minnesota and Wisconsin*, 17. Mayer argues that the true measure of competitiveness is less how many incumbents actually lose, than how many are involved in close races (p. 8).
29. See, for example, Alan I. Abramowitz and Jeffrey A. Segal, *Senate Elections*, 139: "dollar for dollar, spending by challengers and open seat candidates should produce a greater electoral return than spending by incumbents"; Gary C. Jacobson, *The Politics of Congressional Elections*, 130–32 which discusses the correlation between a challenger's level of campaign spending and the probability that a voter will report having contact or familiarity with him or her; Jeffrey Milyo, "The Electoral Effects of Campaign Spending in House Elections"; Alan I. Abramowitz, "Explaining Senate Election Outcomes, 397 which concludes that the "challenger's campaign expenditures are the single most important variable affecting an incumbent senator's chances of being reelected."
30. See Mayer, *Public Financing*, 3–4, which describes Minnesota's system as successful, in part because it has higher spending limits and allows for different levels of expenditures in different types of races—including a 10 percent increase in spending for first-time candidates.

31. Ibid., 2, 17–19, noting that Wisconsin's spending limits have remained the same since 1986.
32. Issacharoff and Karlan, "The Hydraulics" 1,735.
33. Lowenstein, "On Campaign Finance Reform," 351.
34. See Alan Greenblatt, "Politics and Marketing Merge in Parties' Bid for Relevance," 1,969, citing 1997 statistics to show that 48 percent of the electorate, a plurality, identified themselves with neither political party.
35. See S. 25, 105th Cong., § 503(d)(1) (1997), setting a spending limit of $5.5 million in Senate races in the largest states; and H.R. 493, 105th Cong., § 502(b)(1)101 (1997), setting a spending limit of $600,000 in House races.
36. See Bradley A. Smith, "Why Campaign Finance Reform Never Works," citing statistics compiled from FEC reports.
37. See Stephen Ansolabehere and James M. Snyder, Jr., "Money and Institutional Power," 1,704, which finds that increases in the presidential campaign limit have failed to match the similar increases for congressional races because the limits are indexed to different economic indicators.
38. See Mayer, *Public Fiancancing*, 2, comparing Wisconsin's campaign spending limits to those of Minnesota, where higher limits and an indexing system have more effectively fostered competition.
39. The Supreme Court's key decisions on the right to engage in "issue advocacy" are *Buckley v. Valeo*, 79–80, and *Federal Election Commission v. Massachusetts Citizens for Life, Inc.*, 253–54. Recent efforts to regulate "issue advocacy" within the constraints of *Buckley* have been uniformly struck down by the courts. See James Bopp, Jr., "Campaign Finance 'Reform': The Good, the Bad, and the Unconstitutional," citing twenty federal cases that have "adhered faithfully to the 'explicit' or 'express' words of the advocacy test according to its plain terms." The Court has never explicitly ruled on efforts to ban soft money but has implicitly indicated that most soft money cannot be regulated in accordance with the Constitution. See Joel M. Gora, "Campaign Finance Reform: Still Searching Today for a Better Way," 161, noting that there is "not a word in *Buckley*" that suggests that the Court would uphold a total ban on PACs and soft money; and Bradley A. Smith, "Soft Money, Hard Realities: The Constitutional Prohibition on a Soft Money Ban," 182–83, noting that the *Buckley* court held that ads which did not urge the election or defeat of a candidate could not be constitutionally subjected to regulation); see also Issacharoff and Karlan, "The Hydraulics," 1,708–17, 1,735–36, discussing both practical reasons and general constitutional principles that make regulation unlikely to succeed.
40. Samuel Issacharoff et al., *The Law of Democracy: Legal Structure of the Political Process*, 660–61.
41. See, for example, Gora, "Campaign Finance Reform," 184–86, where he argues that meaningful public subsidies and funding of candidates and campaigns will facilitate political opportunity and participation.
42. The only significant group of which I am aware that has consistently urged such an approach is the American Civil Liberties Union. See American Civil Liberties Union, *Policy Guide*, 75–77.

Chapter 6
Money and Speech

1. See generally, Norman Redlich, Bernard Schwartz, and John Attanasio, *Constitutional Law*, 977–1,007.
2. See *Brandenburg v. Ohio*, where speech by a Ku Klux Klan leader is protected; *Miami Herald Publishing Comapany v. Tornillo*, saying that the First Amendment protects the editorial discretion of a newspaper; *Abrams v. United States*, Justice Holmes dissenting, on pamphlets and newspapers; *Gregory v. Chicago*, 112; *Edwards v. South Carolina*, on protest marches.
3. See, for example, Steven H. Shiffrin, "The First Amendment and Economic Regulation: Away from a General Theory of the First Amendment"; *Virginia State Board of Pharmacy v. Virginia Consumer Council*, commercial speech; *Roth v. United States*; *Miller v. California*, on pornography; *Chaplinsky v. New Hampshire*, on "fighting words"; *R.A.V. v. St. Paul*, on "hate speech."
4. *Buckley v. Valeo*, The court of appeals upheld all of the FECA except a requirement that nonpartisan, issue commentary be disclosed. Curiously, such "issue advocacy" had, by 2000, become the major target of campaign finance reform advocates in 1997. See, for example, Political Finance and Lobby Reporter, "Rep. Thomas: 'Issue' Ads Should Be Subject to FECA."
5. J. Skelly Wright, "Politics and the Constitution: Is Money Speech?," 1,005; (hereafter "Is Money Speech?"); J. Skelly Wright, "Money and the Pollution of Politics: Is the First Amendment an Obstacle to Political Equality?"; see also Harold Leventhal, "Courts and Political Thickets," 359–60 (arguing that monetary gifts contain a nonspeech element subject to regulation). On the Supreme Court, Justice Stevens has expressed a similar view. *Nixon v. Shrink Missouri Government PAC* (Justice Stevens Concurring).
6. Wright, "Is Money Speech?" 1,005, 1,009–10 (emphasis in original).
7. *West Virginia Board of Education v. Barnette*, ruling that refusal by Jehovah's Witnesses to salute flag was protected speech; *Tinker v. Des Moines Independent Community School District*, holding that wearing of armbands in an antiwar protest was protected; *Stromberg v. California*, on displaying a flag; *Texas v. Johnson*, on symbolic burning of a U.S. flag.
8. Cases cited in note 7, as well as *National Socialist Party of America v. Skokie*, on the right to parade; *Hurley v. Irish-American Gay, Lesbian, and Bisexual Group of Boston*, on the right of parade organizers not to include a gay-lesbian group in a parade.
9. See *Nixon v. Shrink Missouri Government PAC*, Justice Stevens concurring.
10. Wright, "Is Money Speech?," 1,007–8.
11. Ibid., 1,006–8; Marlene A. Nicholson, "Buckley v. Valeo: The Constitutionality of the Federal Election Campaign Act Amendments of 1974, 1977," 334–35.
12. Laurence Tribe, *American Constitutional Law*, 825–32; Lillian R. BeVier, "Money and Politics: A Perspective on the First Amendment and Campaign Finance Reform," 1,056–57; Dean Alfange, Jr., "Free Speech and Symbolic

Conduct: The Draft Card Burning Case"; John Hart Ely, "Flag Desecration: A Case Study in the Roles of Categorization and Balancing in First Amendment Analysis," 1,496; Melville B. Nimmer, "The Meaning of Symbolic Speech under the First Amendment," 33.

13. Note that a person who yelled "fire" in a crowded theater, in the reasonable belief that there was a fire, would not normally be subject to prosecution.
14. Ely, "Flag Desecration," 1,497.
15. *Hurley v. Irish American Gay, Lesbian, and Bisexual Group of Boston*, 562.
16. Tribe, *American Constitutional Law*, 790–92.
17. BeVier, "Money and Politics," 1,058–59.
18. *Buckley v. Valeo*, 259–60, Justice White, dissenting; Tribe, *American Constitutional Law*, 800–801; Wright, "Is Money Speech," 1,009–10.
19. Tribe, *American Constitutional Law*, 790.
20. Wright, "Is Money Speech?," 1,009. Wright is not alone in this view. See also, for example, Donna A. Farber, "Content Regulation and the First Amendment: A Revisionist View"; Geoffrey R. Stone, "Restrictions of Speech Because of Its Content: The Peculiar Case of Subject-Matter Restrictions," 108.
21. See, for example, Tribe, *American Constitutional Law*, 791.
22. Wright, "Is Money Speech?," 1,008.
23. Ibid.
24. See Daniel H. Lowenstein, "A Patternless Mosaic: Campaign Finance and the First Amendment after Austin," 399.
25. *Buckley v. Valeo*, 19.
26. Wright, "Is Money Speech?," 1,008.
27. *Consolidated Edison Company v. Public Service Commission*, See Tribe, *American Constitutional Law*, 814–21.
28. Wright, "Is Money Speech?," 1,009.
29. BeVier, "Money and Politics," 1,061; Sanford Levinson, "Regulating Campaign Activity: The New Road to Contradiction," 945: "It is worth considering to what extent we in fact support such restrictions because of tacit assumptions about the contents of the views held by the rich." Daniel H. Lowenstein, "On Campaign Finance Reform: The Root of All Evil Is Deeply Rooted," 312.
30. Lowenstein, "Patternless Mosaic," 392; Nicholson, "Buckley v. Valeo," 471.
31. Michael Rezendes, "PAC for Women Faces a Crisis: Emily's List May Lose Fund-raising Tools if Campaign Finance Rules Change"; Francis Wilkinson, "Wrong Fix for Broken Campaign Finance System"; Ruth Marcus, "Trial Lawyers Group Plans Aggressive Political Action; FEC Asked to Allow Endorsement-Donation Setup."
32. Wright, "Money and the Pollution of Politics," 618–19 and n. 63. In Wright's 1976 article, he cites the inability of Congress to pass gun control as another example in which money "thwarted" the will of the majority. Wright, "Is Money Speech?," 1,017.
33. Public Campaign, "Ouch! How Money in Politics Hurts You"; Ann McBride, "Where Soft Money Hits Taxpayers Hard."
34. *Buckley v. Valeo*, 16.

Chapter 7
Money and Corruption

1. *Buckley v. Valeo*, 23–38, upholding contribution restrictions on anticorruption rationale; Ibid., 45–48, rejecting anticorruption rationale as sufficient to uphold expenditure limitations.
2. Fred Wertheimer and Susan W. Manes, "Campaign Finance Reform: A Key to Restoring the Health of Our Democracy," 1,128–30; *Buckley v. Valeo*, 26; Daniel H. Lowenstein, "On Campaign Finance Reform: The Root of All Evil Is Deeply Rooted," 308–9.
3. *Buckley v. Valeo*, 26–27.
4. Ibid., 47, striking down limits on independent expenditures in support of a candidate; ibid., 53, striking down limits on spending from a candidate's personal or family resources; ibid., 55, striking down overall spending limits.
5. Ibid., 20–21; 35, 38.
6. See, for example, *California Medical Association v. Federal Election Commission*; cf. Archibald Cox, "Freedom of Expression in the Burger Court," 62–63.
7. L. A. Powe, "Mass Speech and the Newer First Amendment," 259.
8. See *National Association for the Advancement of Colored People v. Alabama*, 460, and cases cited therein.
9. See, for example, *Federal Election Commission v. National Conservative Political Action Committee*, 494.
10. Quoted in Martin Schram, *Speaking Freely*, 89, 16.
11. Quoted in Wertheimer and Manes "Campaign Finance Reform," 1,128–29.
12. *CNN Larry King Live*, Transcript #99062800V22, June 28, 1999.
13. *Testimony of Dan Coates*, U.S. Congress, Senate, Committee on Rules and Administration.
14. Quoted in Carolyn Skorneck, "Senators Hear Veteran Pols Oppose Limits."
15. Gary C. Jacobson, "Campaign Finance and Democratic Control: Comments on Gottlieb and Lowenstein's Papers," 377; Stephen G. Bronars and John R. Lott, Jr., "Do Campaign Donations Alter How a Politician Votes?" 317; Stephanie D. Moussalli, *Campaign Finance Reform: The Case for Deregulation* 4, 6; Frank Sorauf, *Money in American Elections*, 316; Janet Grenzke, "PAC's and the Congressional Supermarket: The Currency is Complex," 1; Larry Sabato, "Real and Imagined Corruption in Campaign Financing," 159–62; John R. Wright, "PACs, Contributions, Roll Calls: An Organizational Perspective," 411: "The ability of PACs to use their campaign contributions to influence congressional voting is severely constrained. . . . Of the numerous variables that influence the voting behavior of congressmen, the campaign contributions of PACs appear to take effect infrequently." But cf. Richard Hall and Frank Wayman, "Buying Time: Moneyed Interests and the Mobilization of Bias in Congressional Committees," 810: "If money does not necessarily buy votes or change minds . . . it can buy members time."
16. See Moussalli, *Campaign Finance Reform*; Sorauf, *Inside Campaign Finance*; Grenzke, "PAC's and the Congressional Supermarket"; Sabato, "Real and Imagine Corruption"; W. P. Welch, "Campaign Contributions and Legislative

Voting: Milk Money and Dairy Price Supports," 479: "the influence of contributions is 'small,' at least relative to the influences of constituency, party and ideology."

17. See Daniel Ortiz, "The Democratic Paradox of Campaign Finance Reform," 899: "candidates [might] become so beholden to contributors that they follow the contributors' rather than the voters' interests. Everyone, including the Supreme Court, agrees that this is a serious danger. The pivotal questions concern how great a danger it actually presents."

18. Lowenstein, "On Campaign Finance Reform," 325–26; Paul Douglas, *Ethics in Government*, 44.

19. E. Joshua Rosenkranz, "Faulty Assumptions in 'Faulty Assumptions': A Response to Professor Smith's Critiques of Campaign Finance Reform," 894–95.

20. See, for exapmle, Lowenstein, "On Campaign Finance Reform," 328–29, describing campaign contributions as "payments of money to the official for the official's benefit" and concluding that this is the "paradigm case for improper influence."

21. Ibid., 329.

22. See, for example, U.S. Congress, Senate Committee on Governmental Affairs, *Investigation of Illegal or Improper Activities in Connection with the 1996 Federal Election Campaign—Part VIII: Hearings*, statement of Curtis Gans, Director, Center for the Study of the American Electorate, discussing public disinterest in campaign finance "scandals" and concluding that "the American people understand that it takes money to run political campaigns and that, in the absence of total public financing of such campaigns, candidates are going to, and should, solicit funds for those campaigns." See also, Bradley A. Smith, "A Most Uncommon Cause: Some Thoughts on Campaign Finance Reform and a Response to Professor Paul," 833–36, noting that public opinion polls reveal the public's ambivalence on the issue of campaign finance reform; Tarrance Group, "Key Findings from a Nationwide Survey of Voter Attitudes about Campaign Finance Reform" (visited October 18, 1999), finding that 78 percent of respondents oppose tax funding of campaigns.

23. See, for example, Lowenstein, "On Campaign Finance Reform," 329. See generally Daniel H. Lowenstein, "Political Bribery and the Intermediate Theory of Politics," 808–9, 826–28, opining that most campaign contributions constitute bribes.

24. Lowenstein, "On Campaign Finance Reform," 329.

25. *Buckley v. Valeo*, 25–28, citation omitted.

26. See Laurence H. Tribe, *American Constitutional Law*, 834.

27. See, for example, *Jenkins v. Georgia*, holding for independent review as to whether a film was obscene; *Bose Corporation v. Consumers Union*, requiring independent redetermination in libel action.

28. *Landmark Communications, Inc. v. Virginia*, 840–41.

29. *Buckley v. Valeo*, 246, Chief Justice Burger concurring.

30. See, for example, *Whitney v. California*, Chief Justice Brandeis concurring; *Fiske v. Kansas*; *Stromberg v. California*; *Terminiello v. Chicago*; *Cox v. Louisiana*; *Williams v. Rhodes*; *Street v. New York*; *Tinker v. Des Moines School District*; *Brandenberg v. Ohio*; *Broadrick v. Oklahoma*; *Linmark Associates, Inc. v. Township of Willingboro*; *National Socialist Party of America v. Skokie*; *National Bank of Boston v. Bellotti*; *Village of Schaumberg v. Citizens for a Better Environment*; *Consolidated Edison Company v. Public Service Commission*; *Maryland v. Munson*; *Texas v. Johnson*.

   For a general discussion, see Lillian R. BeVier, "Money and Politics: A Perspective on the First Amendment and Campaign Finance Reform," 1,084–90 (1985); See also, Tribe, *American Constitutional Law*, 789–804.

31. 424 U.S., 245–46 (Chief Justice Burger dissenting); Larry J. Sabato and Glenn R. Simpson, Dirty Little Secrets: The Persistence of Corruption in American Politics, 330–35.

32. *Buckley v. Valeo*, 12–60; *Federal Elections Commission v. National Conservative Political Action Committee*; *Federal Elections Commission v. Massachusetts Citizens for Life*; *Austin v. Michigan Chamber of Commerce*; *First National Bank of Boston v. Bellotti*. The distinctions outlined in the above notes are discussed in Bradley A. Smith, "Congress Shall Make No Law . . ."; and in Daniel Hays Lowenstein, "A Patternless Mosaic: Campaign Finance and the First Amendment After Austin," 382–83.

33. Frank J. Sorauf, *Inside Campaign Finance*, 25.

34. Ibid., 148; Wertheimer and Manes, "Campaign Finance Reform," 1,140–41 (on bundling), 1,144–48, 1,156–57.

Chapter 8
Money and Equality

1. *Buckley v. Valeo*, 48–49.

2. Cass R. Sunstein, "Political Equality and Unintended Consequences"; Sunstein, "Words, Conduct, Caste"; Sunstein, *The Partial Constitution*; Sunstein, "Free Speech Now"; Owen M. Fiss, "Why the State?"; Fiss, "Free Speech and Social Structure"; Fiss, "Emerging Media Technology and the First Amendment: In Search of a New Paradigm"; Fiss, "State Activism and State Censorship"; Burt Neuborne, "Toward a Democracy-Centered Reading of the First Amendment"; Neuborne, "Is Money Different?"; Neuborne, "The Supreme Court and Free Speech: Love and a Question"; See also Ronald Dworkin, "The Curse of American Politics," 19; and Dworkin, *Freedom's Law: The Moral Reading of the American Constitution*, 1–31.

3. Richard L. Hasen, "Clipping Coupons for Democracy: An Egalitarian/Public Choice Defense of Campaign Finance Vouchers," 30; Edward Foley, "Equal-Dollars-per-Voter: A Constitutional Principle of Compaign Finance," 1,215–18; Jamin Raskin and Jon Bonifaz, "The Constitutional Imperative and Practical Superiority of Democratically Financed Elections"; Raskin and Bonifaz, "Equal Protection and the Wealth Primary" (hereafter "Wealth Primary"), 278–79.

4. See, for example, Sunstein, "Free Speech Now," 263; Fiss, "Why the State?" 786. Others to argue along similar lines include Dworkin, *Freedom's Law* 1–31; Frederick Schauer, "The Political Incidence of the Free Speech Principle"; and Morton Horowitz, "The Constitution of Change: Legal Fundamentality without Fundamentalism"; see, for example, Sunstein, "Free Speech Now," 267; and Fiss, "Free Speech and Social Structure," 1,414.

5. See, for example, Pruneyard Shopping Center v. Robins; *Hudgens v. National Labor Relative Board*; *Miami Herald Publishing Company v. Tornillo*.

6. See, for example, Foley, "*Equal-Dollars*," 1,227–28; Fiss, "Free Speech and Social Structure," 1,417.

7. See for example, Sunstein, "Free Speech Now," 285–289; Fiss, "State Activism," 2,101, 2,104. Sunstein parts company with Fiss on the latter question. Sunstein also makes clear that the First Amendment, although not limited to political discourse, is most concerned with political speech. Sunstein, *Partial Constitution*, 236–39; cf. Fiss, "Free Speech," 1,423.

8. See *New York Times Company v. Sullivan*, 270; Owen M. Fiss, *The Irony of Free Speech*, 22.

9. Charles Fried, "The New First Amendment Jurisprudence: A Threat to Liberty," 226–27.

10. Ibid., 228.

11. See *Adarand Constructors, Inc. v. Pena*; *City of Richmond v. J. A. Croson Company*.

12. Sunstein, *Partial Constitution*, 209.

13. See, for example, *Johnson v. Federal Communications Commission*, holding that there is no private party right of access to a political debate sponsored by a private party; *Chandler v. Georgia Public Telecommunications Commission*, holding that there is no right of access to broadcast debate; *Kennedy for President Commission v. Federal Communications Commission*, 430–31, holding that a candidate had no "constitutional right of broadcast access to air his views."

14. Sunstein, *Partial Constitution*, 85.

15. See, for example, Robert Nozick, *Anarchy, State and Utopia*. At least one scholar has recently argued that a Nozickian concept of property rights is part of the "innate pre-political aspects of human nature," such that even absent a theory of rights such as that laid out by Nozick, property are "pre-political." John O. McGinnis, "The Original Constitution and Our Origins," 260. My own experience with my young children strongly indicates to me that children have a prepolitical sense of property rights.

16. James D. Gwartney, Richard L. Stroup, and Russell S. Sobel, *Economics: Private and Public Choice*, 722; see also Bruce Bartlett, "A Class Structure That Just Won't Stay Put."

17. Laurence H. Tribe and Michael C. Dorf, *On Reading the Constitution*, 11.

18. Neuborne, "Toward a Democracy-Centered Reading, 1,059.

19. Ibid., 1,071.

20. Neuborne, "The Supreme Court and Free Speech," 809; Neuborne, "Toward a Democracy-Centered Reading," 1,957 n. 13.

21. Neuborne, "Toward a Democracy-Centered Reading," 1,058–59.
22. Ibid., 1,070–71.
23. Ibid., 1,071.
24. J. Skelly Wright, "Politics and the Constitution: Is Money Speech?" 1017; Wright, "Money and the Polution of Politics: Is the First Amendment an Obstacle to Political Equality?" 618–19; Raskin and Bonifaz, "Constitutional Imperative," 1,182–83; See, for example, Foley, "Equal-Dollars-per-Voter," 1,204; Hasen, "Clipping Coupons," 4, 16, 30; Neuborne, "Is Money Different?" 1,612. Fiss, "Why the State?" 790–94.
25. See, for example, Thomas Sowell, "Lack of Knowledge Contributes to the Poor Staying Poor"; Sowell, *The Vision of the Annointed: Self-Congratulation as a Basis for Social Policy*; for a typical view statement of these views, see Mary Ellen Hombs and Mitch Snyder, Homelessness in America: A Forced March to Nowhere.
26. See Fiss, "Why the State?" 791–92.
27. Fiss, "Free Speech," 1,408–10.
28. See, for example, Fried, "The New First Amendment," 252.
29. See John O. McGinnis, "The Once and Future Property-Based Vision of the First Amendment," 122–23.
30. Ibid., 124.
31. Stephen Gottlieb, "The Dilemma of Election Campaign Finance Reform," 216–21; Thomas Gais, *Improper Influence: Campaign Finance Law, Political Interest Groups, and the Problem of Equality*, 173.
32. A copy of the ad is reproduced at 494 U.S. at 714.
33. Dan Balz and Bill McAllister, "The Race for President"; Bernard Goldberg, "Networks Need a Reality Check"; Glen Frankel, "Forbes's Optimism Is Selling: Publishing Heir Prepares for N.Y. Battle with Senate Leader." Because he was spending his own money, Forbes was not subject to federal spending limits. Ruth Marcus and Walter Pincus, "Forbes Spent $18 Million on Race Last Year."
34. See, for example, Gais, *Improper Influence*, 181–82.
35. 424 U.S. at 48–49.
36. This approach was pioneered in the early 1970s in articles by Marlene A. Nicholson, "Campaign Financing and Equal Protection," and Joel Fleishman, "Public Financing of Election Campaigns: Constitutional Constraints on Steps toward Equality of Political Influence of Citizens." However, it is curiously absent from most campaign finance reform literature until resurrected forcefully by Jamin Raskin and Jon Bonifaz in "Equal Protection and the Wealth Primary"; see also Hasen, "Clipping Coupons"; Foley, "Equal Dollars-per-Voter"; Marty Jezer and Ellen Miller, "Money Politics: Campaign Finance and the Subversion of American Democracy"; Marty Jezer, Randy Kehler, and Ben Santuria, "A Proposal for Democratically Financed Elections."
37. See, for example, Hasen, "Clipping Coupons," 6; Foley, Equal-Dollars-per-Voter," 331; Raskin and Bonifaz, "Constitutional Imperative," 1,190. Though Raskin and Bonifaz stop short of the outright abolition of private

contributions, they would effectively end private campaign finance through a de facto ban on any contribution in excess of $5.

38. Hasen, "Clipping Coupons," 21, 23–24. Hasen's proposal includes a formula that would encourage voters to spread their vouchers around to several groups rather than giving to one or two candidates or groups; A similar proposal has been made by Bruce Ackerman, "Crediting the Voters: A New Beginning for Campaign Finance."

39. See, for example, Hasen, "Clipping Coupons," 22; Richard L. Hasen, "Campaign Finance Laws and the Rupert Murdoch Problem."

40. See, for example, Foley, "Equal-Dollars-per-Voter," 1,253.

41. Ronald M. Dworkin and Burt Neuborne, "Statement in Support of Overturning Buckley v. Valeo."

42. Raskin and Bonifaz, "Constitutional Imperative," 1,189–1,201. A more detailed description of the plan can be found in Jezer, Kehler, and Santuria, "Proposal."

43. Raskin and Bonifaz, "Wealth Primary," 306 n. 180, 290–91.

44. Ibid., 280, 306–12.

45. Ibid., 307–9.

46. See also *Nixon v. Condon*, striking down a state law that gave the party the right to determine who was qualified to vote.

47. *Terry v. Adams*, 470–72 (Justice Frankfurter concurring).

48. Raskin and Bonifaz, "Wealth Primary," 309, citing each proposition, respectively, to *Terry v. Adams*, at 469 (in which Justice Black, for the Court, argued that the state abused the Fifteenth Amendment right of due process by allowing its electoral machinery to ratify the racially exclusionary duplication of its election that constituted the Jaybird Association primary); 481 (Justice Clark concurring); and at 473 (Justice Frankfurter concurring). This idea is not entirely new with Raskin and Bonifaz. Twenty years ago, Marlene Nicholson similarly argued that for purposes of mandating campaign finance reform through judicial fiat, state action could be found in that "campaign financing. . . can be viewed as a very significant part of the 'machinery' for choosing officials." Nicholson, "Campaign Financing," 831.

49. U.S. Bureau of the Census, *A Report of the Seventeenth Decennial Census of the United States: Census of Population 1950*, V.I "Characteristics of the Population Part 43, Texas."

50. *Terry v. Adams*, 494 (Justice Minton dissenting). See, for example, John C. Kester, "Constitutional Restrictions on Political Parties," 738, saying Terry "went too far." Cf. Daniel Hays Lowenstein, "Associational Rights of Major Political Parties: A Skeptical Inquiry," 1748–52, discussing the problematic aspects of the white primary cases for both prior and later jurisprudence; noting that overruling them would be harmonic with later cases on party rights; suggesting that the cases really had little practical effect, and that their overruling would be unlikely to have any detrimental consequences on voting rights; and suggesting that the public/private distinction at issue in the white primary cases is not helpful when discussing the regulation of political parties.

51. Raskin and Bonifaz, "Wealth Primary," 309–10 (citing *Terry*, 345 U.S. 473–74); ibid., 273.

52. *Terry v. Adams*, 476 (emphasis added).
53. *Rendell Baker v. Kohn*; *San Francisco Arts and Athletics, Inc. v. United States Olympic Committee*.
54. Raskin and Bonifaz, "Wealth Primary," 307.
55. Laurence H. Tribe, *American Constitutional Law*, 1,451.
56. *San Antonio Independent School District v. Rodriguez*. See generally, Tribe, *American Constitutional Law*, 1,465.
57. Raskin and Bonifaz, "Wealth Primary," 281, (citing *Harper v. Board of Election*); Raskin and Bonifaz, "Constitutional Imperative," 1,162 n. 4 (citing *Reynolds v. Sims*).
58. Raskin and Bonifaz, "Wealth Primary," 279–80, 297–98.
59. Ibid., 288.
60. See, for example, ibid., 275 n. 12, discussing inadequate spending for federal poverty programs and unequal income distribution; 301 discussing inequality of wealth and income; Raskin and Bonifaz, "Constitutional Imperative," 1,163–64, dismantling the regime of plutocracy; 1,179–80, citing "the dominance of wealthy interests in the political process"; 1,180 n. 69; 1,185, citing the need for more government action on "health care, environmental degradation, urban poverty" and raising the minimum wage; and 1,203: "The time has come to abolish the tyranny of private wealth."
61. Fried, "New First Amendment," 252.
62. Raskin and Bonifaz, "Wealth Primary," 280, 282–83.
63. *Bullock v. Carter*, 144.
64. *Lubin v. Parish*, 715, 718–19.
65. See, for example, Tribe, *American Constitutional Law*, 1,662.
66. See Bradley A. Smith, "Judicial Protection of Ballot Access Rights," 201 n. 172.
67. Both men are quoted in Stuart Taylor, "The President's Least Favorite Nominee."

Chapter 9
Unfree Speech

1. See Robert J. Dinkin, *Campaigning in America*, 40; Herbert E. Alexander, *Financing Politics: Money, Elections, and Political Reform*, 78: "the exact costs of . . . early forays into personal campaigning . . . are not known"); George Thayer, *Who Shakes the Money Tree?* 31–32.
2. See, for example, Thayer, *Who Shakes the Money Tree?* 28. See also Chilton Williamson, *American Suffrage: From Property to Democracy 1760–1860*.
3. See Chandler Davidson, "The Voting Rights Act: A Brief History," 21.
4. *Guinn v. United States*, on grandfather clauses; *Nixon v. Herndon*, striking down state statute limiting primary election to whites; *Smith v. Allwright*, striking down internal party rule limiting primary to white voters; *Carrington v. Rash*, ruling against bans on military voting; *Harper v. Virginia Board of Elections*, on poll taxes; and *Dunn v. Blumstein*, on residency requirements.

5. See Filip Palda, *How Much Is Your Vote Worth?*, 9–10 (data from 1972–1992); 1998 FEC Reports, available at http://www.fec.gov. Overall, congressional candidates spent $740.4 million in the 1998 campaigns, a decline of about 3 percent in spending.

6. David B. Magleby and Candice J. Nelson, *The Money Chase: Congressional Campaign Finance Reform*, 43; Karl-Heinz Nassmacher, "Comparing Party and Campaign Finance in Western Democracies," 245.

7. Dinkin, *Campaiging in America* 49–53, 95–198; Alexander *Financing Politics*, 78. This trend had begun in the elections of 1828, 1832, and 1836. See Nathan Miller, *Stealing from America: A History of Corruption from Jamestown to Reagan*, 116–17.

8. Louise Overacker, *Money in Elections*, 28.

9. Dinkin, *Camapaigning in America*, 167.

10. Magleby and Nelson, *The Money Chase*, 62. See, for example, Alexander, *Financing Politics*, 85.

11. Herbert E. Alexander and Anthony Corrado, *Financing the 1992 Election*, 127. The parties were each given $55.2 million in public funding to finance the general election. Compliance funds may be raised separately from that amount. It has been argued that these funds are used for regular campaign activity, not mere compliance. Ibid., 126–27, noting postelection complaints filed with the Federal Elections Commission by the Center for Responsive Politics. The $11 million figure does not include substantial compliance costs by defeated presidential primary candidates, nor, of course, for thousands of other federal, state, and local offices that are subject to various campaign finance laws. See generally Palda, *How Much Is Your Vote Worth?*, 20–23.

12. Robert J. Samuelson, "The Price of Politics."

13. See, for example, Magleby and Nelson, *The Money Chase*, 40–41; Alexander and Corrado, *Financing the 1992 Elections*, 3–4; Bradley A. Smith, "Faulty Assumptions and Undemocratic Consequences of Campaign Finance Reform," 1,059–60.

14. Palda, *How Much Is Your Vote Worth?*, 96, noting that political spending has risen at roughly the same rate as government expenditures.

15. Filip Palda, "The Determinates of Campaign Spending: The Role of the Government Jackpot."

16. John R. Lott, Jr., "A Simple Explanation for Why Campaign Expenditures Are Increasing: The Government Is Getting Bigger." During the period studied, per-capita federal budget expenditures rose from $4,219 to $5,320, after adjusting for inflation.

17. See Richard Epstein, "Property, Speech, and the Politics of Distrust," 56; Lillian R. BeVier, "Campaign Finance Reform: Specious Arguments, Intractable Dilemmas," 1,258, 1,265–66.

18. See *Nixon v. Shrink Missouri Government PAC*, 914, Justice Kennedy, concurring.

19. Disclosure is not without its problems. It can also have a chilling effect on speech; see *McIntyre v. Ohio Elections Commission*; *Brown v. Socialist Workers '74 Campaign Committee*; and National Association for the Advancement

of *Colored People v. Alabama*. It also smothers speech by subjecting small players to heavy regulation. For that reason, some have suggested that disclosure levels should be set at a relatively high level. Larry J. Sabato and Glenn R. Simpson, *Dirty Little Secrets: The Persistence of Corruption in American Politics*, 332.

20. See, for example, Jamin Raskin and Jon Bonifaz, "Equal Protection and the Wealth Primary," 275 n. 12, 301; Raskin and Bonifaz, "The Constitutional Imperative and Practical Superiority of Democratically Financed Elections," 1,163–64, 1,179–80, 1,185, 1,203. Most of the campaign finance "reform" lobbying groups are generally identified with the political left, including Common Cause. Groups such as U.S. Pirg and Citizen Action, in particular, have consistently called for a greater government role in the economic and substantial increases in government spending and taxation. A most notable exception is the American Civil Liberties Union, which, though generally identified with the political left, has fought long and hard against heavy political regulation.

21. See S. 25, Sec. 101(e); H.R. 493, Sec. 101(f) (1st Sess., 105th Cong.). S. 25, Sec. 105; and eight times larger in the House version, H.R. 493, Sec. 104 and Sec. 202. Section 202 of H.R. 493 limits the percentage of contributions that can exceed $250 to just 25 percent of the total "voluntary" spending limit. There is no exception for a noncomplying candidate. Thus a candidate who spends over the limit is restricted to receiving $250 contributions, whereas a complying candidate, in addition to having the spending limit raised, may accept contributions up to $2,000 without limit.

22. See, for example, Alan I. Abramowitz, "Explaining Senate Election Outcomes"; Gary C. Jacobson, "The Effects of Campaign Spending in House Elections: New Evidence for Old Arguments"; Palda, *How Much Is your Vote Worth?*, 48–50; Steven D. Levitt, "Congressional Campaign Finance Reform," 9; Levitt, "Using Repeat Challengers to Estimate the Effect of Campaign Spending on Election Outcomes in the U.S. House"; Jeffrey Milyo, *The Electoral Effects of Campaign Spending in House Elections: A Natural Experiment Approach*.

23. See S. 25, Sec. 201, 105th Congress.

24. See H.R. 493, Sec. 101; S. 25, Sec. 101(e) (105th Cong., 1st. Sess).

25. H.R. 493, Sec. 202, would limit most contributions to just $250. See also *Carver v. Nixon*, striking down $300 Missouri state limit on contributions; *Day v. Holahan*, striking down $100 state limit on contributions; *National Black Police Association v. District of Columbia Board of Elections*, striking down $200 District limit.

26. Smith, "Faulty Assumptions," 1,072–73, 1,075–76; Thomas Gais, *Improper Influence*, 173–74; See, for example, Vincent Blasi, "Free Speech and the Widening Gyre of Fund-Raising: Why Campaign Spending Limits May Not Violate the Constitution after All."

27. Lisa Rosenberg, *A Bag of Tricks: Loopholes in the Campaign Finance System*, 7–8.

28. See Robert Dreyfuss, "Harder Than Soft Money", 30, 32–34; Deborah Beck, Paul Taylor, Jeffrey Stranger, and Douglas Rivlin, "Issue Advocacy Advertising During the 1996 Campaign."

29. A quick Lexis search turned up hundreds of such references. See, for example, Jerome Kuhnhenn, "Congress Refocuses on Fund-Raising in Kansas Races as House Republicans Look at National, State Democratic Panels," on "so-called issue ads"; San Antonio Express-News, "Disguised Attack Ads Used by Both Parties," "sham issue ads"; Russell Feingold, "Letter to the Editor: Get Campaign Finance Reform Facts," 17 on "phony issue ads"; *U.S. Congress, House, Committee on the Judiciary, Subcommittee on the Constitution, Hearing on Issue Advocacy, statement of Don Simon on "campaign ads masquerading as issue ads."*

30. *Buckley v. Valeo*, 39–40, 46.

31. Ibid., 41.

32. Ibid., 43, quoting *Thomas v. Collins*.

33. Ibid., 43–44 and 52; Justice White dissented from the Court's holding that struck down section 608(e)'s limit on independent expenditures; ibid., 259 (opinion of Justice White, concurring in part and dissenting in part). White does not, however, address that portion of the Court's opinion that interprets 608(e) as applying, in any case, only to "express advocacy," and instead focuses solely on whether Congress can limit expenditures generally. All of his discussion seems to focus on ads expressly supporting a candidate, and is not inconsistent with the majority's holding on the issue advocacy question; ibid., 259–65. It is interesting to note that this portion of White's opinion, in which he would have upheld expenditure limits, fails to cite a single case in support of his position. This observation was brought to my attention by Alan Morrison, "Watch What You Wish For: The Perils of Reversing Buckley v. Valeo," 38, 41.

34. See, for example, *Monitor Patriot Company v. Roy*: "It can hardly be doubted that the constitutional guarantee has its fullest and most urgent application precisely to campaigns for political office"; *Mills v. Alabama*: "There is practically universal agreement that a major purpose of [the First] Amendment was to protect the free discussion of governmental affairs." Though many have suggested that the First Amendment has other purposes (see, for example, Laurence H. Tribe, *American Constitutional Law*, 785–89 and sources therein cited), I know of no one arguing that political discussion is not protected by the First Amendment.

35. *Buckley v. Valeo*, 42.

36. Ibid., 45.

37. See *Federal Election Commission v. Massachusetts Citizens for Life, Inc.*; *Maine Right to Life Committee v. Federal Election Commission*; *Federal Election Commission v. Christian Action Network, Inc.*; *Faucher v. Federal Election Commission*; *Federal Election Commission v. Central Long Island Tax Reform Immediately Committee*; *Federal Election Commission v. Colorado Republican Federal Campaign Committee*; *Federal Election Commission v. Survival Education Fund*; *Federal Election Commission v. National Organi-*

zation For Women; Federal Election Commission v. American Federation of State, County and Muncipal Employees.

See also Federal Election Commission v. National Conservative Political Action Committee, 497, which held that the First Amendment prohibits limits on independent expenditures that expressly advocate the election or defeat of a candidate, and noting in dicta "the fact that candidates and elected officials may alter or reaffirm their own positions on issues in response to political messages . . . can hardly be called corruption, for one of the essential features of democracy is the presentation to the electorate of varying points of view"; Clifton v. Federal Election Commission, which held that the Federal Election Commission's efforts to regulate "issue advocacy" as "contributions" exceeded its powers under FECA, and stated, "we do not take Congress to have authorized rules that sacrifice First Amendment interests"; Federal Election Commission v. GOPAC, Inc., 858–62, which held that where a group's "ultimate major purpose was to influence the election of Republican candidates for the House of Representatives," but the group did not support candidates for federal office with direct contributions or advocacy, application of FECA regulations to the group would be contrary to Buckley's holding on issue advocacy.

Even Federal Election Commission v. Furgatch, a case often cited by proponents of greater regulation, supports Buckley's narrow definition of express advocacy.

And it is worth noting that even before Buckley was decided, the Second Circuit had held that issue advocacy could not be made subject to campaign finance disclosure requirements passed as part of Federal Election Commission in 1971. United States v. National Committee for Impeachment.

38. H.R. 493, Sec. 251(b).
39. Elections Board v. Wisconsin Manufacturers and Commerce.
40. Alexander and Corrado, Financing the 1992 Elections, 111–13; 147–48; See for example, Rosenberg, A Bag of Tricks, 3–6.
41. Colorado Republican Federal Campaign Committee v. Federal Election Commission, 2,316. See Eu v. San Francisco City Democratic Central Committee, striking down a state law that prohibited party officials from making primary endorsements; Geary v. Renne, striking down a state law that banned party endorsements in nonpartisan races, See also Tashjian v. Republican Party of Connecticut, upholding a party's right to hold an open primary in violation of state law; Democratic Party of the United States v. La Follette, upholding the right of a political party to seat delegates at its convention when seating those delegates would violate state law because the delegates had not pledged to support the winner of the state primary; Duke v. Massey, holding that a political party has a right to define its membership and views by excluding a candidate from primary ballot.
42. See Richard Briffault, "Campaign Finance, the Parties, and the Court: A Comment on Colorado Republican Federal Campaign Committee v. Federal Elections Commission," 114–16.

43. Ronald Dworkin and Burt Neuborne, Letter to John McCain and Russell Feingold, September 22, 1997. Lexis and Westlaw searches reveal that from its founding in 1995 through March of 2000, when this was written, the Brennan Center had been on losing side in seven of nine reported campaign finance cases in which it had participated as counsel for the parties or amicus parties, which reached final judgment.

44. Ibid., 3, referring to *Austin v. Michigan State Chamber of Commerce*, 657–61.

45. *Austin*, 714 (appendix to opinion of Justice Kennedy dissenting), which reprints the advertisement in question.

46. *First National Bank of Boston v. Bellotti*, 777, 790.

47. *Citizens against Rent Control v. City of Berkeley*, 299. See also *C and C Plywood Corporation v. Henson*, striking down a statute that prohibited corporate contributions to a group that supported or opposed ballot measures, on First Amendment grounds.

48. Both are quoted in Stuart Taylor, "The President's Least Favorite Nominee."

49. See Rasmussen Research, "Seventy Percent Want Spending Limits: Most Want More Limits on Incumbents" by a 56 percent to 25 percent margin, voters oppose "public funding" of congressional campaigns); Ed Goeas and William Stewart, "Key Findings from a Nationwide Survey of Voter Attitudes about Campaign Finance Reform" (by 78 percent to 17 percent margin, voters oppose "taxpayer-financed" campaigns).

50. Eric Pianin and Juliet Eilperin, "Applying Brakes to Gas Tax Cut: House GOP Leaders Doubt Its Effectiveness," quoting Representative Bud Shuster.

51. Clifford Brown, Lynda W. Powell, and Clyde Wilcox, *Serious Money: Fundraising and Contributing in Presidential Nominating Campaigns*, 23–24.

52. See Edward B. Foley, "Equal-Dollars-per-Voter: A Constitutional Principle of Campaign Finance," 1,252, advocating a rule that would "prohibit newspapers from using their resources to publish editorials that support or oppose a candidate or ballot initiative"; Richard Hasen, "Campaign Finance Laws and the Rupert Murdoch Problem," saying that "Political equality will be limited so long as the media are exempt from otherwise applicable campaign finance regulations."

53. See L. A. Powe, Jr., "Boiling Blood," 1,670: "The influence of the press comes from its choices of coverage: which stories [or issues] and how presented [including photography]."

54. See Bradley A. Smith, "The Sirens' Song: Campaign Finance Regulation and the First Amendment," 28–41, noting that there will always be loopholes and that the potential for corruption will always exist.

55. See, for example, George Stigler, "The Theory of Economic Regulation."

56. For an enlightening look at the creative ways in which campaign laws are evaded, see Sabato and Simpson, *Dirty Little Secrets*.

57. See Richard Hasen, "Clipping Coupons for Democracy: An Egalitarian/Public Choice Defense of Campaign Finance Vouchers"; see also Foley, "Equal-

Dollars-per-Voter"; and Bruce Ackerman, "Crediting the Voters: A New Beginning for Campaign Finance."

58. See, for example, Hasen, "Clipping Coupons," 22–23.

59. See, for example, Robert Norton Smith, "Please Stop Thinking about Tomorrow"; Elizabeth McDonald, "The Kennedys and the IRS"; *Red Lion Broadcasting Company v. Federal Communications Commission*; Sabato and Simpson, *Dirty Little Secrets*, 311 and 403 n.3; Tim Weiner, "Historian Wins Long Battle to Hear More Nixon Tapes"; Neal A. Lewis, "Whitewater Counsel Examining Use of FBI to Get GOP Files"; Rowan Scarborough, "NRA Won't Release Members' Names: IRS Demands Confidential List," noting a suspiciously high number of audits since 1994 of conservative political groups critical of the president.

60. Quoted in Sabato and Simpson, *Dirty Little Secrets*, 327.

61. Hasen, "Clipping Coupons," at 23, "Political activity not directly endorsing or opposing a candidate would not be subject to any limits," which indicates that he would allow most, if not all, issue advocacy.

62. See Brent Larkin, "Five Sure Bets Not So Sure," See Joe Hallett, "Voinovich Defends Not Appearing with Dole"; Voinovich was elected to the Senate in 1998.

63. See, for example, Foley, "Equal-Dollars-per-Voter," 1,249–50.

64. See *United States v. Congress of Industrial Organizations*.

65. *United States Chamber of Commerce v. Federal Election Commission*, 69.

66. Hasen, "Clipping Couplons," 25–26 n. 111.

67. See BeVier, "Campaign Finance Reform," 1,274–75, commenting on role of interest groups in overcoming collective action problems; Palda, *How Much Is Your Vote Worth?*, 31–32, saying that campaign advertising increases voters' knowledge of both issues and candidates, with message repetition being an important part of that effort; and citing the work of Jean Crete, "Television, Advertising and Canadian Elections."

68. Hasen, "Clipping Coupons."

69. Foley, "Equal-Dollars-per-Voter," 1,252.

70. See, for example, Michael Wines, "The Presidential Race: Pools and Stars," describing allegations of media bias by Media Research Center; see also William Claberson, "Increasingly, Reporters Say They're Democrats," saying that news reporters are more likely to vote Democratic than the general populace; this may skew selection of and reporting on issues. See also Levinson, "Regulating Campaign Activity," 947.

71. See, for example, Foley, "Equal-Dollars-per-Voter," 1,252. Perhaps an even greater problem is a "well-disguised" effort to persuade voters to support or oppose a candidate.

72. Ibid., 1,252–53.

73. See, for example, Hasen, "Clipping Coupons," 15–16; *The Federalist No. 10* (James Madison).

74. BeVier, "Campaign Finance Reform."

75. Ronald Dworkin, *Freedom's Law*, 17; see also Dworkin, "The Curse of American Politics."
76. Owen Fiss, "Free Speech and Social Structure," 1,425.
77. *Buckley v. Valeo*, at 48–49; Daniel D. Polsby, "Buckley v. Valeo: The Special Nature of Political Speech."

Chapter 10
Real Equality, Real Corruption, Real Reform

1. See, for example, Jamin Raskin and Jon Bonifaz, "The Constitutional Imperative and Practical Superiority of Democratically Financed Elections," 1,163–64; 1,179–80; 1,203; Marty Jezer and Ellen Miller, "Money Politics: Campaign Finance and the Subversion of American Democracy," 474; John S. Shockley, "Direct Democracy, Campaign Finance, and the Courts: Can Corruption, Undue Influence, and Declining Voter Confidence Be Found?" 427–28.
2. See, for example, Adam Smith, *The Wealth of Nations*, 23.
3. William Wisely, *A Tool of Power: The Political History of Money*, 2–3.
4. David W. Adamany and George E. Agree, *Political Money*, 3.
5. See Bradley A. Smith, "Faulty Assumptions and Undemocratic Consequences of Campaign Finance Reform," 1,077–79. The political landscape is also littered with wealthy, free-spending, unsuccessful candidates, such as Lewis Lehrman, Steve Forbes, Ron Lauder, and Michael Huffington.
6. Adamany and Agree, *Political Money*, 3.
7. Richard Hasen, "Clipping Coupons for Democracy: An Egalitarian/Public Choice Defense of Campaign Finance Vouchers": 26–27 ("it is . . . necessary in order to have a workable system"; Edward B. Foley, "Equal-Dollars-per-Voter: A Constitutional Principle of Campaign Finance," 1,248–49: "Ultimately . . . the most defensible argument for excluding donations of time . . . is, candidly, a pragmatic one.").
8. Marty Jezer et al. "A Proposal for Democratically Financed Congressional Elections," 341, citing Philip M. Stern, *The Best Congress Money Can Buy*, 101, which purports to quote former Congressman Michael Barnes.
9. George Orwell, *Animal Farm*, 123, quoted in *Quote It! Memorable Legal Quotations*, 35.
10. See Sanford Levinson, "Regulating Campaign Activity: The New Road to Contradiction?" 945–50.
11. See Smith, "Faulty Assumptions," 1,077–81. For a more detailed discussion of the manner in which campaign contributions help to prevent legislative "shirking," see Lillian BeVier, "Campaign Finance Reform: Specious Arguments, Intractable Dilemmas," 1,273–76.
12. Adamany and Agree, *Political Money*, 3.
13. Richard Briffault, "Public Funding and Democratic Elections," 575.
14. Ibid.
15. Robert L. Bartley, "Despite Polls, History Favors Dole," citing a poll by Freedom Forum on the views of journalists; Wall Street Journal, "Profile of the

Electorate," on general views of electorate; Chicago Tribune, "Hollywood Not Doling Out Dollars for Republicans," regarding dominant ideologies among Hollywood celebrities; Richard Pipes, *Property and Freedom*, 292, saying that fewer than 5 percent of humanities faculty identify themselves as conservative; James Lindgren, "Measuring Diversity," showing that only 0.5 percent of women on law faculties are Republicans, and over 80 percent of all faculty self-identify as Democrats; Deborah Jones Merritt, "Research and Teaching on Law Faculties, an Empirical Exploration," 780 n. 54, saying that over 80 percent percent of law faculty are Democrats; Phil Kuntz, "PACs Flip-Flop Again, Sending More Money to Democrats in Congress Than to Republicans."

16. James D. Gwartney, Richard L. Stroup, and Russell S. Sobel, *Economics: Private and Public Choice*, 722.

17. *Reynolds v. Sims*, 557; *Kramer v. Union Free School District*; *Harper v. Virginia Board of Elections*.

18. U.S. Congress, Senate, Committee on Rules and Administration, *Hearings on Campaign Finance Reform*, Statement of Lillian R. BeVier. Professor BeVier uses substantially the same language in "Campaign Finance Reform," 1,267.

19. See, for example, Jamin Raskin and Jon Bonifaz, "Equal Protection and the Wealth Primary," 273–74; Foley, "Equal-Dollars-per-Voter," 1,213; John S. Shockley, "Money in Politics: Judicial Roadblocks to Campaign Finance Reform," 680–82; J. Skelly Wright, "Money and the Pollution of Politics: Is the First Amendment an Obstacle to Political Equality?" 627–28; Marlene Nicholson, "Campaign Financing and Equal Protection"; Joel Fleishman, "Public Financing of Election Campaigns: Constitutional Constraints on Steps toward Equality of Political Influence of Citizens."

20. *Reynolds v. Sims*, 557; *Avery v. Midland County Texas*; *Kilgarlin v. Hill*; *Swann v. Adams*; *Young Men's Christian Association v. Lomenzo*.

21. See, for example, *Munro v. Socialist Workers' Party*, holding that a ballot access law was constitutional even though it adversely affected the ability of minor parties to compete.

22. Jezer et al., "Proposal" 360. Similarly, Hasen argues that political outcomes should not be determined by "the dollars in one's pocket." Hasen, "Clipping Coupons," 59.

23. See, for example, Foley, "Equal-Dollars-per-Voter," 1,213 (equal dollars per voter is an "essential precondition" of democracy); 1,225 ("a bedrock principle of constitutional democracy"); 1,226 ("society must accept that equal-dollars-per-voter . . . is an essential precondition of democratic government."); 1,257 ("our nation's constitutional democracy rests upon the bedrock principle that no citizen, as a consequence of her wealth, should have any greater opportunity to participate in the electoral process than any other citizen").

24. *United States v. Carolene Products Company*, 152 n. 4.

25. *Buckley v. Valeo*, 48–49.

26. *Newshour with Jim Lehrer*, October 18, 1996.

27. Larry J. Sabato and Glenn R. Simpson, *Dirty Little Secrets: The Persistence of Corruption in American Politics.*

28. Jack D. Atchison, *Legal Extortion: The War against Lincoln Savings and Charles Keating,* 160.

29. *Buckely v. Valeo,* 245–46, Chief Justice Burger, concurring in part and dissenting in part.

30. Ibid., 67.

31. Ibid., 236–37, 245–46, Chief Justice Burger, concurring in part and dissenting in part; Sabato and Simpson, *Dirty Little Secrets,* 330–35; Stephanie Moussalli, *Campaign Finance Reform: The Case for Deregulation,* 20; Bradley A. Smith, "Money Talks: Speech, Corruption, Equality and Campaign Finance," 61.

32. See Herbert E. Alexander, *Financing Politics: Money, Elections, and Political Reform,* 21–22; the disclosure of the donations was not revealed until after the 1972 elections, due to uncertainty about whether FECA's disclosure provisions applied to contributions made before passage of FECA.

33. *Buckley v. Valeo,* 64–66.

34. Sabato and Simpson, *Dirty Little Secrets,* 332.

35. *McIntyre v. Ohio Elections Commission,* 357.

36. In *Burroughs v. United States,* the Court upheld an indictment under the Federal Corrupt Practices Act for failing to disclose properly information on contributions, but the law was not challenged on First Amendment grounds.

37. *Buckley v. Valeo,* 237; Burt Neuborne, "Toward a Democracy-Centered Reading of the First Amendment," 1,068.

38. See *Buckley v. Valeo,* 73.

39. Steve Stephens, "Free-Speech Views Hinder Federal Election Commission Candidate."

40. Ian Ayres and Jeremy Bulow, "The Donation Booth: Mandating Donor Anonymity to Disrupt the Market for Political Influence."

41. *New York Times Company v. Sullivan.*

42. Cf. *The Federalist No. 62,* 381 (James Madison).

Bibliography

Court Decisions

Abrams v. United States, 250 U.S. 616 (1919).
Adarand Constructors, Inc. v. Pena, 515 U.S. 200 (1995).
Austin v. Michigan State Chamber of Commerce, 494 U.S. 652 (1990).
Avery v. Midland County Texas, 390 U.S. 474 (1968).
Bates v. Little Rock 361 U.S. 516 (1960).
Bose Corporation v. Consumers Union, 466 U.S. 485 (1984).
Brandenburg v. Ohio, 395 U.S. 444 (1969).
Broadrick v. Oklahoma, 413 U.S. 601 (1973).
Brown v. Socialist Workers '74 Campaign Committee, 459 U.S. 87 (1982).
Buckley v. American Constitutional Law Foundation, 525 U.S. 182 (1999).
Buckley v. Valeo, 519 F. 2nd 821 (D.C. Cir. 1975), affirmed in part and reversed in part, 424 U.S. 1 (1976).
Bullock v. Carter, 405 U.S. 134 (1972).
Burroughs v. United States, 290 U.S. 534 (1934).
C & C Plywood Corporation v. Henson, 583 F. 2d 421 (5th Cir. 1978).

California Medical Association v. Federal Election Commission, 453 U.S. 182 (1981).

Carrington v. Rash, 380 U.S. 89 (1965).

Carver v. Nixon, 72 F. 3d 633 (8th Cir. 1995).

Chandler v. Georgia Public Telecommunications Commission, 917 F. 2d 486 (11th Cir. 1990).

Chaplinsky v. New Hampshire, 315 U.S. 568 (1942).

Citizens against Rent Control v. City of Berkeley, 454 U.S. 290 (1981).

City of Richmond v. J. A. Croson Company, 488 U.S. 469 (1989).

Clements v. Fashing, 457 U.S. 957 (1982).

Clifton v. Federal Election Commission, 114 F. 3d 1309 (1997).

Colorado Republican Federal Campaign Committee v. Federal Election Commission, 518 U.S. 604 (1996).

Communist Party v. Subversive Activities Control Board, 367 U.S. 1 (1961).

Consolidated Edison Company v. Public Service Commission, 447 U.S. 530 (1980).

Cox v. Louisiana, 379 U.S. 536 (1965).

Day v. Holahan, 34 F. 3d. 1356 (8th Cir. 1994).

Democratic Party of the United States v. La Follette, 450 U.S. 107 (1981).

Duke v. Massey, 87 F. 3d 1226 (11th Cir. 1996).

Dunn v. Blumstein, 405 U.S. 330 (1972).

Edenfield v. Fane, 507 U.S. 761 (1993).

Edwards v. South Carolina, 372 U.S. 229 (1963).

Elections Board v. Wisconsin Manufacturers and Commerce, 227 Wis. 2d 650 (1999), certiorari denied 120 S.Ct. 408 (1999).

Eu v. San Francisco County Democratic Central Committee, 489 U.S. 214 (1989).

Faucher v. Federal Election Commission, 928 F. 2d 468 (1st Cir. 1991), certiorari denied 502 U.S. 820 (1991).

Federal Election Commission v. American Federation of State, County and Municipal Employees, 471 F. Supp. 315 (D.D.C. 1979).

Federal Election Commission v. Central Long Island Tax Reform Immediately Committee, 616 F. 2nd 45 (2nd Cir. 1980), en banc.

Federal Election Commission v. Christian Action Network, Inc., 92 F. 3d 1178 (4th Cir. 1996), summarily affirming 894 F. Supp. 947 (W.D. Va. 1995).

Federal Election Commission v. Colorado Republican Federal Campaign Committee, 839 F. Supp. 1448 (D. Colo. 1993), reversed on other grounds 59 F. 3rd 1015 (10th Cir. 1995), and vacated on other grounds 518 U.S. 604 (1996).

Federal Election Commission v. Furgatch, 807 F. 2d 857 (9th Cir. 1987), certiorari denied 484 U.S. 850 (1987).

Federal Election Commission v. GOPAC, Inc., 917 F. Supp. 851(D.D.C. 1996).

Federal Election Commission v. Massachusetts Citizens for Life, Inc., 479 U.S. 238 (1986).

Federal Election Commission v. National Conservative Political Action Committee, 470 U.S. 480 (1985).

Federal Election Commission v. National Organization for Women, 713 F. Supp. 428 (D.D.C. 1989).

Federal Election Commission v. Survival Education Fund, No. 89 Civ. 0347, 1994 WL 9658 (S.D.N.Y. 1994), affirmed in part and reversed in part on other grounds, 65 F. 3rd 285 (2nd Cir. 1995).

First National Bank of Boston v. Bellotti, 435 U.S. 765 (1978).

Fiske v. Kansas, 274 U.S. 380 (1927).

Gable v. Patton, 142 F. 3d 940 (6th Cir. 1998), certiorari denied 525 U.S. 1177 (1999).

Geary v. Renne, 911 F. 2d 280 (9th Cir. 1990), vacated on other grounds, 501 U.S. 312 (1991).

Gibson v. Florida Legislative Commission, 372 U.S. 539 (1963).

Greater New Orleans Broadcast Association v. United States, 527 U.S. 173 (1999).

Gregory v. Chicago, 394 U.S. 111 (1969).

Guinn v. United States, 238 U.S. 347 (1915).

Harper v. Virginia Board of Elections, 383 U.S. 663 (1966).

Hudgens v. National Labor Relations Board, 424 U.S. 507 (1976).

Hurley v. Irish-American Gay, Lesbian, and Bisexual Group of Boston, 515 U.S. 557 (1995).

Jenkins v. Georgia, 418 U.S. 153 (1974).

Johnson v. Federal Communications Commission, 829 F. 2d 157 (D.C. Cir. 1987).

Kennedy for President Committee v. Federal Communications Commission, 636 F. 2d 417 (D.C. Cir. 1980).

Kilgarlin v. Hill, 386 U.S. 120 (1967).

Kramer v. Union Free School District, 395 U.S. 621 (1969).

Landmark Communications, Inc. v. Virginia, 435 U.S. 829 (1978).

Linmark Associates, Inc. v. Township of Willingboro, 431 U.S. 85 (1977).

Louisiana ex rel. Gremillion v. NAACP, 366 U.S. 293 (1961).

Lubin v. Panish, 415 U.S. 709 (1974).

Maine Right to Life Committee v. Federal Election Commission, 98 F. 3d 1 (1st Cir. 1996), certiorari denied 522 U.S. 810 (1997).

Maryland v. Munson, 467 U.S. 947 (1984).

McIntyre v. Ohio Elections Commission, 514 U.S. 334 (1995).

Miami Herald Publishing Company v. Tornillo, 418 U.S. 241 (1974).

Miller v. California, 413 U.S. 15 (1973).

Mills v. Alabama, 384 U.S. 214 (1966).

Monitor Patriot Company v. Roy, 401 U.S. 265 (1971).

Munro v. Socialist Workers' Party, 479 U.S. 189 (1986).

National Association for the Advancement of Colored People v. Alabama, 357 U.S. 449 (1958).

National Bank of Boston v. Bellotti, 435 U.S. 765 (1978).

National Black Police Association v. District of Columbia Board of Elections, 924 F. Supp. (D. D.C. 1996).

National Socialist Party of America v. Skokie, 432 U.S. 43 (1977).

New York Times Company v. Sullivan, 376 U.S. 254 (1964).

Nixon v. Condon, 286 U.S. 73 (1932).

Nixon v. Herndon, 273 U.S. 537 (1927).

Nixon v. Shrink Missouri Government PAC, 120 S. Ct. 897 (2000).

Perkins v. Moss, 100 N.Y. Supp. 427 (1906).

Pestrak v. Ohio Elections Commission, 926 F. 2d 573 (6th Cir. 1991), certiorari dismissed 502 U.S. 1022 (1991).

Pruneyard Shopping Center v. Robins, 447 U.S. 74 (1980).

R.A.V. v. St. Paul, 505 U.S. 377 (1992).

Red Lion Broadcasting Company v. Federal Communications Commission, 395 U.S. 367 (1969).

Rendell Baker v. Kohn, 457 U.S. 830 (1982).

Reno v. American Civil Liberties Union, 521 U.S. 844 (1997).

Reynolds v. Sims, 377 U.S. 533 (1964).

Roth v. United States, 354 U.S. 476 (1957).

Rubin v. Coors Brewing Company, 514 U.S. 476 (1995).

San Antonio Independent School District v. Rodriguez, 411 U.S. 1 (1973).

San Francisco Arts and Athletics, Inc. v. United States Olympic Committee, 483 U.S. 522 (1987).

Smith v. Allwright, 321 U.S. 649 (1944).

Street v. New York, 394 U.S. 576 (1969).

Stromberg v. California, 283 U.S. 359 (1931).

Swann v. Adams, 385 U.S. 440 (1967).

Talley v. California, 362 U.S. 60 (1960).

Tashijan v. Republican Party of Connecticut, 479 U.S. 208 (1986).

Terminello v. Chicago, 337 U.S. 1 (1949).

Terry v. Adams, 345 U.S. 461 (1953).

Texas v. Johnson, 491 U.S. 397 (1989).

Thomas v. Collins, 323 U.S. 516 (1945).

Tinker v. Des Moines Independent Community School District, 393 U.S. 503 (1969).

United States v. Carolene Products Company, 304 U.S. 144 (1938).

United States v. Congress of Industrial Organizations, 335 U.S. 106 (1948).

United States v. National Committee for Impeachment, 469 F. 2d 1135 (2nd Cir. 1972).

United States v. Newberry, 256 U.S. 232 (1921).

United States v. O'Brien, 391 U.S. 367 (1968).

United States v. United Auto Workers, 352 U.S. 567 (1957).

United States Chamber of Commerce v. Federal Election Commission, 69 F. 3d 600 (D.C. Cir. 1995).

Village of Schaumberg v. Citizens for a Better Environment, 444 U.S. 620 (1980).

Virginia State Board of Pharmacy v. Virginia Consumer Council, 413 U.S. 748 (1976).

West Virginia Board of Education v. Barnette, 319 U.S. 624 (1943).

Whitney v. California, 274 U.S. 357 (1927).

Williams v. Rhodes, 393 U.S. 23 (1968).

Young Men's Christian Association v. Lomenzo, 377 U.S. 633 (1964).

Other Works

Abramowitz, Alan I. "Explaining Senate Election Outcomes." *American Political Science Review* 82.2 (1988): 385–404.

Abramowitz, Alan I., and Jeffrey A. Segal. *Senate Elections.* Ann Arbor: University of Michigan Press, 1992.

Ackerman, Bruce. "Crediting the Voters: A New Beginning for Campaign Finance." *American Prospect* 13.4 (1993): 71–89.

Adamany, David W., and George E. Agree. *Political Money.* Baltimore: Johns Hopkins University Press, 1975.

Alexander, Herbert E. *Financing Politics: Money, Elections, and Political Reform.* 4th ed. Washington D.C.: CQ Press, 1992.

Alexander, Herbert E., and Anthony Corrado. *Financing the 1992 Election.* Armonk, N.Y.: M. E. Sharpe, 1995.

Alfange, Dean, Jr. "Free Speech and Symbolic Conduct: The Draft Card Burning Case." *Supreme Court Review* 1968: 1–53.

Allen, Paula Kane. "Fellow Freshman Focus on Campaign Reform." *Bangor Daily News*, 26 April 1997, A1.

American Civil Liberties Union. *Policy Guide.* New York: American Civil Liberties Union, 1993.

Anderson, Annelise. *Political Money: The New Prohibition.* Stanford: Hoover Institution, 1997.

Ansberry, Clare. "The Best Beef Jerky Has Characteristics Few Can Appreciate." *Wall Street Journal*, 4 April 1995, A1, A4.

Ansolabehere, Stephen, and Shanto Iyengar. *Going Negative: How Political Advertisements Shrink and Polarize the Electorate.* New York: Free Press, 1995.

Ansolabehere, Stephen, and James M. Synder, Jr. "Money and Institutional Power." *Texas Law Review* 77.5 (1999): 1,673–1,704.

Askin, Frank J. "Political Money and Freedom of Speech: Kathleen Sullivan's Seven Deadly Sins—An Anti-toxin." *University of California-Davis Law Review* 31.4 (1998): 1,065–82.

Atchison, Jack D. *Legal Extortion: The War against Lincoln Savings and Charles Keating.* Salt Lake City: Northwest, 1995.

Ayres, Ian, and Jeremy Bulow. "The Donation Booth: Mandating Donor Anonymity to Disrupt the Market for Political Influence." *Stanford Law Review* 50.3 (1998): 837–91.

Bailey, Holly. "Top Gun." *Capitol Eye*, 9 November 1999, 1.

Balz, Dan. "Why Consumers Care about Campaign Finance Reform." Available at www. commmoncause.org/publications/nov99/consumers.html, November 1999.

Balz, Dan, and Bill McAllister. "The Race for President." *Washington Post*, 23 February 1996, A13.

Bartlett, Bruce. "A Class Structure That Just Won't Stay Put." *Wall Street Journal*, 20 November 1991, A16.

Bartley, Robert. "Despite Polls, History Favors Dole." *Wall Street Journal*, 23 May 1996, A14.

Beck, Deborah, Paul Taylor, Feffrey Stranger, and Douglas Rivlin. "Issue Advocacy Advertising during the 1996 Campaign." Philadelphia: Annenberg Public Policy Center, 16 September 1997.

BeVier, Lillian R. "Campaign Finance Reform: Specious Arguments, Intractable Dilemmas." *Columbia Law Review* 94.1 (1994): 1,258–80.

———. "Money and Politics: A Perspective on the First Amendment and Campaign Finance Reform." *California Law Review* 73.1 (1985): 1,045–90.

Blasi, Vincent. "Free Speech and the Widening Gyre of Fund-Raising: Why Campaign Spending Limits May Not Violate the First Amendment after All." *Columbia Law Review* 94.1 (1994): 1,281–1,385.

Bopp, James Jr. "Campaign Finance 'Reform': The Good, the Bad, and the Unconstitutional." *Heritage Foundation Backgrounder* 1,308 (19 July 1999), 1–8.

Briffault, Richard. "Public Funding and Democratic Elections." *University of Pennslyvania Law Review* 148.2 (2000): 563–90.

———. "Campaign Finance, the Parties, and the Court: A Comment on Colorado Republican Federal Campaign Committee v. Federal Election Commission." *Constitutional Commentary* 14 (1997): 91–126.

———. "The Federal Election Campaign Act and the 1980 Election." *Columbia Law Review* 84.8 (1984): 2,083–2,110.

Bronars, Stephen G., and John R. Lott, Jr. "Do Campaign Donations Alter How a Politician Votes? Or, Do Donors Support Candidates Who Value the Same Things That They Do?" *Journal of Law and Economics* 40.2 (1997): 317–50.

Brown, Clifford, Lynda W. Powell, and Clyde Wilcox. *Serious Money: Fundraising and Contributing in Presidential Nomination Campaigns.* New York: Cambridge University Press, 1995.

Burke, Debra. "Twenty Years after the Federal Election Campaign Act Amendments of 1974: Look Who's Running Now." *Dickinson Law Review* 99.2 (1995): 357–92.

Burke, Edmund. "The English Constitutional System." In Hanna F. Pitkin, ed., *Representation.* New York: Atherton Press, 1969.

Burke, Thomas. "The Concept of Corruption in Campaign Finance Law." *Constitutional Commentary* 14.1 (1997): 127–49.

Cain, Bruce. "Moralism and Realism in Campaign Finance Reform." *University of Chicago Legal Forum* 1995 (1995): 111–40.

Cass, Ronald A., "Money, Power, and Politics: Governance Models and Campaign Finance Regulation." *Supreme Court Economic Review* 6 (1998): 1–59.

"Celebrity Hearings: Much Show, Little Go." *San Antonio Express-News*, 11 July 1994, available at 1994 WL 3558496.

Center for Responsive Politics. "Banking Deregulation." Available at http://www.opensecrets.org/news/banks/index/htm.

Chicago Tribune. "Hollywood Not Doling Out Dollars for Republicans." *Chicago Tribune*, 9 April 1996, evening update edition, 2.

Claberson, William. "Increasingly, Reporters Say They're Democrats." *New York Times*, 18 November 1992, A20.

Coates, Dan. Interview by Larry King. *CNN Larry King Live.* Transcript #99062800V22, 28 June 1999.

Cole, David. "First Amendment Antitrust: The End of Laissez-Faire in Campaign Finance." *Yale Law and Policy Review* 9.1 (1991): 236–55.

Cole, Donald B. *The Presidency of Andrew Jackson.* Lawrence: University of Kansas Press, 1993.

Coleman, John J., and Paul F. Manna. "Congressional Campaign Spending and the Quality of Democracy." *Journal of Politics* (forthcoming August 2000).

Collins, Carville B. "Maryland Campaign Finance Law: A Proposal for Reform." *Maryland Law Review* 47.2 (1988): 524–56.

Common Cause. "Channeling Influence: The Broadcast Lobby and the $70-Billion Free Ride." Press release available at www.commoncause.com, April 1977.

———. "National Rifle Association Gives Large Amounts of Soft PAC Money." Press release available at www.commoncause.com, 26 April 1999.

Congressional Quarterly. *Congressional Campaign Finances: History, Facts and Controversy.* Washington, D.C.: Congressional Quarterly, 1992.

"Constitutional Implications of Campaign Finance Reform." Colloquium. *Adminstrative Law Review* (American University) 8 (1994): 161–203.

Cox, Archibald. "Freedom of Expression in the Burger Court." *Harvard Law Review* 94.1 (1980): 1–73.

Crain, W. Mark, et al. "Laissez-faire in Campaign Finance." *Public Choice* 56 (1988): 201–12.

Crete, Jean. "Television, Advertising, and Canadian Elections." In Frederick J. Fletcher, ed., *Media and Voters in Canadian Election Campaigns.* Toronto: Dundurn, 1991.

Davidson, Chandler. "The Voting Rights Act: A Brief History." In Bernard Grofman and Chandler Davidson, eds., *Controversies in Minority Voting.* Washington D.C.: Brookings Institution, 1992.

Dinkin, Robert J. *Campaigning in America.* Contributions in American History Series 135. New York: Greenwood, 1989.

Donnay, Patrick D., and Graham P. Ramsden. "Public Financing of Legislative Elections: Lessons from Minnesota." *Legislative Study Quarterly* 20.2 (1995): 351–62.

Dorf, Michael C. "Integrating Normative and Descriptive Constitutional Theory." *Georgetown Law Journal* 85 (1997): 1,756–1,822.

Douglas, Paul H. *Ethics in Government.* Cambridge: Harvard University Press, 1952.

Drew, Elizabeth. *Politics and Money: The New Road to Corruption.* New York: Macmillan, 1983.

Dreyfuss, Robert. "Harder Than Soft Money." *American Prospect* 9.36 (January-February 1998): 30–45.

Dubois, Philip, and Floyd F. Feeney. *Improving the California Initiative Process: Options for Change.* Berkeley: University of California Policy Seminar, 1992.

Dworkin, Ronald. "The Curse of American Politics." *New York Review,* 17 October 1996, 19.

Dworkin, Ronald. *Freedom's Law: The Moral Reading of the American Constitution.* Cambridge: Harvard University Press, 1996.

Dworkin, Ronald, and Burt Neuborne. "Letter to John McCain and Russell Feingold." New York: Brennan Center for Justice, 22 September 1997.

———. "Statement in Support of Overturning Buckley v. Valeo." New York: Brennan Center for Justice, 1997.

Elsner, Alan. "Running for the White House Will Take Megabucks This Time." *San Francisco Chronicle,* 1 February 1995, A9.

Ely, John Hart. "Flag Desecration: A Case Study in the Roles of Categorization and Balancing in First Amendment Analysis." *Harvard Law Review* 88.7 (1975): 1,482–1,507.

Epstein, Richard. "Property, Speech, and the Politics of Distrust." In Geoffrey R. Stone et al., eds. *The Bill of Rights in the Modern State.* Chicago: University of Chicago Press, 1992.

"E.T.: Prototypical '80s Celeb." *Gannett News Service,* 29 December 1989.

Farber, Daniel A. "Content Regulation and the First Amendment: A Revisionist View." *Georgetown Law Journal* 68.4 (1980): 727–88.

Federal Election Commission. *Advisory Opinion 1978–10 (George Van Riper, Executive Director of the Kansas Republican Party).* Washington, D.C., August 29, 1978.

———. *Advisory Opinion 1998–22 (Leo Smith).* Washington, D.C., November 22, 1998.

———. *Advisory Opinion 1999–06 (National Rural Letter Carrier's Association).* Washington, D.C., April 30, 1999.

———. *Advisory Opinion 1999–9 (Bill Bradley for President, Inc).* Washington, D.C., June 10, 1999.

———. *Budget Request for Fiscal Year 2000.* Available at http://www.fec.gov/pages/budcont.htm.

Feingold, Russell. "Letter to the Editor: Get Campaign Finance Reform Facts." *Milwaukee Journal and Sentinel,* 29 October 1997, 17.

Felknor, Bruce L. *Political Mischief: Smear, Sabotage and Reform in U.S. Elections.* New York: Praeger, 1992.

Fiss, Owen M. "Emerging Media Technology and the First Amendment: In Search of a New Paradigm." *Yale Law Journal* 104.7 (1995): 1,613–18.

———. "Free Speech and Social Structure." *Iowa Law Review* 71.5 (1986): 1,405–25.

———. *The Irony of Free Speech.* Cambridge: Harvard University Press, 1996.

———. "State Activism and State Censorship." *Yale Law Journal* 100.7 (1991): 2,087–2,106.

———. "Why the State?" *Harvard Law Review* 100.4 (1987): 781–94.

Fleishman, Joel. "Public Financing of Election Campaigns: Constitutional Constraints on Steps toward Equality of Political Influence of Citizens." *University of North Carolina Law Review* 52 (1972): 349–416.

Fleishman, Joel L., and Pope McCorkle. "Level-Up Rather Than Level Down: Towards a New Theory of Campaign Finance." *Journal of Law and Politics* 1.2 (1984): 211–85.

Foley, Edward. "Equal-Dollars-per-Voter: A Constitutional Principle of Campaign Finance." *Columbia Law Review* 94.1 (1994): 1,204–57.

Frankel, Glen. "Forbes's Optimism Is Selling: Publishing Heir Prepares for N.Y. Battle with Senate Leader." *Washington Post*, 28 February 1996, A1.

Fried, Charles. "The New First Amendment Jurisprudence: A Threat to Liberty." In Geoffrey R. Stone, Richard A. Epstein, and Cass R. Sunstein, eds., *The Bill of Rights in the Modern State*. Chicago: University of Chicago Press, 1992.

Fritz, Sara, and Dwight Morris. "Federal Election Panel Not Enforcing Limit on Campaign Donations." *Los Angeles Times*, 15 September 1991, A1, A8–9.

Fund, John H. *Term Limitation: An Idea Whose Time Has Come*. Washington, D.C.: Cato Institute, 1990.

Gais, Thomas. *Improper Influence: Campaign Finance Law, Political Interest Groups, and the Problem of Equality*. Ann Arbor: University of Michigan Press, 1996.

Gardner, John. *In Common Cause*. New York: W. W. Norton, 1972.

Gates, Max. "FTC Targets Buyer's Guide Violations." *Automotive News*, 27 March 1995, 46.

Gibbs, Nancy. "The Wake-Up Call." *Time*, 3 February 1997, 22.

Goeas, Ed, and William Stewart. "Key Findings from a Nationwide Survey of Voter Attitudes about Campaign Finance Reform." Tarrance Group, 1998. Available at www.tarrance.com/polls/campfin.htm.

Goldberg, Bernard. "Networks Need a Reality Check." *Wall Street Journal*, 13 February 1996, A14.

Gora, Joel M. "Campaign Finance Reform: Still Searching Today for a Better Way." *Journal of Law and Policy* 6.1 (1997): 137–61.

Gottlieb, Stephen. "The Dilemma of Election Campaign Finance Reform." *Hofstra Law Review* 18.1 (1989): 216–300.

Green, Donald, and Jonathan Krasno. "Salvation for the Spendthrift Incumbent: Reestimating the Effects of Campaign Spending in House Elections." *American Journal of Political Science* 32.4 (1988): 884–907.

Greenblatt, Alan. "Politics and Marketing Merge in Parties' Bid for Relevance." *Congressional Quarterly Weekly Reporter* 55.32 (1997): 1,967–69.

Grenzke, Janet. "PAC's and the Congressional Supermarket: The Currency Is Complex." *American Journal of Political Science* 33.1 (1989): 1–24.

Gwartney, James D., Richard L. Stroup, and Russell S. Sobel. *Economics: Private and Public Choice*. Fort Worth: Dryden, 1999.

Hall, Richard, and Frank Wayman. "Buying Time: Moneyed Interests and the Mobilization of Bias in Congressional Committees." *American Political Science Review* 84.3 (1990): 797–820.

Hallett, Joe. "Voinovich Defends Not Appearing with Dole." *Cleveland Plain Dealer*, 12 September 1996, A1.

Hasen, Richard L. "Campaign Finance Laws and the Rupert Murdoch Problem." *Texas Law Review* 77.7 (1999): 1,627–66.

———. "Clipping Coupons for Democracy: An Egalitarian/Public Choice Defense of Campaign Finance Vouchers." *California Law Review* 84.7 (1996): 1–60.

Heard, Alexander. *The Costs of Democracy*. Chapel Hill: University of North Carolina Press, 1960.

Hersch, Philip L., and Gerald S. McDougall. "Campaign War Chests as a Barrier to Entry in Congressional Races." *Economy Inquiry* 630 (1994): 630–40.

Hendee, David. "Defending the Sugar Program." *Omaha World Herald*, 17 July 1995, 1.

Hombs, Mary Ellen, and Mitch Synder. *Homelessness in America: A Forced March to Nowhere*. 2nd ed. Washington, D.C.: Community for Creative Non-Violence, 1983.

Horowitz, Morton. "The Constitution of Change: Legal Fundamentality without Fundamentalism." *Harvard Law Review* 107.1 (1993): 30–117.

Issacharoff, Samuel, and Pamela S. Karlan. "The Hydraulics of Campaign Finance Reform." *Texas Law Review* 77.5 (1999): 1,705–38.

Issacharoff, Samuel, et al. *The Law of Democracy: Legal Structure of the Political Process*. Westbury, N.Y.: Foundation Press, 1998.

Jackson, Brooks. *Honest Graft: The Business of Money in Politics*. New York: Alfred A. Knopf, 1988.

Jacobson, Gary C. "Campaign Finance and Democratic Control: Comments on Gottlieb and Lowenstein's Papers." *Hofstra Law Review* 18.1 (1989): 369–84.

———. "The Effects of Electoral Campaign Spending in Congressional Elections." *American Political Science Review* 72 (1978): 469–91.

———. "The Effects of Electoral Campaign Spending in House Elections: New Evidence for Old Arguments." *American Journal of Political Science* 34.2 (1990): 334–62.

———. *The Electoral Origins of Divided Government: Competition in U.S. House Elections, 1946–1988*. Boulder, Colo.: Westview, 1990.

———. "Enough Is Too Much: Money and Competition in House Elections." In Kay Scholzman, ed., *Elections in America*. Boston: Allen and Unwin, 1987.

———. "Money and Votes Reconsidered: Congressional Elections 1972–1982." *Publisher's Choice* 47 (1985): 17.

———. *Money in Congressional Elections*. New Haven: Yale University Press, 1980.

———. "Money in the 1980 and 1982 Congressional Elections." In Michael J. Malbin, ed., *Money and Politics in the United States: Financing Elections in the 1980s*. Chatham, N. J.: Chatham House, 1994.

———. *The Politics of Congressional Elections*. 3rd ed. New York: Longman, 1992.

Jezer, Marty, and Ellen Miller. "Money Politics: Campaign Finance and the Subversion of American Democracy." *Notre Dame Journal of Legal Ethics and Public Policy* 8.2 (1994): 467–98.

Jezer, Marty, Randy Kehler, and Ben Santuria. "A Proposal for Democratically Financed Elections." *Yale Law and Policy Review* 11.2 (1994): 333–60.

Johnson, Timothy D. *Winfield Scott: The Quest for Military Glory*. Lawrence: University of Kansas Press, 1998.

Jones, Ruth S. "Contributing as Participation." In Margaret Latus Nugent and John R. Johannes, eds., *Money, Elections, Democracy.* Boulder, Colo.: Westview, 1990.

Kamber, Victor. *Poison Politics: Are Negative Campaigns Destroying Democracy?* New York: Plenum, 1997.

Kester, John C. "Constitutional Restrictions on Political Parties." *Virginia Law Review* 60.4 (1974): 735–92.

Kozinski, Alex, and Eugene Volokh. "A Penumbra Too Far." *Harvard Law Review* 106.3 (1993): 1,638–57.

Kuhnhenn, Jerome. "Congress Refocuses on Fund-Raising in Kansas Races as House Republicans Look at National State Democratic Panels." *Kansas City Star,* 20 November 1997, A5.

Kuntz, Phil. "PACs Flip-Flop Again, Sending More Money to Democrats in Congress Than to Republicans." *Wall Street Journal,* 23 May 1996, A16.

La Pierre, D. Bruce. "Campaign Contribution Limits: Pandering to Public Fears about 'Big Money' and Protecting Incumbents." *Administrative Law Review* 52.2 (2000): 687–742.

Larkin, Brent. "Five Sure Bets Not So Sure." *Cleveland Plain Dealer,* 20 October 1996, C1.

Leventhal, Harold. "Courts and Political Thickets." *Columbia Law Review* 77.3 (1977): 345–87.

Levinson, Sanford. "Electoral Regulation: Some Comments." *Hofstra Law Review* 18.2 (1989): 411–20.

———. "Regulating Campaign Activity: The New Road to Contradiction." *Michigan Law Review* 83.4 (1985): 939–53.

Levit, Kenneth J. "Campaign Finance Reform and the Return of Buckley v. Valeo." *Yale Law Journal* 103.5 (1993): 469–503.

Levitt, Steven D. "Congressional Campaign Finance Reform." *Journal of Economic Perspectives* 9.1 (1995): 183–93.

———. "Using Repeat Challengers to Estimate the Effects of Campaign Spending on Election Outcomes in the U.S. House." *Journal of Political Economics* 102.4 (1994): 777–98.

Lewis, Charles. *The Buying of the President.* New York: Avon, 1996.

———. *The Buying of the President 2000.* New York: Avon, 2000.

Lewis, Neal A. "Whitewater Counsel Examining Use of FBI to Get GOP Files." *New York Times,* 11 June 1996, A1.

Lindgren, James. "Measuring Diversity." Speech to National Association of Scholars, Washington, D.C., 5 January 1997.

Lott, John R. Jr. "Brand Names and Barriers to Entry in Political Markets," *Public Choice* 52.1 (1986): 87–98.

———. "The Effect of Nontransferable Property Rights on the Efficiency of Political Markets: Some Evidence." *Journal of Public Economy* 32.2 (1987): 231–45.

———. "Explaining Challengers' Campaign Expenditures: The Importance of Sunk Non-transferable Brand Name." *Public Finance Quarterly* 17.1 (1989): 108–25.

Lott, John R., Jr. "A Simple Explanation for Why Campaign Expenditures Are Increasing: The Government Is Getting Bigger." Manuscript, 25 March 1996.

Lowenstein, Daniel Hays. "Associational Rights of Major Political Parties: A Skeptical Inquiry." *Texas Law Review* 71.7 (1993): 1,741–92.

———. *Election Law: Cases and Materials*. Durham, N.C.: Carolina Academic Press, 1995.

———. *Election Law, Cases and Materials: Teacher's Manual*. Durham, N.C.: Carolina Academic Press, 1995.

———. "On Campaign Finance Reform: The Root of All Evil Is Deeply Rooted." *Hofstra Law Review* 18.2 (1989): 301–67.

———. "A Patternless Mosaic: Campaign Finance and the First Amendment after Austin." *Capital University Law Review* 21.2 (1992): 381–428.

———. "Political Bribery and the Intermediate Theory of Politics." *UCLA Law Review* 32.4 (1985): 784–851.

Lowenstein, Daniel H., and Richard Hasen. *Election Law Supplement, 1999–2000*. Durham, N.C.: Carolina Academic Press, 1999.

Lowenstein, Daniel H., and Robert M. Stern. "The First Amendment and Paid Initiative Petitions Circulators: A Dissenting View and a Proposal." *Hastings Consitutional Law Quarterly* 17.1 (1989): 175–224.

Magleby, David B., and Candice J. Nelson. *The Money Chase: Congressional Campaign Finance Reform*. Washington, D.C.: Brookings Institution, 1990.

Malbin, Michael J. "Most GOP Winners Spent Enough Money to Reach Voters." *Political Finance and Lobby Reporter*, 11 January 1995, 8–9.

Marcus, Ruth. "Trial Lawyers Group Plans Aggressive Political Action; FEC Asked to Allow Endorsement-Donation Setup." *Washington Post*, 21 March 1996, A6.

Marcus, Ruth, and Walter Pincus. "Forbes Spent $18 Million on Race Last Year." *Washington Post*, 6 February 1996, A1.

Mason, David, and Stephan Schwalm. "Advantage Incumbents: Clinton's Campaign Finance Proposal." *Heritage Foundation Backgrounder*, 11 June 1993, 2–5.

Mayer, Kenneth R. *Public Financing and Electoral Competition in Minnesota and Wisconsin*. New York: W. W. Norton, 1998.

Mayer, Kenneth R., and John M. Wood. "The Impact of Public Financing on Electoral Competitiveness: Evidence from Wisconsin, 1964–1990." *Legislative Study Quarterly* 20.1 (1995): 69–86.

McBride, Ann. Interview by Jim Lehrer on *Newshour with Jim Lehrer*, 18 October, 1996.

———. "Where Soft Money Hits Taxpayers Hard." *Palm Beach Post*, 23 July 1998, E1.

McDonald, Elizabeth. "The Kennedys and the IRS." *Wall Street Journal*, 28 January 1997, A16.

McGinnis, John O. "The Once and Future Property-Based Vision of the First Amendment." *University of Chicago Law Review* 63.1 (1996): 49–132.

———. "The Original Constitution and Our Origins." *Harvard Journal of Law and Public Policy* 19.2 (1996): 251–62.

Merritt, Deborah Jones. "Research and Teaching on Law Faculties, an Empirical Exploration." *Chicago-Kent Law Review* 73.3 (1998): 765–822.

Mill, John Stuart. "Considerations on Representative Government." In Mill, *Principles of Political Economy, with Some of Their Applications to Social Philosophy.* 3 vols. Oxford: Oxford University Press, 1975.

Miller, James C. III. *Monopoly Politics.* Stanford: Hoover Institution, 1999.

Miller, Nathan. *Stealing from America: A History of Corruption from Jamestown to Reagan.* New York: Paragon, 1992.

Milyo, Jeffrey. *The Electoral Effects of Campaign Spending in House Elections: A Natural Experiment Approach.* Los Angeles: Citizens Research Foundation, 1998.

———. "The Electoral Effects of Incumbent Wealth." *Journal of Law and Economics* 42.3 (1999): 699–720.

Moister, Stanley. "Public Found to Be More Cynical Than Press." *Los Angeles Times,* 22 May 1995, A11.

Moore, Jennifer. "Campaign Finance Reform in Kentucky." *Kentucky Law Journal* 85.3 (1997): 723–65.

Moore, Martha T. "Main Goal: Carry Banner of Supply Side Economics." *USA Today,* 6 September 1995, B4.

Morris, Dwight. "Federal Election Panel Not Enforcing Limit on Campaign Donations." *Los Angeles Times,* 15 September 1991, A1.

Morrison, Alan. "Watch What You Wish For: The Perils of Reversing Buckley v. Valeo." *American Prospect* 18.1 (1998): 38–44.

Mott, Stewart R. "Independent Fundraising for an Independent Candidate." *New York University Review of Law and Social Change* 10.1 (1981): 135–44.

Mousalli, Stephanie D. *Campaign Finance Reform: The Case for Deregulation.* Tallahassee, Fla.: James Madison Center, 1990.

Murray, Robert K. *The Harding Era: Warren G. Harding and His Administration.* Minneapolis: University of Minnesota Press, 1969.

Mutch, Robert. *Campaigns, Congresses and Courts: The Making of Federal Campaign Finance Law.* New York: Praeger, 1988.

Nagle, John Copeland. "The Recusal Alternative to Campaign Finance Litigation." *Harvard Journal on Legislation* 37.1 (2000): 69–103.

Nahra, Kirk J. "Political Parties and Campaign Finance Laws: Dilemmas, Concerns, and Opportunities." *Fordham Law Review* 56.1 (1987): 53–110.

Nassmacher, Karl-Heinz. "Comparing Party and Campaign Finance in Western Democracies." In Arthur B. Gunlicks, ed., *Campaign and Party Finance in North America and Western Europe.* Boulder, Colo.: Westview, 1993.

Neuborne, Burt. *Campaign Finance Reform and the Constitution: A Critical Look at Buckley v. Valeo.* New York: Brennan Center for Justice, 1997.

———. "Is Money Different?" *Texas Law Review* 77.7 (1999): 1,609–26.

———. "The Supreme Court and Free Speech: Love and a Question." *St. Louis University Law Review* 42.3 (1998): 789–812.

———. "Toward a Democracy-Centered Reading of the First Amendment." *Northwestern University Law Review* 93.6 (1999): 1,055–73.

Nicholson, Marlene A. "Buckley v. Valeo: The Constitutionality of the Federal Election Campaign Act Amendments of 1974." *Wisconsin Law Review* 1977 .2 (1977): 323–74.

———. "Campaign Financing and Equal Protection." *Stanford Law Review* 26.5 (1974): 815–53.

———. "Continuing the Dialogue on Campaign Finance Reform: A Response to Roy Schotland." *Capital University Law Review* 21.2 (1992): 463–88.

Nimmer, Melville B. "The Meaning of Symbolic Speech under the First Amendment." *UCLA Law Review* 21.1 (1973): 29–53.

Nozick, Robert. *Anarchy, State, and Utopia.* New York: Basic Books, 1974.

Ornstein, Norman J., et al. *Vital Statistics on Congress, 1997–1998.* Washington, D.C.: Government Printing Office, 1998.

Ortiz, Daniel. "The Democratic Paradox of Campaign Finance Reform." *Stanford Law Review* 50.3 (1998): 893–914.

Orwell, George. *Animal Farm.* New York: Harcourt Brace, 1946.

Overacker, Louise. *Money in Elections.* New York: Arno, 1932.

Palda, Filip. "The Determinates of Campaign Spending: The Role of the Government Jackpot." *Economic Inquiry,* 1 October 1992, 627.

———. *How Much Is Your Vote Worth?* San Francisco: ICS Press, 1994.

Paul, Jeremy. "Campaign Reform for the 21st Century: Putting Money Where Mouth Is." *University of Connecticut Law Review* 30.3 (1998): 779–815.

Pianin, Eric, and Juliet Eilperin. "Applying Brakes to Gas Tax Cut: House GOP Leaders Doubt Its Effectiveness." *Washington Post,* 15 March 2000, A4.

Pipes, Richard. *Property and Freedom.* New York: Alfred A. Knopf, 1992.

Political Finance and Lobby Reporter. "Late Money Key to House Races." *Political Finance and Lobby Reporter,* 11 January 1995, 3, 5–6.

———. "Money in House Seat Turnovers." *Political Finance and Lobby Reporter,* 23 November 1994, 3, 4.

———. "Rep. Thomas: Issue Ads Should Be Subject to FECA." *Political Finance and Lobby Reporter,* 29 January 1997, 5.

———. "Senate Candidates Add $31.5 Million to Their Own Election Campaigns." *Political Finance and Lobby Reporter,* 24 October 1994, 1.

Pollock, James K., Jr. *Party Campaign Funds.* New York: Alfred A. Knopf, 1926.

Polsby, Daniel D. "Buckley v. Valeo: The Special Nature of Political Speech." *Supreme Court Review* 1976: 1–43.

Powe, L. A. "Boiling Blood." *Texas Law Review* 77.7 (1999): 1,667–72.

———. "Mass Speech and the Newer First Amendment." *Supreme Court Review* 1982: 243–84.

Public Campaign. "Clean Money Campaign Reform Annotated Model Legislation: Comment to §103 (A)(2)." Available at http://www.publiccampaign.org, 29 October 1999.

———. "Insurance v. Assurance." Available at http://www.publiccampaign.org/ ouch.html#insurance, 2 February 2000.

———. "Ouch! How Money in Politics Hurts You." Available at http.//www. publiccampaign.org/ouch.html, June 2000.

Rada, Elizabeth, et al. "Access to the Ballot." *Urban Law* 13.5 (1981): 793–814.

Rakove, Jack. *Original Meanings: Politics and Ideas in the Making of the Constitution.* New York: Alfred A. Knopf, 1996.

Raskin, Jamin, and Jon Bonifaz. "The Constitutional Imperative and Practical Superiority of Democratically Financed Elections." *Columbia Law Review* 94.4 (1994): 1,160–1,203.

———. "Equal Protection and the Wealth Primary." *Yale Law and Policy Review* 11.4 (1993): 273–332.

Rasmussen Research. "Seventy Percent Want Spending Limits: Most Want More Limits on Incumbents." Available at http://www.rasmussen.poll.com, 25 September 1999.

Redlich, Norman, Bernard Schwartz, and John Attanasio. *Constitutional Law.* 3rd ed. New York: Matthew Bender, 1996.

Rezendes, Michael. "PAC for Women Faces a Crisis: Emily's List May Lose Fund-Raising Tools if Campaign Finance Rules Change." *Boston Globe*, 24 June 1996, A5.

Roberts, Roxanne. "The Remote Controllers." *Washington Post*, 10 June 1995, B1.

Roeder, Edward. "Big Money Won the Day Last November." *Cleveland Plain Dealer*, 25 December 1994, C1, C4.

Rosenberg, Lisa. *A Bag of Tricks: Loopholes in the Campaign Finance System.* Washington, D.C.: Center for Responsive Politics, 1996.

Rosenkranz, E. Joshua. "Faulty Assumptions in 'Faulty Assumptions': A Response to Professor Smith's Critiques of Campaign Finance Reform." *Connecticut Law Review* 30.3 (1998): 867–96.

Rothman, David J. *Politics and Power: The United States Senate 1869–1901.* Cambridge: Harvard University Press, 1969.

Rowe, Jonathan. "The View of You from the Hill." *Columbia Journalism Review*, July 1994: 47.

Saad, Lydia. "No Public Outcry for Campaign Finance Reform." Gallup Poll, 22 February 1999. Available at http://www.gallup.com/poll/releases/pr970222.asp.

Sabato, Larry. "Real and Imagined Corruption in Campaign Financing." In A. James Reichley, ed., *Elections American Style.* Washington, D.C.: Brookings Institution, 1987.

Sabato, Larry J., and Glenn R. Simpson. *Dirty Little Secrets: The Persistence of Corruption in American Politics.* New York: Times Books, 1996.

Salit, Jacqueline. "Breaking Bread with the Devils of Politics." *Newsday*, 3 October 1999, B4.

Samuelson, Robert J. "The Price of Politics." *Newsweek*, 28 August 1995, 65.

San Antonio Express-News. "Disguised Attack Ads Used by Both Parties." Editorial, 5 October 1997, 2K.

Scarborough, Rowan. "NRA Won't Release Members' Names: IRS Demands Confidential List." *Washington Times*, 3 February 1997, A4.

Schauer, Frederick. "The Political Incidence of the Free Speech Principle." *University of Colorado Law Review* 64.4 (1993): 935–58.

Schotland, Roy. "Proposals for Campaign Finance Reform: An Article Dedicated to Being Less Dull Than Its Title." *Capital University Law Review* 21.2 (1992): 429–62.

Schram, Martin. *Speaking Freely: Former Members of Congress Talk about Money in Politics.* Washington, D.C.: Center for Responsive Politics, 1995.

Shannon, Jasper P. *Money and Politics.* New York: Random House, 1959.

Shapiro, Martin. "Corruption, Freedom and Equality in Campaign Financing." *Hofstra Law Review* 18.2 (1989): 385–95.

Shiffrin, Steven H. "The First Amendment and Economic Regulation: Away from a General Theory of the First Amendment." *Northwestern University Law Review* 78.5 (1983): 1,212–83.

Shockley, John S. "Direct Democracy, Campaign Finance, and the Courts: Can Corruption, Undue Influence, and Declining Voter Confidence Be Found?" *Miami Law Review* 39.3 (1986): 377–468.

———. "Money in Politics: Judicial Roadblocks to Campaign Finance Reform." *Hastings Constitutional Law Quarterly* 10.3 (1983): 679–720.

Simon, Donald. "Beyond Post-Watergate Reform: Putting an End to the Soft Money System." *Journal of Legislation* 24.1 (1998): 167–78.

———. "Channeling Influence: The Broadcast Lobby and the $70 Billion Free Ride: Statement of Common Cause from the Executive Vice President." Available at http://www.commoncause.com, 2 April 1997, 1–4.

Skorneck, Carolyn. "Senators Hear Veteran Pols Oppose Limits." *Orange County Register*, 15 May 1997, A14.

Smith, Adam. *The Wealth of Nations.* New York: Modern Library, 1937.

Smith, Bradley A. "Congress Shall Make No Law . . ." *Washington Times*, 29 December 1994, A19.

———. "Faulty Assumptions and Undemocratic Consequences of Campaign Finance Reform." *Yale Law Journal* 105.4 (1996): 1,049–92.

———. "Judicial Protection of Ballot Access Rights." *Harvard Journal on Legislation* 28.1 (1991): 167–218.

———. "Money Talks: Speech, Corruption, Equality, and Campaign Finance." *Georgetown Law Journal* 86.1 (1997): 45–100.

———. "A Most Uncommon Cause: Some Thoughts on Campaign Finance Reform and a Response to Professor Paul." *Connecticut Law Review* 30.3 (1998): 831–66.

———. "The Sirens' Song: Campaign Finance Regulation and the First Amendment." *Journal of Law and Policy* 6.1 (1999): 1–44.

———. "Soft Money, Hard Realities: The Constitutional Prohibition on a Soft Money Ban." *Journal of Legislation* 179.2 (1998): 179–200.

———. "Why Campaign Finance Reform Never Works." *Wall Street Journal*, 19 March 1997, A19.

Smith, Robert Norton. "Please Stop Thinking about Tomorrow." *New Times Times*, 19 January 1997, A15.

Somin, Ilya. "Voter Ignorance and the Democratic Ideal." *Critical Review* 12.4 (1998): 413–47.

Sorauf, Frank J. *Inside Campaign Finance: Myths and Realities*. New Haven: Yale University Press, 1992.

———. *Money in American Elections*. Glenview Ill.: Scott, Foresman, 1988.

———. "Politics, Experience, and the First Amendment: The Case of American Campaign Finance." *Columbia Law Review* 94.4 (1994): 1,348–68.

Sowell, Thomas. "Lack of Knowledge Contributes to the Poor Staying Poor." *St. Louis Dispatch*, 1 August 1996, B7.

———. *The Vision of the Annointed: Self-Congratulation as a Basis for Social Policy*. New York: Basic Books, 1995.

Stephens, Steve. "Free-Speech Views Hinder FEC Candidate." *Columbus Dispatch*, 14 June 1999, B1.

Stern, Philip. *The Best Congress Money Can Buy*. New York: Pantheon, 1988.

Stigler, George. "The Theory of Economic Regulation." *Bell Journal of Economic and Management Science* 2 (1971): 3.

Stone, Geoffrey R. "Restrictions of Speech Because of Its Content: The Peculiar Case of Subject-Matter Restrictions." *University of Chicago Law Review* 46.1 (1978): 81–153.

Strauss, David A. "Corruption, Equality, and Campaign Finance Reform." *Columbia Law Review* 94.4 (1994): 1,369–89.

———. "What is the Goal of Campaign Finance Reform?" *University of Chicago Legal Forum* 1995: 141–62.

Sullivan, Kathleen. "Political Money and Freedom of Speech." *University of California-Davis Law Review* 30.3 (1997): 663–90.

———. "Political Money and Freedom of Speech: A Reply to Frank Askin." *University of California-Davis Law Review* 31.4 (1998): 1,083–90.

Sunstein, Cass R. "Free Speech Now." In Geoffrey R. Stone, Richard A. Epstein, and Cass R. Sunstein, eds., *The Bill of Rights in the Modern State*. Chicago: University of Chicago Press, 1992.

———. *The Partial Constitution*. Cambridge: Harvard University Press, 1993.

———. "Political Equality and Unintended Consequences." *Columbia Law Review* 94.4 (1994): 1,390–1,414.

———. "Words, Conduct, Caste." *University of Chicago Law Review* 60.3 (1993): 795–844.

Sydnor, Charles S. *Gentlemen Freeholders*. Chapel Hill: University of North Carolina Press, 1952.

Tarrance Group. "Key Findings from a Nationwide Survey of Voter Attitudes about Campaign Finance Reform." Available at http://www.tarrance.com/polls/campfin.htm, 1998.

Taylor, Stuart. "The President's Least Favorite Nominee." *National Journal* 9 (28 February 2000): 598–99.

Thayer, George. *Who Shakes the Money Tree?* New York: Simon and Schuster, 1973.

Tribe, Laurence. *American Constitutional Law*. 2d ed. Mineola, N.Y.: Foundation Press, 1988.

Tribe, Laurence, and Michael C. Dorf. *On Reading the Constitution*. Cambridge: Harvard University Press, 1991.

U.S. Bureau of the Census. *A Report of the Seventeenth Decennial Census of the United States: Census of Population 1950*. Washington, D.C., 1952.

U.S. Congress. House. *Resolution 493*. 105th Cong, 1st sess. 21 January 1997.

———. Committee on the Judiciary. Subcommittee on the Constitution. *Hearing on Issue Advocacy*. 105th Cong., 1st Sess. 18 September 1997.

U.S. Congress. Senate. *Clean Elections Act of 1999*. 106th Cong., 2nd sess., S. 982.

———. *Resolution 25*. 105th Cong., 1st sess., 21 January 1997.

———. Committee on Governmental Affairs. *Investigation of Improper Activites in Connection with the 1996 Federal Election Campaign*. Part VIII, 105th Cong., 2nd sess., 1997.

———. Committee on Rules and Administration. *Hearings on Campaign Contribution Limits*. 106th Cong., 2nd sess., 24 March 1999.

———. Committee on Rules and Administration, *Hearings on Campaign Finance Reform*. 104th Cong., 2nd sess., 8 May 1996.

———. Committee on Rules and Administration, *Testimony of Dan Coates*. 106th Cong., 1st sess., 24 May 1999.

Van Natta, Don, Jr. "Spending by Candidate May Pass $3 Billion." *Portland Press Herald*, 8 October 1999, A1.

Wall Street Journal. "Profile of the Electorate." *Wall Street Journal*, 28 June 1996, R6.

———. "Sony's Statemanship." Editorial. *Wall Street Journal*, 20 June 1995, A22.

Weiner, Tim. "Historian Wins Long Battle to Hear More Nixon Tapes." *New York Times*, 13 April 1996, A12.

Welch, W. P. "Campaign Contributions and Legislative Voting: Milk Money and Dairy Price Supports." *Western Political Quarterly* 35.4 (1982): 478–95.

Wertheimer, Fred, and Randy Huwa. "Campaign Finance Reform: Past Accomplishments, Future Challenges." *New York University Review of Law and Social Change* 10.1 (1981): 43–65.

Wertheimer, Fred, and Susan Manes. "Campaign Finance Reform: A Key to Restoring the Health of Our Democracy." *Columbia Law Review* 94.4 (1994): 1,126–59.

Wilkinson, Francis. "Wrong Fix for Broken Campaign Finance System." *Houston Chronicle*, 7 June 1996, A6.

Williamson, Chilton. *American Suffrage: From Property to Democracy 1760–1860*. Princeton: Princeton University Press, 1960.

Wines, Michael. "The Presidential Race: Pools and Stars." *New York Times*, 16 September 1997, B7.

Winter, Ralph K. "The History and Theory of Buckley v. Valeo." *Journal of Law and Policy* 6 (1997): 93–109.

Wisely, William. *A Tool of Power: The Political History of Money*. New York: John Wiley and Sons, 1977.

Wright, John R. "PACs, Contributions, Roll Calls: An Organizational Perspective." *American Political Science Review* 79 (1985): 400–12.

Wright, J. Skelly. "Politics and the Constitution: Is Money Speech?" *Yale Law Journal* 85.8 (1976): 1,001–20.

———. "Money and the Pollution of Politics: Is the First Amendment an Obstacle to Political Equality?" *Columbia Law Review* 82.4 (1982): 609–45.

Zodrow, George. "Economic Analysis of Capital Gains Taxation: Realizations, Revenues, Efficiency, and Equity." *Tax Law Review* 48.4 (1993): 419–525.

Zuckerman, Edward. "Money Didn't Matter for Most Challengers Who Won." *Political Finance and Lobby Reporter*, 23 November 1994, 1, 4.

———. "Speechless in D.C." *Political Finance and Lobby Reporter*, 9 November 1994, 1, 2.

Index